RESPONSIBILITY TO PROTECT AND SOVEREIGNTY

Law, Ethics and Governance Series

Series Editor: Charles Sampford, Director, Key Centre for Ethics, Law, Justice and Governance, Griffith University, Australia

Recent history has emphasised the potentially devastating effects of governance failures in governments, government agencies, corporations and the institutions of civil society. 'Good governance' is seen as necessary, if not crucial, for economic success and human development. Although the disciplines of law, ethics, politics, economics and management theory can provide insights into the governance of organisations, governance issues can only be dealt with by interdisciplinary studies, combining several (and sometimes all) of those disciplines. This series aims to provide such interdisciplinary studies for students, researchers and relevant practitioners.

Recent titles in the series

Protection of Refugees and Displaced Persons in the Asia Pacific Region
Edited by
Angus Francis and Rowena Maguire
ISBN 978-1-4094-5540-0

Intellectual Liberty
Natural Rights and Intellectual Property
Hugh Breakey
ISBN 978-1-4094-4711-5

Health Workforce Governance
Improved Access, Good Regulatory Practice, Safer Patients
Edited by Stephanie D. Short and Fiona McDonald
ISBN 978-1-4094-2921-0

Ethics and Socially Responsible Investment
A Philosophical Approach
William Ransome and Charles Sampford
ISBN 978-0-7546-7581-5

Idealism and the Abuse of Power
Lessons from China's Cultural Revolution
Zhuang Hui-yun
ISBN 978-0-7546-7208-1

Responsibility to Protect and Sovereignty

Edited by

CHARLES SAMPFORD

Griffith University, Australia

and

RAMESH THAKUR

The Australian National University, Australia

Routledge

Taylor & Francis Group

LONDON AND NEW YORK

First published 2013 by Ashgate Publishing

2 Park Square, Milton Park, Abingdon, Oxon OX14 4RN
711 Third Avenue, New York, NY 10017, USA

Routledge is an imprint of the Taylor & Francis Group, an informa business

First issued in paperback 2016

British Library Cataloguing in Publication Data
A catalogue record for this book is available from the British Library

The Library of Congress has cataloged the printed edition as follows:
Responsibility to protect and sovereignty / edited By Charles Sampford and Ramesh Thakur.
pages cm. – (Law, ethics and governance)
Includes bibliographical references and index.
ISBN 978-1-4094-3782-6 (hardback)
1. Responsibility to protect (International law) 2. Intervention (International law) 3. Sovereignty. I. Sampford, C. J. G. (Charles J. G.) editor of compilation. II. Thakur, Ramesh Chandra, 1948- editor of compilation.
KZ4082.R47 2013
341.4'8 –dc23

2013020318

ISBN 978-1-4094-3782-6 (hbk)
ISBN 978-1-138-24592-1 (pbk)

Contents

List of Cases

2004 US App. LEXIS 10162 (US Court of Appeals for the 9th Circuit).

East Timor (Portugal v Australia) (Judgment) [1995] ICJ Rep 90.

Hagi-Mohammed v Minister for Immigration and Multicultural Affairs [2001] FCA 1156.

Knezevic v Ashcroft, 367 F.3d 1206.

S v Federal Ministry of the Interior, Austrian Administrative Court, 26 January 1994, 93/01/0034.

Salibian v Canada [1990] FCJ 454 (Canada, Federal Court of Appeal).

List of Contributors

Kevin Boreham is a Barrister and Solicitor of the High Court and the Supreme Court of the Australian Capital Territory (ACT). Kevin has been teaching at the ANU (Australian National University) College of Law since 2002. Kevin's first career was as an officer of the Australian Department of Foreign Affairs and Trade. He served in Australia's diplomatic missions in Colombo, Hanoi, Manila, Tehran and New York, where he was Australian Deputy Permanent Representative to the United Nations from 1987–89.

Hugh Breakey is a Postdoctoral Fellow at the Institute for Ethics, Governance and Law and the Key Centre for Ethics, Law, Justice and Governance at Griffith University, Australia. He is the Vice President of the Australian Association for Professional and Applied Ethics. He researches in the area of moral, political and legal philosophy, particularly in application to security, property and intellectual rights. His first book, *Intellectual Liberty: Natural Rights and Intellectual Property*, was published in 2012 by Ashgate. He has published in top law, philosophy, ethics and international policy journals, including *The Modern Law Review*, *The Philosophical Quarterly*, *Social Theory and Practice* and *Global Responsibility to Protect*.

Clinton Fernandes is a Senior Lecturer in Strategic Studies with the School of Humanities and Social Sciences at UNSW @ ADFA, Canberra. His principal research area is international relations and strategy. He was consulting historian on the film *Balibo*.

Angus Francis is co-coordinator of the International Refugee Law Working Group of the International Association for the Study of Forced Migration; a member of the Southern Refugee Legal Aid Network; and a Member of the Refugee and Immigration Legal Service (Brisbane).

Paul Harpur BBus (HRM), LLB (Hons), LLM, PhD, Solicitor of the High Court of Australia (non-practicing), Lecturer at the TC Beirne School of Law, The University of Queensland. He has published widely in the areas of law, human rights and occupational health and safety.

Hitoshi Nasu joined the ANU College of Law in December 2006. Prior to his appointment to the ANU, he was a part-time lecturer at the University of Sydney, teaching international law. His scholarly interests are public international law, migration law, international peace and security law, international humanitarian law and UN law. He has published widely in these fields.

Charles Sampford became the Foundation Dean of Law at Griffith University in 1991. He later became Director of the National Institute for Law, Ethics and Public Affairs, which was incorporated into the Key Centre for Ethics, Law, Justice and Governance (KCELJAG) at Griffith University, Queensland, Australia. He is presently Director of the Institute for Ethics, Governance and Law (IEGL), a joint initiative of the United Nations University, Griffith University, Queensland University of Technology and in association with the Australian National University. He is also Convenor of the ARC Governance Research Network (GovNet) and President of the International Institute for Public Ethics. Earlier positions included Senior Visiting Research Fellow at St John's College Oxford and a Senior Fulbright Award to Harvard.

Ramesh Thakur is Director of the Centre for Nuclear Non-Proliferation and Disarmament (CNND) in the Crawford School, Australian National University, and Adjunct Professor in the Institute of Ethics, Governance and Law at Griffith University. He was Vice Rector and Senior Vice-Rector of the United Nations University (and Assistant Secretary-General of the United Nations) from 1998–2007.

Spencer Zifcak is Professor and Director of the Institute of Legal Studies at Australian Catholic University. He has held appointments as Visiting Fellow at Trinity College Dublin, Wolfson College Oxford, Faculty of Law at New York University and at the UNESCO Centre for Human Rights Education in Bratislava, Slovakia. In 2010, he took up the position of Benjamin Meaker Visiting Professor, Institute of Advanced Studies, University of Bristol (UK). Professor Zifcak holds appointments as a Director of the public policy think-tank, the Australia Institute, and is a Director of the newly established Centre for Dialogue at La Trobe University in Melbourne. He is a Vice-President of Liberty and a legal member of the Mental Health Review Tribunal of Victoria.

Acknowledgement

The research was supported under an Australian Research Council Grant (LP100200672) – Enhancing the Protection of Civilians in Conflict through Civil-Military Collaboration in Peace Operations. The views expressed are those of the authors and are not necessarily those of the Australian Research Council.

List of Abbreviations

9/11	11 September 2001
ABC	Australian Broadcasting Corporation
ADF	Australian Defence Force
AETA	Australia-East Timor Association
ALP	Australian Labor Party
ANAO	Australian National Audit Office
BBC	British Broadcasting Corporation
CARICOM	Caribbean Community and Common Market
CAVR	Commission for Reception, Truth and Reconciliation (known by its Portuguese initials)
CNN	Cable News Network
DC	District of Columbia
DFAT	Department of Foreign Affairs and Trade
ECOSOC	Economic and Social Council
ECOWAS	Economic Community of West African States
ETISC	East Timor Ireland Solidarity Campaign
EU	European Union
Fretilin	Frente Revolucionaria de Timor-Leste Independente
FRY	Federal Republic of Yugoslavia
G8	Group of Eight (Member countries of the Security Council)
GA	General Assembly
GDP	Gross Domestic Product
HLP	High Level Panel
ICC	International Criminal Court
ICG	International Crisis Group
ICISS	International Commission on Intervention and State Sovereignty
ICJ	International Court of Justice

ICRC	International Committee of the Red Cross
ICTY	International Criminal Tribunal for the Former Yugoslavia
IDP	Internally Displaced Persons
IHL	International Humanitarian Law
IICK	Independent International Commission on Kosovo (or the Goldstone Commission)
IMF	International Monetary Fund
INTERFET	International Force – East Timor
ISHR	International Service for Human Rights
JAG	Judge Advocate General
KLA	Kosovo Liberation Army
LTTE	Liberation Tigers of Tamil Eelam
MINURCAT	United Nations Peacekeeping Mandate Central African Republic
MINUSTAH	United Nations Peacekeeping Mandate Haiti
MONUC	United Nations Peacekeeping Mandate Democratic Republic of Congo
NAM	Non-Aligned Movement
NATO	North Atlantic Treaty Organization
NGO	Non-Government Organization
OCHA	United Nations Office for the Coordination of Humanitarian Affairs
OIC	Organization of the Islamic Conference
OSCE	Organization for Security and Cooperation in Europe
P–5	Permanent Members of United Nations Security Council (China, France, Russian Federation, United Kingdom and United States of America)
PoC	Protection of Civilians
R2P	Responsibility to Protect
SC	Secretary-General
SFOR	Stabilization Force
SSB	Single Side Band
UDHR	Universal Declaration of Human Rights
UN	United Nations

UNAMA	United Nations Peacekeeping Mandate Afghanistan
UNAMET	United Nations Mission in East Timor
UNAMID	United Nations Peacekeeping Mandate Darfur
UNGA	United Nations General Assembly
UNHCR	United Nations High Commission for Human Rights
UNMIL	United Nations Peacekeeping Mandate Liberia
UNMIS	United Nations Peacekeeping Mandate Sudan
UNOCI	United Nations Peacekeeping Mandate Cote d'Ivoire
UNSC	United Nations Security Council
US	United States of America
WEOG	Western Europe and Others Group

Chapter 1
Introduction

Charles Sampford

The Responsibility to Protect was born in 2001, widely debated and discussed and then anointed by the United Nations World Leaders Summit in 2005 which adopted it through an omnibus General Assembly resolution.[1]

The responsibility to protect attempts to address questions about the relative duties/obligations/responsibilities[2] of sovereign states, other states and the international community to prevent and terminate mass violence against civilian victims. The International Commission on State Sovereignty and Intervention (ICISS) and its report, *The Responsibility to Protect*, cites three specific responsibilities:[3]

1. *the responsibility to prevent* – to address both the root causes and direct causes of internal conflict;
2. *the responsibility to react* – to respond to situations of compelling human need with appropriate measures; and
3. *the responsibility to rebuild* – to provide, particularly after a military intervention, full assistance with recovery, reconstruction and reconciliation, addressing the causes of the harm the intervention was designed to halt or avert.[4]

The responsibility to protect norm/principle/doctrine,[5] dubbed 'R2P',[6] was limited by the World Summit to the most serious persecution of civilian populations including genocide, war crimes, crimes against humanity and ethnic cleansing.

R2P provides the vital conceptual breakthrough in the long-held debate over state sovereignty vs humanitarian intervention. International debates over how to respond to atrocities such as Rwanda or in Sudan had tended to focus on the rights

1 That Resolution (also called the High-level Plenary Meeting) was passed in September 2005 and adopted the rule of law in domestic affairs and the rule of law in international affairs.

2 The stronger word 'duty' is not so often used even though it is the correlative of the right of the human being to be protected.

3 International Commission on Intervention and State Sovereignty (2001).

4 International Commission on Intervention and State Sovereignty (2001), p. xi.

5 The nuanced distinctions between these terms are as often used to obscure as they do to clarify the writer's position.

6 A form of abbreviation that should appeal to the mobile phone without usable keypad popular at the time.

of states – of other states to militarily 'intervene' across sovereign borders and the right of the home state to treat such matters as an internal affair. The rights and needs of those to be protected were not so central.[7] But the international concern was raised by mass attacks on civilians by militaries, militias and terrorist groups as part of a deliberate war strategy or in facilitation and support of 'rogue elements'. Such attacks included killing, rape as a tool of war, forced displacement and the intimidation. Such attacks are supported by dualistic thinking that dehumanises civilian populations.[8] Violence against civilians can come about because of non-conflict lawlessness, coups and reaction to insurgent activity; the result can be genocide.

The requirement for protection of civilians (PoC) is central to international humanitarian law (IHL), human rights law and refugee law. PoC has emerged as the central goal of many international missions and a key principle for the United Nations (UN) and many member states. It has led to seven reports by the United Nations Secretary General,[9] five UN Security Council (UNSC) resolutions,[10] and eight presidential statements.[11] Eight UN mandates have placed protection of civilians at the centre of their missions.[12] Specific measures include: extending the mandate of UN peacekeeping operations to permit peacekeepers to protect civilians under imminent threat of violence; highlighting the protection needs of especially vulnerable groups (women, children, refugees and internally displaced persons, humanitarian workers); pushing for compliance with international human rights, international humanitarian and refugee law; ensuring better conflict prevention; stressing the multi-disciplinary nature of peace-building; seeking greater co-operation with regional actors; maintaining the separation of combatants and armed elements from civilians in internally displaced persons (IDP) and

7 National Council of Churches Australia (n.d.), *What is 'R2P', the responsibility to protect?*, available at: http://www.ncca.org.au/cws/protect/r2p (accessed 20 October 2012).

8 Slim (2008).

9 Secretary-General (1999); Secretary-General (2001); Secretary-General (2002); Secretary-General (2004); Secretary-General (2005); Secretary-General (2007); Secretary-General (2009).

10 UN Security Council Resolution S/RES/1265 (1999); UN Security Council Resolution S/RES/1296 (2000); UN Security Council Resolution S/RES/1674 (2006); UN Security Council Resolution S/RES/1738 (2006); UN Security Council Resolution S/RES/1894 (2009).

11 UN Security Council (1996); UN Security Council (2002); UN Security Council (2003); UN Security Council (2004); UN Security Council (2004, 20 July); UN Security Council (2005); UN Security Council (2009); UN Security Council (2009).

12 UN Peacekeeping Mandate Darfur (UNAMID); UN Peacekeeping Mandate Afghanistan (UNAMA); UN Peacekeeping Mandate Central African Republic (MINURCAT); UN Peacekeeping Mandate Cote d'Ivoire (UNOCI); UN Peacekeeping Mandate Democratic Republic of Congo (MONUC); UN Peacekeeping Mandate Haiti (MINUSTAH); UN Peacekeeping Mandate Liberia (UNMIL); UN Peacekeeping Mandate Sudan (UNMIS).

refugee camps; working on disarmament and demobilisation; and ensuring timely intervention in cases of genocide, crimes against humanity and war crimes.[13]

Where international assistance is provided, it is recognised that a range of civil and military organisations will be required to deliver the necessary protection but that co-ordinating the efforts of such agencies can be enormously difficult.[14] There are indications that the UN and member states acknowledge the importance and prevalence of the protection of civilians[15] and are committed to its full and effective implementation. In July 2009, the Departments of Peacekeeping Operations and Field Support launched *A New Partnership Agenda: Charting a New Horizon for UN Peacekeeping*.[16] Recommendation 12 proposed the development of a clear and comprehensive guidance on implementation of protection of civilian mandates in peacekeeping.

Protection – of Whom, from What

A key problem for the protection of civilians (PoC) in armed conflict is the lack of an agreed-upon definition or framework of protection, both between and within various groups of actors (military, government, regional and international organisations and humanitarian/private/non-government organisations). While it will most likely be impossible (or even desirable) to achieve an agreed-upon definition, considering the range of actors for co-ordination, to better understanding and training between groups may enable improved relations and co-operation,[17] it is recognised that protection may have different meanings depending on context, culture,[18] the missions of agencies and NGOs and the disciplines of those involved.

Working in collaboration with over 50 human rights organisations, the International Committee of the Red Cross (ICRC) has sought to define protection via a framework including three linked types of action: responsive, remedial and building an environment that promotes respect for the rights of individuals.[19] The ICRC's meaning, 'all activities aimed at obtaining full respect for the rights of the individual in accordance with the letter and spirit of the relevant bodies of law', seems to go beyond protection to promoting rights and better societies.

---

13 Secretary-General (1999); Secretary-General (2001); Secretary-General (2004); UN Security Council Resolution S/RES/1265 (1999); UN Security Council Resolution S/RES/1296 (2000); UN Security Council Resolution S/RES/1674 (2006); UN Security Council Resolution S/RES/1738 (2006).

14 UN Secretary General (2006).

15 UN General Assembly (2009).

16 UN Departments of Peacekeeping Operations and Field Support (2009).

17 Holt and Taylor (2009); International Committee of the Red Cross (ICRC) (September 2008).

18 Luck (August 2008).

19 Angelo Gnaedinger (Director-General ICRC) (9 May 2007); Caverzasio (2001).

However worthy those goals, it would be hard to get agreement of the host and/or UN Security Council if missions were drawn so broadly given limited resources. In any case, broad and uncertain meanings are likely to make operationalising PoC difficult to impossible.[20] Unfortunately, the perceived need for international assistance often overlooks the potential contribution of those being protected[21] so that assistance is seen as creating new protection systems rather than fixing and enhancing existing 'protection systems'.

There is a relationship, although contested,[22] between PoC and R2P through the common denominator of civilian protection.[23] They may 'differ in terms of scope but while PoC is all-inclusive in protecting civilians under imminent threat of physical violence, R2P is limited to what are defined as the four main atrocity crimes. R2P emerged to provide a more robust framework for protection in such situations than that offered by PoC'.[24] There is international resistance to R2P because some see it as legitimising military intervention.[25] Recent events in the Middle East have proved to be somewhat of a watershed. Resolution 1973 is the first Security Council resolution authorising military intervention for the purposes of protecting civilians in the name of the Responsibility to Protect ('R2P') principle.[26]

The Authors and Their Analyses

The book sets out to examine and question:

- UN debates with respect to the doctrine both before and after the resolutions' adoption;
- Official attitude to a humanitarian intervention by nation states;
- What takes place after any intervention;
- The ability of the Security Council to access reliable information and whether the United Nations should adopt new processes to ensure the Security Council has sufficient evidence to enable it to make the important judgment about whether or not genocidal activities or ethnic cleansing are occurring in a target State;
- Whether there is a need for finding a closer operational link between the responsibility to prevent and the responsibility to react and a normative link

20 Bellamy (2009); Stamnes (2009).

21 Bonwick (2006); Luck (August 2008).

22 J. Harald Sande Lie (2008).

23 Holt and Berkman (2006).

24 J. Harald Sande Lie (2008), p. 5.

25 See Adebajo and Fakier (2007); Bellamy (2009); Benjamin (2009); Bessler and Seki (2006); J. Harald Sande Lie (2008).

26 UN Security Council Resolution S/RES/1973 (2011). For a fuller discussion, see Chapter by Angus Francis in this book.

between the responsibility to protect and principles of international law;
- If R2P has little potency as a framework for international decision-making in response to mass atrocity crimes;
- 'How, in short, do we build an international system that responds to threats like mass murder and mass ethnic cleansing in the absence of a central authority?'

In Chapter 2, Spencer Zifcak argues that while the R2P doctrine was readily accepted by UN member states in principle, the R2P doctrine had only sparsely been applied in practice. All that changed with the arrival of the Libyan and Syrian crises. Early in 2011, the doctrine faced the sternest test of its practical application in response to the Libyan and then the Syrian uprisings. He describes the two conflicts with a view to analysing and assessing the realities of pillar 3 international intervention so as to evaluate the political and legal standing of R2P in their wake.

Over the last few years, Security Council members have increasingly asserted that it is *the primary responsibility of the State to protect its civilians* – or *R2PC*. The phrase appears in Council Resolutions, Secretary-General Reports and Council Open Debates on the protection of civilians. Hugh Breakey argues in Chapter 3 that Council members have a shared conception of R2PC, and that it is an inventive amalgamation of different aspects of International Humanitarian Law, International Human Rights Law and the Responsibility to Protect.

Chapter 4 is a critical evaluation of Australia's intervention in East Timor. Clinton Fernandes argues that Australian policymakers were forced to send in a peacekeeping force under the pressure of a tidal wave of public outrage. Although the episode has since been reconstructed as a remarkable success of humanitarian intervention, the historical record indicates that the Australian Government worked assiduously to prevent international intervention in East Timor until the bitter end. The chapter shows that – whatever the merit or otherwise of the 'Responsibility to Protect' doctrine – the East Timor case cannot be used to invoke it except by ignoring the historical record. He concludes with the following observation:

> [T]he deployment of troops to East Timor is often portrayed as a fine example of the 'Responsibility to Protect' in action. By contrast, the historical record shows that it was activists who upheld the R2P principle despite long-standing, ferocious opposition from many states.

Paul Harpur, in Chapter 5, analyses the process followed by the United Nations Security Council to determine if there is an R2P situation. In particular, the chapter analyses the ability of the Security Council to access reliable information and whether the United Nations should adopt new processes to ensure that the Security Council has sufficient evidence to enable it to make the important judgment about whether or not genocidal activities or ethnic cleansing are occurring in a target State.

In Chapter 6, Hitoshi Nasu argues that the concept of the responsibility to protect, as agreed upon by world leaders in 2005, is too restrictive and qualifies their commitment to the responsibility to prevent. He argues that it is dubious whether the intensity and the character of the violence in East Timor and Kosovo in 1999 would have been enough to shift the responsibility to protect to the international community. The chapter addresses this conceptual gap, emphasising the need for finding a closer operational link between the responsibility to prevent and the responsibility to react as well as a normative link between the responsibility to protect and principles of international law.

Kevin Boreham, in Chapter 7, analyses the United Nations Human Rights Council's response to mass atrocity crimes in the Darfur region of Sudan. He argues that the practice of the Human Rights Council in dealing with Darfur proves that the Responsibility to Protect (R2P) is not an emerging norm of customary international law and, secondly, R2P has little potency as a framework for international decision-making in response to mass atrocity crimes. He contends that R2P may even have been counter-productive in the case of Darfur.

The Independent International Commission on Kosovo chaired by Richard Goldstone famously found the intervention 'illegal' but 'legitimate'. In Chapter 8, I challenge that distinction as flawed in principle and in application to Kosovo. I argued that their concept of legitimacy is flawed and the formulation 'illegal but legitimate' was doubly so. This is not because an illegal action may not be morally justifiable (even morally compelling) but that it is an inaccurate, confusing and dangerous mode of argument. I then address the justification of the Kosovo intervention and argue that is not made out. I end by placing the illegal but legitimate formula in the context of the subsequent debates about R2P and the recognition of the need to develop international law.

In Chapter 9, Angus Francis highlights some of the issues that arise when considering the relationship between the R2P principle and refugee protection. While the issues are particular to this context, they illustrate that the pressing question facing the future implementation of the R2P principle, as expressed by Thakur and Weiss, is: 'How, in short, do we build an international system that responds to threats like mass murder and mass ethnic cleansing in the absence of a central authority?'[27]

Finally, in Chapter 10, Ramesh Thakur examines Responsibility to Protect both in retrospect and prospect. He asks:

> Is R2P well-meaning enough to be attractive for its promise of making a difference, yet so vague as to be potentially threatening by being open to abuse? Is it in danger of falling prey to the fatal organisational paradox syndrome, where the effort to preserve the fragile diplomatic consensus in the international community is privileged over the call to protect vulnerable populations that led to the consensus being forged in the first place? That is, can the global consensus on R2P, necessary for the world to be able to translate it from noble principle to actual deeds, be

---

27 Thakur and Weiss (2009).

> stopped from fraying only at the cost of the integrity of R2P that precludes the need to act? Alternatively, is R2P a norm in search of a self-justifying crisis?

He concludes by arguing that:

> R2P is much more fundamentally about building state capacity than undermining state sovereignty. The scope for military intervention under its provenance is narrow and tight. The instruments for implementing its prevention and reconstruction responsibilities on a broad front are plentiful. R2P is principally about protecting developing country peoples by collective international means.

References

A. Adebajo and Y. Fakier (2007) *Africa's Responsibility to Protect*, Police Advisory Group Seminar Report.

A. Gnaedinger (Director-General ICRC) (9 May 2007) *Protection of civilians in conflict – the ICRC perspective: Statement at Humanitarian and Resident Coordinators' Retreat, Geneva*, available at http://www.icrc.org/eng/resources/documents/statement/children-statement-140507.htm (accessed 27 July 2010).

A.J. Bellamy (2009) *The R2P*, Polity.

A.J. Bellamy (2009) 'Realizing the Responsibility to Protect', 10, *International Studies Perspectives* 111.

D. Benjamin (2009) *Changing Norms in International humanitarian Law*, paper presented to the Annual Convention of the International Studies Association, available at http://www.allacademic.com//meta/p_mla_apa_research (accessed 20 December 2010).

M. Bessler and K. Seki (2006) 'Civil-Military Relations in Armed Conflicts: A Humanitarian Perspective', 3, *Liaison*.

A. Bonwick (2006) 'Who really protects civilians?', 16, *Development in Practice* 227.

S. Caverzasio (2001) *Strengthening Protection in War: A search for professional standards*, ICRC.

V.K. Holt and G. Taylor (2009) *Protecting Civilians in the Context of UN Peacekeeping Operations*, United Nations.

V.K. Holt and T.C. Berkman (2006) *The Impossible Mandate? Military Preparedness, the Responsibility to Protect and Modern Peace Operations*, Stimson Center.

International Commission on Intervention and State Sovereignty (2001) *The Responsibility to Protect*, available at http://www.iciss.ca/report-en.asp (accessed 15 November 2012).

International Committee of the Red Cross (ICRC) (September 2008) *Enhancing Protection for Civilians in Armed Conflict and Other Situations of Violence*, available at http://www.unhcr.org/refworld/docid/499ad7692.html (accessed 15 November 2012).

J. Harald Sande Lie (2008) *The Responsibility to Protect and Peace Operations*, National Institute of International Affairs (NUPI) Report, available at http://globalr2p.org/pdf/R2P-4-Sande%20Lie.pdf (accessed 15 November 2012).

E. Luck (2008, August) 'The United Nations and the Responsibility to Protect', in *Policy Analysis Brief*, The Stanley Foundation.

Secretary-General (1999) *Report to the Security Council S/1999/957*, available at www.un.org/Docs/sc/reports/ (accessed 12 November 2012).

Secretary-General (2001) *Report to the Security Council S/2001/331*, available at www.un.org/Docs/sc/reports/ (accessed 12 November 2012).

Secretary-General (2002) *Report to the Security Council S/2002/1300*, available at www.un.org/Docs/sc/reports/ (accessed 12 November 2012).

Secretary-General (2004) *Report to the Security Council S/2004/431*, available at www.un.org/Docs/sc/reports/ (accessed 12 November 2012).

Secretary-General (2005) *Report to the Security Council S/2005/740*, available at www.un.org/Docs/sc/reports/ (accessed 12 November 2012).

Secretary-General (2007) *Report to the Security Council S/2007/643*, available at www.un.org/Docs/sc/reports/ (accessed 12 November 2012).

Secretary-General (2009) *Report to the Security Council S/2009/277*, available at www.un.org/Docs/sc/reports/ (accessed 12 November 2012).

H. Slim (2008) *Killing Civilians: Method, Madness, and Morality in War*, Columbia University Press.

E. Stamnes (2009) 'Speaking 'R2P' and the prevention of mass atrocities', 1, *Global Responsibility to Protect*.

R. Thakur and T. Weiss (2009) 'R2P: From Idea to Norm and Action', 1, *Global Responsibility to Protect* 1.

UN Departments of Peacekeeping Operations and Field Support (2009) *A New Partnership Agenda: Charting a New Horizon for UN Peacekeeping*, United Nations, available at http://www.un.org/en/peacekeeping/documents/newhorizon.pdf (accessed 15 November 2012).

UN General Assembly (2009) *Report of the Special Committee on Peacekeeping Operations and Its Working Group A/63/19 of 24*, available at http://www.nvio.no/gfx/articles/c34rapport%20a63/19.pdf (accessed 15 November 2012).

UN Peacekeeping Mandate Darfur (UNAMID) (n.d.) 'African Union/United Nations Hybrid operation in Darfur', available at http://www.un.org/en/peacekeeping/missions/unamid/ (accessed 15 November 2012).

UN Peacekeeping Mandate Afghanistan (UNAMA) 'United Nations Assistance Mission in Afghanistan', available at http://unama.unmissions.org/default.aspx (accessed 15 November 2012).

UN Peacekeeping Mandate Central African Republic (MINURCAT) 'United Nations Mission in the Central African Republic and Chad', available at http://www.un.org/en/peacekeeping/missions/minurcat/ (accessed 15 November 2012).

UN Peacekeeping Mandate Cote d'Ivoire (UNOCI) 'United Nations Operation in Côte d'Ivoire', available at http://www.un.org/en/peacekeeping/missions/unoci/.

UN Peacekeeping Mandate Democratic Republic of Congo (MONUC) 'United Nations Organization Mission in the Democratic Republic of the Congo', available at http://www.un.org/en/peacekeeping/missions/monuc/ (accessed 15 November 2012).

UN Peacekeeping Mandate Haiti (MINUSTAH) 'United Nations Stabilization Mission in Haiti', available at http://www.un.org/en/peacekeeping/missions/minustah/ (accessed 15 November 2012).

UN Peacekeeping Mandate Liberia (UNMIL) 'United Nations Mission in Liberia', available at http://www.un.org/en/peacekeeping/missions/unmil/ (accessed 15 November 2012).

UN Peacekeeping Mandate Sudan (UNMIS) 'United Nations Mission in the Sudan', available at http://www.un.org/en/peacekeeping/missions/unmis/ – (accessed 15 November 2012).

UN Secretary General (2006) *United Nations Integrated Missions Planning Process (IMPP), Guidelines Endorsed by the Secretary-General, 13 June 2006: Approved through Decision 2006/26 of 14 June 2006*, available at http://www.undg.org (accessed 15 November 2012).

UN Security Council (1996) *Statement by the President of the Security Council S/PRST/1996/6*, available at http://www.un.org/Docs/sc/unsc_pres_statements (accessed 15 November 2012).

UN Security Council (2002) *Statement of the President of the Secuirty Council S/PRST/2002/6*, available at http://www.un.org/Docs/sc/unsc_pres_statements (accessed 15 November 2012).

UN Security Council (2003) *Statement by the President of the Security Council S/PRST/2003/27*, available at http://www.un.org/Docs/sc/unsc_pres_statements (accessed 15 November 2012).

UN Security Council (2004) *Statement by the President of the Security Council S/PRST/2004/46*, available at http://www.un.org/Docs/sc/unsc_pres_statements (accessed 15 November 2012).

UN Security Council (2004, 20 July) *Statement by the President of the Security Council S/PRST/2004/27*, United Nations, available at http://www.un.org/Docs/sc/unsc_pres_statements (accessed 15 November 2012).

UN Security Council (2005) *Statement by the President of the Security Council S/PRST/2005/25*, available at http://www.un.org/Docs/sc/unsc_pres_statements (accessed 15 November 2012).

UN Security Council (2009) *Statement by the President of the Security Council S/PRST/2009/1*, available at http://www.un.org/Docs/sc/unsc_pres_statements (accessed 15 November 2012).

UN Security Council (2009) *Statement by the President of the Security Council S/PRST/2009/9*, available at http://www.un.org/Docs/sc/unsc_pres_statements (accessed 15 November 2012).

UN Security Council Resolution S/RES/1265 (1999), available at http://www.un.org/en/ga/resolutions.shtml (accessed 15 November 2012).

UN Security Council Resolution S/RES/1296 (2000), available at http://www.un.org/en/ga/resolutions.shtml (accessed 15 November 2012).

UN Security Council Resolution S/RES/1674 (2006), available at www.un.org/en/ga/63/resolutions.shtml (accessed 15 November 2012).

UN Security Council Resolution S/RES/1738 (2006), available at http://www.un.org/en/ga/resolutions.shtml (accessed 15 November 2012).

UN Security Council Resolution S/RES/1894 (2009) 11 November, available at http://www.un.org/en/ga/resolutions.shtml (accessed 15 November 2012).

UN Security Council Resolution S/RES/1973 (2011), available at http://www.un.org/en/ga/resolutions.shtml (accessed 15 November 2012).

Chapter 2
Falls the Shadow: The Responsibility to Protect from Theory to Practice[1]

Spencer Zifcak

Between the idea
And the reality
Between the Motion and the act
Falls the *Shadow*

T.S. Eliot[2]

Introduction

Few in the international political and diplomatic communities could have imagined the international standing and influence that the new doctrine of the responsibility to protect (R2P) would succeed in attaining in the decade since it was first conceived.[3] Formulated first in the report of the International Commission on Intervention and State Sovereignty in 2001 in response to widespread criticism of the idea of humanitarian intervention, the core principles of R2P were set down and accepted by UN General Assembly only four years later at the World Leader's Summit in September 2005. It was then formally recognised and incorporated by the UN Security Council in a series of resolutions that followed. In each of these resolutions, the Council reaffirmed the responsibility of sovereign states and the international community to take all necessary steps to prevent populations from genocide, crimes against humanity, war crimes and ethnic cleansing.[4]

Subsequently, in 2009, UN Secretary-General, Ban Ki-Moon issued his first report on the implementation of R2P. The report was a detailed encapsulation and explication of the new doctrine's principal parameters. It drew heavily on the work of ICISS but its cast was more pragmatic. In elaborating upon it, a three-pillar approach to its implementation was proposed.

1 This chapter is based in significant part on interviews I conducted with 21 senior diplomats in Permanent Missions to the UN and in the UN Secretariat in New York in November 2011. I would like to thank all these interviewees for their remarkable insights and very generous assistance.

2 T.S. Eliot (1925).

3 ICISS (2011).

4 UNSC (2006); UNSC (2009); UNSC (2011a); UNSC (2011b); UNSC (2011c); UNSC (2012a); UNSC (2012b).

In the first, the nation in which a humanitarian disaster is in prospect must assume responsibility for taking timely and appropriate measures to prevent it. For this, early warning and awareness of the possibility of crisis was crucial. The second pillar involved a calibrated response by the international community to an emergent threat that the nation in question had failed to avert. Here, concerted and directed assistance in the form of development aid, foreign investment, technical assistance, economic incentives, rapid police responsiveness, and more general capacity building was crucial. Under the third pillar, these measures could be supplemented on the cusp of mass atrocity by 'soft' coercion imposed by the international community. This might include fact-finding missions, the deployment of peacekeepers, the imposition of arms embargoes, the application of diplomatic and economic sanctions or the creation of safe-havens and no-fly zones. Then, when all else has failed, the Security Council may authorise military intervention as the measure of last resort.

While all this was readily accepted by UN member states in principle, the R2P doctrine had only sparsely been applied in practice. The preceding UN Secretary-General, Kofi Annan, had called it in aid when conducting his mediation in Kenya in 2008, following the tribal killings that had occurred following the country's intensely contested election. Beyond that, however, R2P had yet to be tested in practice. In particular, its most controversial pillar – coercive intervention by the international community to put an end to imminent or actual commission of crimes against humanity – had not been tried. All that changed with the arrival of the Libyan and Syrian crises. Early in 2011, therefore, the doctrine faced the sternest test of its practical application in response to the Libyan and then the Syrian uprisings. In this chapter, therefore, I describe the two conflicts with a view to analysing and assessing the realities of pillar 3 international intervention so as to evaluate the political and legal standing of R2P in their wake.

I Libya

The rebellion against the Gaddafi regime had commenced in February 2011, following closely upon revolutionary changes that were occurring in Tunisia and Egypt. However, whereas in those countries the autocrats in charge had reacted with a measure of restraint, Gaddafi declared war on the Libyan uprising. Soon, the number of protestors killed climbed from the hundreds to more than a thousand. As the Gaddafi forces gained strength and territory, so the opposition weakened to the extent that it appeared that Benghazi, the city at the epicentre of the rebellion, would fall. It was at that point that Gaddafi threatened the disaffected population there with extinction.

In response to the rapidly disintegrating situation in Libya, the relevant organs of the UN laid the ground for the subsequent intervention in a series of condemnatory actions.

The Human Rights Council convened a Special Session on the situation of human rights in the Libyan Arab Jamahiriya on 25 February 2011. Introducing the Session, the High Commissioner for Human Rights described the Libyan descent into violence and chaos as shocking and brutal. It represented a callous and worsening disregard for the rights and freedoms of the Libyan people, she said, that had been characteristic of the Libyan leadership for more than four decades.[5] On the same day, the Council adopted resolution S-15/1.[6] The resolution expressed deep concern as to the deteriorating situation and strongly condemned reported human rights violations including indiscriminate attacks on civilians, extrajudicial killings, arbitrary arrests and detention and torture of peaceful demonstrators. It called on the Libyan government to 'meet its responsibility to protect its population and to put an end immediately to all human rights violations. The General Assembly suspended Libya on 1 March.

It was highly significant, immediately before the Human Rights Council met, that the key regional organisations traditionally sympathetic to Middle Eastern and North African regimes joined the chorus of international protest and made recommendations for immediate ameliorative action.[7] Between 20 and 23 February, the Council of the League of Arab States, the Secretary-General of the Organization of Islamic Conference and the Peace and Security Council of the African Union all issued statements condemning the descent into violence in Libya and calling for the establishment of immediate talks between the contending parties to arrange a ceasefire and work towards a mediated solution of the conflict.[8] The Arab League went one step further and suspended Libya's membership of the League.[9]

The Security Council met to consider the Libyan crisis on 26 February. At this meeting the Council adopted resolution 1970.[10] The resolution expressed grave concern about the Libyan conflict. It deplored the gross and systematic violation of human rights in the country. It welcomed the condemnation by the Arab League, the African Union and the Organization of the Islamic Conference. It condemned the deliberate killing of civilians and it recalled the Libyan authorities' responsibility to protect its population. The resolution demanded an immediate end to hostilities; the observance of human rights; access for human rights monitors; and safe passage for humanitarian and medical workers and supplies into the country. It also set in place a set of coercive measures. It imposed an arms embargo; a travel ban on key figures in the Libyan administration; a freeze on their assets overseas; and it called for a review of progress with respect to these measures within 120 days.

Regional organisations became even more vocal as the violence escalated. The OIC came in behind the Arab League and also endorsed the creation of a no-fly

5 UN Human Rights Council (2011c).
6 UN Human Rights Council (2011b).
7 Bellamy (2011a), p. 263.
8 UNSC (2011d); Organisation of Islamic Conference (2011).
9 Williams (2011), p. 248.
10 UNSC (2011a).

zone. It stopped short, however, of endorsing foreign military intervention on the ground. On 12 March, the Arab League again intervened forcefully to call upon the Security Council to establish a no-fly zone and to create safe areas exposed to shelling.[11] It urged the Council to set in place measures to protect the civilian population from widespread human rights abuse and declared that the existing Libyan authorities had lost all legitimacy.

The Security Council met again on 17 March to review the situation and determine what further action was required. The outcome of its deliberations was the path breaking resolution 1973.[12] The resolution deplored the failure of the Libyan authorities to comply with resolution 1970, expressed grave concern at the deteriorating human rights situation and escalating violence in the country and reiterated the responsibility of the Libyan government to protect the Libyan population. It recalled the condemnation of the Libyan regime by the Arab League, the African Union and the OIC and their demand for the creation of a no-fly zone and the creation of safe havens for civilians under threat of shelling. Following from this, the Council for the first time authorised coercive military intervention in a sovereign state without the consent of that State's governing authorities. Resolution 1973 strengthened and extended the arms embargo, asset freeze and travel restrictions imposed in resolution 1970. Most importantly, however, it authorised the use of force by a coalition of nations under NATO's umbrella in two separate ways.

First, the Security Council resolved that 'all necessary measures' could be taken to protect civilians and civilian populated areas under threat of attack. The measures, however, could not include the deployment of any 'foreign occupation force of any form on any part of Libyan territory'. Secondly, the Council determined that a no-fly zone should be established over Libya in order to protect civilians and authorised the NATO coalition to take 'all necessary measures' to enforce the ban on flights. The aim of all these measures was to force the Libyan regime to desist from grievous abuses of human rights and humanitarian law, abuses which by that time had clearly assumed the status of crimes against humanity. The designation of crimes against humanity having been determined, the responsibility to protect could be invoked by the Security Council to shape an international military intervention designed to prevent the occurrence of existing and probable atrocities.

Two days after resolution 1973 was adopted, a military coalition under the umbrella of NATO began bombing Libyan government positions from which attacks upon civilians were likely to be launched. This was the most obvious military measure taken to protect civilians but the intervention was multifaceted. The United States took out Libya's integrated air defence system to deprive it of the capacity to launch air strikes on Benghazi and elsewhere. A coalition of 14 NATO countries and four partner nations was created to combine both naval and aerial forces. France and Britain flew 40 per cent of the sorties. Spain, the Netherlands, Turkey, Greece and Romania supported the intervention by enforcing the no-fly zone and the arms embargo at sea.

11 UNSC (2011b).
12 UNSC (2011b).

However, when it became clear two months after the initial aerial intervention that Libyan government resistance in other parts of the country was stronger than had been anticipated, NATO began to attack a wider range of targets in the Libyan capital, Tripoli, and elsewhere that had been identified as 'command and control' centres. On the weekend of 1 May the Gaddafi family compound was hit, killing the leader's second youngest son and three of his grandchildren.[13] Russia described the attack as a 'disproportionate use of force … leading to detrimental consequences and the death of innocent civilians'.[14]

As the fighting continued, reservations of a different kind began to be expressed from two different sources. Libyan fighters on the ground began to complain that the NATO bombing campaign was insufficient and misdirected.[15] Rebels in the West and the port city of Misrata complained that without more intensive and extensive NATO bombardment, they lacked the firepower and military discipline to take charge on the ground.[16] At the same time, NATO's military leadership became increasingly convinced that civilian protection could not be achieved unless the Libyan leadership was destroyed.[17] With government forces still in charge of significant territory in the west of the country, including in the capital Tripoli, the prospect of a stalemate emerged with the country divided between rebels in the east and Colonel Gaddafi still in charge in the west.[18] To the rebels on the ground and NATO commanders leading attacks in the air, any such partition was anathema.[19]

The question then became whether more muscular NATO intervention, for example through the destruction of infrastructure including government buildings, the electricity grid and fuel dumps, and the deliberate targeting of Libyan commanders including Colonel Gaddafi, could properly be regarded as falling within the UN 'civilian protection' mandate. In the end, the NATO strategy morphed progressively into one that embraced regime change. The argument made in defence of this expanded understanding was that the protection of civilians could not be achieved unless military victory was complete. On any account, this was to stretch the terms of resolution 1973 to their absolute limit but it sufficed to underpin and rationalise NATO's subsequent intensification of the war that, together with the bravery of the Libyans on the ground, finally brought the conflict substantially to an end in late August 2011.

On 16 September, the Security Council adopted resolution 2009.[20] This resolution established the mandate for a UN Support Mission in Libya (UNMISIL). It lifted the arms embargo to enable the transfer of arms intended solely for security

13 Muammar Gaddafi son killed by NATO air strike – Libyan government (2011).
14 UNSC (2011e).
15 Nordland (2011), p. 10.
16 Chivers and Kirkpatrick (2011), p. 10.
17 NATO (2011).
18 Burns (2011a).
19 Burns (2011b), p. 8.
20 UNSC (2011f).

or disarmament assistance to the new Libyan authorities and for the protection of UN humanitarian and diplomatic personnel. It lifted the asset freeze on the Libyan National Oil Corporation and Zuetina Oil Company to permit revenues from oil to flow again, and lifted the ban on flights on Libyan commercial aircraft, in order to facilitate normal economic activity. The priority areas for UNMISIL were to restore security and public order and to promote the rule of law; to undertake the task of constitution-making and to promote national reconciliation; to promote and protect human rights and to support transitional justice; and to take immediate steps towards the pursuit of economic recovery. The Council agreed to recognise the National Transitional Council as the official representative at the UN of the Libyan nation.

The international community had exercised its 'responsibility to protect' but the 'responsibility to rebuild' remained an obligation and challenge of formidable proportions.[21]

The Responsibility to Protect after Libya

The Libyan intervention had presented considerable dangers for the future of the doctrine of the responsibility to protect. Being the first military intervention the purpose of which was to protect a nation's civilian population against gross human rights abuses committed by their government, the risks attached to failure were considerable. If the intervention were to fail, the entire doctrine may well have been called into question or, even, fallen into desuetude.

In the event, the objective of protecting Libyan civilians against the grave human rights abuses threatened by their government was achieved. The citizens of Benghazi were spared the massacre that in all likelihood had awaited them. Then, the remainder the of the country fell to Libyan rebels, assisted forcefully by the NATO coalition, thus ensuring that Colonel Gaddafi could not regain control and that, at least for the foreseeable future, the civilian population would be safe under the umbrella of the government of the former opposition National Transitional Council.

The fact of military victory on the ground was sufficient to justify the conclusion that the Libyan R2P operation succeeded.[22] This is despite the strong protests as to its methods, lodged not without reason, by those members of the Security Council who abstained from the vote on resolution 1973.[23] However, it was not just the military win that seemed to secure R2P as an international political doctrine of very considerable importance. The Libyan success had a number of novel aspects each of which consolidated the doctrine's gains.

Unlike prior humanitarian interventions, the Libyan one proceeded with the authorisation of the UN Security Council. This was not a unilateral intervention by

21 Pelham (2011a).

22 Thakur (2011), p. 13; Evans (2011).

23 UNSC (2011g).

Western forces such as that which had created such enormous legal controversy in Kosovo. The Libyan intervention fell squarely within the terms of the UN Charter.

The Security Council acted following preceding, strong action by the Human Rights Council. It had condemned outright the human rights abuses being committed in Libya and, still in the early days of the conflict, recommended that the General Assembly expel Libya from the Council.[24]

The role of Regional Organisations was even more important.[25] The Arab League in particular, took firm action against Libya, condemning the government's attitudes and actions and expelling the country from its membership. In this it was joined by the Peace and Security Council of the African Union and the Organization of the Islamic Conference. Buttressed by the support of these regional bodies, and following the League's recommendation that a no-fly zone be imposed as one means of staunching the bloodshed, the Security Council was in a far stronger position to act without courting the criticism of selectivity.[26]

Success in Libya came without the imposition of 'boots on the ground'. Resolution 1973 had explicitly excluded the deployment of forces of occupation. That exclusion had been critical to its adoption. Yet, despite that prohibition, military means had been found to achieve the protection of Libyan civilians from the depredations of their government, and to set the country on the road to security, national reconciliation and economic recovery.

Nevertheless, at the same time, the intervention revealed significant weaknesses in the manner of its implementation. These became immensely important in subsequent Security Council deliberations with respect to debate with respect to external intervention in Syria. The most severe criticism of the Libyan case related to 'mission creep'.[27] Those members of the Security Council who abstained from the vote on resolution 1973 attacked forcefully what they saw as the abuse of the Council's mandate. In their view there was no way in which the relevant resolution could have permitted the transformation of the mission from the protection of civilians to the objective of regime change. Russia, China, India and Brazil all objected strongly to the alteration of NATO's military stance from the relative neutrality of civilian protection to evident partiality in taking the rebel side.[28] [29]

Secondly, deep reservations were expressed as to the legality of the transformation. Here, the argument was that resolution 1973 could not be stretched to cover actions such as intervention in a civil war, the assassination of a government's leadership and the overthrow of the regime.[30] Security Council

24 UN Human Rights Council (2011a).

25 UNSC (2011b).

26 Bellamy (2011a), p. 266.

27 Pattison (2011), p. 271.

28 For example, UNSC (2011e). See Mr Churkin (Russian Federation) and Mr Baodong (China).

29 See further, Evans (2012a).

30 See Mr. Mashabane (South Africa), UNSC (2011h).

endorsement was critical to underpin the legality of the intervention, particularly as it took place without Libyan consent, but the actions of the coalition forces appeared to take the intervention well beyond the resolution's terms and, therefore, in all probability, beyond what the UN Charter could be interpreted to allow.

Thirdly, the nature of the military campaign raised starkly the question of whether it could have taken a different form and still been as effective. If so, then evidently, a more targeted and limited form of military intervention should have been preferred.

Arguments of this kind raise perhaps the most difficult of all questions concerning an R2P military intervention. In every case a military assessment will need to be made as to the minimum force required to achieve a mission's core objective – that is, the protection of the civilian population from genocide, crimes against humanity and other gross human rights abuse. That assessment may not always be containable within the terms of a Security Council mandate determined in advance. And it will rarely be practicable or sensible to go back to the Council for an extension of the mandate in the midst of war. In that circumstance, one has little choice but to accept that conditions on the ground may, in the end, trump all other considerations.[31]

Given these different and competing political perspectives on the Libyan intervention, it has remained difficult to encapsulate the standing of the R2P doctrine at its close with any great certainty. At the risk of over simplification, however, the following propositions may tentatively be proposed:

- The Libyan intervention can be considered as a successful application of the responsibility to protect because the military campaign succeeded in protecting Libyan citizens from the commission of further and certain crimes against humanity and grave human rights abuse.
- In so doing, the intervention lent legitimacy and weight to the appropriateness of Pillar 3 intervention in emergency circumstances.
- Further, in this regard, it solidified the view that the application of Pillars 1, 2 and 3 need not proceed sequentially. From time to time, there will be desperately urgent cases in which Pillar 3 intervention must be the first option to be considered not the last.
- The intervention confirmed the absolutely central role of the Security Council in providing authorisation, on behalf of the international community, for military intervention to take place in emergency circumstances. Such authorisation lends essential political legitimacy and legal force to any intervention that may be contemplated within R2P's rubric.
- The intervention also established the crucial role that can and should be played by recognised regional organisations in determining whether an intervention may be appropriate and if so, what form it might best take. Without the backing of relevant regional organisations, it is far less likely

31 Gwertzman (2011).

that the Security Council will be moved to endorse a Pillar 3 incursion upon the sovereignty of a state, not least so as to avoid the charge of selective implementation.

- The Libyan intervention demonstrated clearly, however, that much work remains to be done in determining the nature and limits of military strategy and tactics in the implementation of a Pillar 3 intervention. There is little doubt, for instance, that the Security Council will be more minded than previously to define the parameters of an intervention much more precisely.

II Syria

Protests in Syria followed those that had occurred in Tunisia and Egypt. In February 2011, demonstrations against the government occurred initially in relation to issues such as poverty, inequality, restrictions upon freedom of speech, the desire for democracy and the demand that human rights be respected. In mid-March, large but peaceful protests commenced in Dar'a after a group of children accused of painting anti-government graffiti on public buildings were detained and tortured by government intelligence agents. Syrian armed forces responded violently however, attacking protesters and firing on at a funeral procession. After this, the protests spread rapidly to other cities including Damascus, Homs, Hama and Idlib.[32] On 30 March, the President of Syria, Bashar Al-Assad, denounced the cumulative protests, alleging that Syria was facing a grand conspiracy by imperialist forces. Internal conspirators, he said, were spreading lies about the government, inciting sectarian tension and using violence against government security forces.[33] The problem was not with his government but with 'armed terrorist gangs'.

On 16 April, President Al-Assad, in a tactic designed to placate the protesters, swore in a new government,[34] lifted the state of emergency that had been in place since 1963,[35] abolished the High Security Court, and recognised the right to peaceful protest while strictly regulating it. One week later, on 22 April, the largest demonstrations yet seen occurred across the country. Protesters accused the government of providing too little too late.[36] More than one hundred were killed by government forces in the immediate aftermath of the demonstrations.

As the protests endured, the Government deployed the army backed by armoured personnel vehicles to quell them. The first systematic military deployment occurred on 25 April in Dar'a.[37] From that time, protests continued and expanded

32 UN Human Rights Council (2011d), p. 27.
33 UN Human Rights Council (2011d), p. 30.
34 Mroue (2011).
35 Stack (2011), p. 10.
36 Blanford (2011), p. 21.
37 UN Human Rights Council (2011d), p. 28.

across the country and the reaction of the military forces became increasingly violent. The protest movement responded to the repression by shifting its focus from demanding reforms to the regime to advocating its removal,[38] thus reflecting the calls that had been heard in other parts of the region.[39]

The April demonstrations marked a significant alteration in the form and intensity of governmental repression. Sources regarded as reliable by the Office of the UN High Commissioner for Human Rights (OHCHR) reported the use of artillery fire against unarmed civilians, door-to-door arrest campaigns, the obstruction of medical personnel seeking to care for the injured, raids against hospitals, clinics and mosques, the arrest of medical personnel and the purposeful destruction of medical supplies.[40] Electricity, water and communications systems in the city were cut. The OHCHR received information of mass, arbitrary arrests and the torture of protesters, lawyers, journalists, human rights defenders and others.

By the end of May, the UN reported that government forces had killed 850 people and some 8000 had been arbitrarily detained. Media reports at the time indicated that mass graves had been found in Dar'a with a further death toll of 1100.[41] On the 25 May, France, Germany, Portugal and the United Kingdom introduced a draft resolution into the Security Council condemning the government crackdown.[42] The draft resolution recalled the Syrian Government's responsibility to protect its citizens, stressed the need for those responsible for government sponsored violence to be brought to account and called for an end to killings, arbitrary detention, disappearances and torture. It demanded that the siege of Dar'a cease and that all media and communications restrictions be lifted. It urged the Syrian government to co-operate with an investigative commission that the Human Rights Council had proposed.

Intensive discussion then ensued among Security Council members as to an amended form of the European resolution. Russia, China, India, Brazil and South Africa expressed their concern that a Council resolution should not seek to dictate the content of the reform program that the Syrian government should undertake. That, they felt, was essentially an internal matter. They sought also to remove what they saw as muscular language in the resolution. In doing so, they wished to avoid any suggestion in the resolution's terms that the Council's involvement may presage any form of external military intervention.

On the 21 July the Secretary General's Special Advisers on the Prevention of Genocide and the Responsibility to Protect issued a statement on Syria.[43] They observed that the scale and ferocity of the violence in Syria indicated that

38 Blanford (2011), p. 21.
39 Barry (2012), p. 8.
40 UNSC (2011i).
41 Ali (2011), p. 24.
42 Europeans on UN council offer Syria resolution (2011).
43 Deng and Luck (2011); UN Human Rights Council (2011d).

crimes against humanity may have been committed there. More in hope than anticipation, they urged the Syrian government to fulfil its responsibility to protect its population and to ensure that its security forces complied with their obligations under international human rights law. Meanwhile, negotiations on the draft Security Council resolution were foundering. The killings and the torture intensified.[44]

Five months after negotiations on the European resolution had begun, France, Germany, Portugal and the United Kingdom introduced their final, amended draft resolution for discussion and adoption.[45] In summary, the resolution recalled the Syrian government's responsibility to protect its population; regretted the Government's lack of progress in introducing its promised reforms; and expressed its deep concern with respect to the deteriorating political situation in Syria and the prospect of a further escalation of violence. The resolution demanded an immediate end to the violence; the restoration of freedom of expression and assembly; the cessation of the use of lethal force against civilians; and the government's support for the alleviation of the humanitarian crisis that had resulted from the continuing conflict. It called for an inclusive Syrian led political process, conducted free from fear and intimidation, to address the legitimate concerns of Syria's population. As in the Libyan case, the resolution called for the Arab League to use its influence to end the violence. Significantly, the European draft dropped paragraphs concerning the imposition of sanctions but conveyed an intention to introduce such measures should Syria not comply with the resolution's terms within a designated time.

On the 4 October, the Security Council rejected the resolution. Nine members voted in its favour, four – Brazil, India, Lebanon and South Africa abstained – and two – China and Russia voted against it, exercising their veto.[46] The arguments advanced for the adoption of the resolution are reasonably well understood, having to do principally with the protection of Syrian civilians. What is of more interest for present purposes was the content and character of those mounted against it.[47]

In the debate following the resolution's defeat, Russia set down four.[48] First, the resolution did not pay sufficient respect to Syria's national sovereignty and territorial integrity and to the principle of non-intervention into its domestic affairs. Secondly, in Russia's view, the resolution was founded upon the logic of confrontation. It should, instead, reflect a clear preference for even-handed dialogue amongst the Syrian parties aimed at achieving peace and national agreement concerning the reforms necessary to advance the country's social and political life. Thirdly, Russia asserted that the violence in Syria was inflicted by both sides. Adopting the stance of the Syrian President, it asserted that the Syrian Government was confronted by a radical opposition of extremist bent that relied

44 For example see, UN Human Rights Council (2011d), p. 80.

45 UNSC (2011j).

46 United Nations Department of Public Information (2011).

47 Libya Bitten, Syria Shy (2012).

48 See Mr Churkin (Russian Federation), UNSC (2011k).

upon terrorist tactics to advance its cause. Fourthly, and crucially, Russia was intensely critical of the Libyan intervention and its possible implications for Syria. As to that intervention, the Russian Permanent Representative, Mr Churkin, said that the Council's mandate in Libya had turned into the opposite of what had been intended:

> The demand for a quick ceasefire turned into a fully-fledged civil war … The situation in relation to the no-fly zone has morphed into the bombing of oil refineries, television stations, and other civilian sites. The arms embargo has morphed into a naval blockade in western Libya … today the tragedy of Benghazi has spread to other western Libyan towns … These types of model should be excluded from global practices once and for all.[49]

As the death toll continued to rise alarmingly, the Arab League chose again to enter the fray. On 16 November, the League suspended Syria from its membership and gave the regime three days in which to comply with the terms of a detailed initiative or else it would face economic and political sanctions. The sanctions were subsequently imposed. The key elements of the initiative were the demand that there be an immediate cessation of the violence and the withdrawal of Syrian military forces from the streets. On the 22 December, 150 Arab League monitors arrived in Syria and deployed throughout the country to determine the extent to which the Syrian authorities were complying with the League's initiative.[50] As at the end of 2011, their presence had not had any impact in reducing the violence whatsoever and they were subsequently withdrawn.

The independent international commission of inquiry established by the Human Rights Council presented its report on 23 November. On any account it was a devastating critique of the actions of the Syrian regime. It concluded that gross violations of human rights by the Syrian military and security forces had occurred in Syria since the commencement of the protests in March 2011.[51] The violations were such as to persuade the commission that the Syrian Government had been responsible for the commission of crimes against humanity.[52] The Commission concluded grimly that:

> The sheer scale and consistent pattern of attacks by military and security forces on civilians and civilian neighbourhoods and the widespread destruction of property could only be possible with the approval or complicity of the state. According to international law, when certain crimes are committed as part of a widespread or systematic attack against civilians and the perpetrators know that their conduct is part of this attack, such offences constitute crimes against humanity.

49 UNSC (2011k).
50 Fordham (2011), p. 12.
51 UN Human Rights Council (2011d), p. 1.
52 UN Human Rights Council (2011d), p. 100.

> The commission is thus gravely concerned that crimes against humanity of murder, torture, rape or other forms of sexual violence of comparable gravity, imprisonment or other severe deprivation of liberty, enforced disappearances of persons and other inhumane acts of a similar character have occurred ...[53]

The matter returned to the Security Council on 12 December 2011. On that day, the High Commissioner for Human Rights updated the Council in informal session as to the state of the conflict. She told the Council that since March it was estimated that more than 5000 people had been killed. Tens of thousands had been arrested. Fourteen thousand were believed to have been arbitrarily detained. More than twelve thousand had fled across the border and tens of thousands more had been internally displaced. The Syrian Government's ruthless repression could drive the country into a fully fledged civil war. She concluded that, in the light of the Syrian Government's manifest failure to exercise its responsibility to protect its citizens, the international community should take urgent and effective measures to protect the Syrian people.[54]

Throughout January, Security Council members met again to engage in frantic negotiations towards the adoption of a new, consensus resolution. The foundation for the negotiations was a draft resolution that had been presented to the Council by the Arab League.[55] The League's draft was assertive and controversial. At its heart lay a plan for a transition of power in Syria. The plan called for the formation of a national unity government in Syria; the delegation by the Syrian President to his Vice-President of the responsibility to form and then cooperate with the national unity government; and for the new government to hold transparent and free parliamentary and presidential elections under international and Arab supervision. The draft resolution also urged the Syrian government to fully cooperate with the Arab League's observer mission; it encouraged all States in the region to impose economic sanctions upon the Assad regime; and it proposed that the regime's implementation of a Security Council resolution be reviewed within fifteen days of its adoption. Should the Council determine that the government continued to be non-compliant, the League proposed that the Council should consider the adoption of further measures to pressure it to halt the violence.

The Arab League draft ran across Russia's interests in two important respects.[56] First, it constituted an external demand for President Assad to stand aside. To Russian eyes, this would constitute a substantial incursion upon Syrian sovereignty. Secondly, Russia was wary of the idea that the Council might take further, unspecified, measures against the regime. For Russia this smacked of an invitation for external military intervention on the Libyan model. That was a red line that the Russian government would not permit the international community to cross.

53 UN Human Rights Council (2011d), p. 107.
54 Office of the High Commissioner for Human Rights (2011).
55 UN draft resolution on Syria (2012).
56 Syria: a Soviet hangover turned headache (2012).

The rapid deterioration in Syria prompted a cross-section of the Council's members to bring a new draft resolution forward for consideration.[57] The new resolution presented to the Council by Morocco, and supported by eighteen other nations, went some considerable distance to allay Russian and Chinese concerns. The detailed steps towards a transition of power in Syria, contained in the Arab League draft, were removed in favour of a general statement of support for the League's initiative. The reference to encouraging states to impose sanctions upon Syria disappeared. It demanded that, in accordance with the Arab League's December plan of action, Syrian authorities should withdraw all military and militia forces from cities and towns and allow full and unhindered access to League and Arab State institutions. The resolution's preambular provisions stated explicitly that nothing in the resolution authorised coercive measures to be taken against Syria pursuant to Article 42 of the UN Charter.

The vote on the resolution was scheduled for 4 February 2012. On the evening of 3 February, the Syrian authorities launched the first of many rocket attacks upon the city of Homs. Rebel held suburbs of the city were shelled relentlessly without regard for any distinction between rebel fighters and civilians. At least two hundred and ten people were killed and hundreds more were wounded in one weekend of shelling. It was the bloodiest weekend of violence in the eleven months since the uprising began. The total number of Syrian people killed climbed past six thousand. The draft Security Council resolution was put to the vote on the morning of 4 February. Thirteen Council members voted in favour of it. Russia and China vetoed it.

Immediately after the vote was taken, Council members engaged in perhaps the most acrimonious debate since the end of the Cold War. The French Ambassador summarised the mood amongst the resolution's backers:

> This is a sad day for the Council; it is a sad day for the Syrians; and it is a sad day for all the friends of democracy … history has compounded our shame because today is the anniversary of the Hama massacre (in 1982) and falls only one day after another massacre in Homs. The father killed on a mass scale, the son has followed in his footsteps. Horror would appear to be hereditary in Damascus.[58]

The Russian and Chinese delegations were unmoved. They described the resolution as unbalanced, because it failed to condemn both the Syrian authorities and the armed rebels in equal measure. They accused Western nations, by means of the resolution, of masking intent to seek regime change in Damascus. The Russian Ambassador counter-attacked:

> … from the very beginning of the Syrian crisis some influential members of the international community, including some sitting at this table, have undermined

57 UNSC (2012c).

58 See Mr Araud (France), UNSC (2012e).

> any possibility of a political settlement, calling for regime change, encouraging opposition towards power, indulging in provocation and nurturing the armed struggle … (no) account has been taken of our proposals that along with the withdrawal of Syrian armed forces from the cities there should be an end to attacks by armed groups on State institutions and neighbourhoods.[59]

The Security Council had arrived at an impasse. The Syrian death toll passed eight thousand.

Ten days later, in a concerted effort to break the deadlock, the UN General Assembly and the Arab League took the initiative and recommended the appointment of former UN Secretary-General, Kofi Annan, as their Joint Special Envoy to Syria.[60] On 21 March, the Security Council unanimously endorsed Mr Annan's appointment and his six point plan to bring an end to the violence and effect a governmental transition that met with the approval of the Syrian people. The plan called for all sides to work with the envoy in the establishment of an inclusive political process to address the Syrian people's concerns; to commit to end the fighting so that a sustained cessation of all forms of violence could be achieved; to ensure the provision of needed humanitarian assistance; to intensify the pace and scale of the release of people who had been arbitrarily detained; to ensure freedom of movement for journalists; and to respect the freedom of association and the right of the people to demonstrate peacefully.[61]

The Syrian Government responded on 25 March by agreeing to observe the terms of the six-point plan, in particular by commencing the withdrawal of military concentrations, and ceasing the use of heavy weapons, in and around populations centres. On 12 April, Annan reported that the parties appeared to be observing the cessation of fire.[62] Given that tentative assurance, the Security Council decided to establish a UN Supervision Mission in Syria (UNMISIS). Its mandate was to monitor the cessation of the violence and to support the full implementation of the Annan plan.[63]

However, short-lived hope gave way to palpable dismay when reports were received of a massacre in the town of Houla on 25 May. One hundred and eight people were executed there, including 32 children. Survivors buried their dead two days later as eye witnesses confirmed that the killings had been initiated by government sponsored militia. They had gone from house to house to find and extinguish their victims. Annan declared that those responsible must be held accountable and he urged the Syrian government to take bold steps to signal that it was serious in its intention to resolve the crisis peacefully. President al-Assad, however, did nothing. He did not remove his tanks and heavy weapons from populated areas and his

59 See Mr Churkin (Russian Federation), UNSC (2012e).
60 UN General Assembly (2012).
61 UNSC (2012f).
62 UNSC (2012g).
63 UNSC (2012d).

forces continued to shell towns, fire at protesters and arrest opposition activists in their thousands.[64] He blamed the Houla massacre on 'armed terrorists'.[65] In parallel, Russia stepped up its arms sales to the regime, while Saudi Arabia and Qatar began providing weaponry to the opposition.[66] The Annan plan was already in deep trouble but remained the only diplomatic initiative on the table. On 15 July, the International Committee of the Red Cross declared that Syria was in a state of civil war.

That same day, another massacre followed in Tremseh. Between 100 and 200 people were killed in the town, the deaths arising from sustained shelling and the deployment of tanks and helicopters after which house to house searches and executions were carried out by loyalist militia.[67] UN Secretary-General, Ban Ki-moon, remarked that the attacks cast serious doubts on the Assad regime's commitment to the Annan peace plan and he warned members of the Security Council that, failing more concerted and unified action, its stalemate could provide a licence for further massacres. A Syrian foreign ministry spokesperson asserted that there had been no massacre but what had occurred was a response by regular military forces against heavily armed groups that did not want a political solution.[68] Mr Annan expressed his shock and alarm. In a letter to the President of the Security Council, Annan wrote that 'Tragically, we now have another grim reminder that the Council's resolutions continue to be flouted … I recommended that the Council should insist on implementation of its decisions and send a message to all that there will be consequences for non-compliance. This is imperative and could not be more urgent in light of unfolding events'. Because the situation was deteriorating rapidly, the UN Monitors were withdrawn from Syria in fear that they might be targeted by either side. The scale and intensity of the fighting between government and rebel forces in Damascus and Aleppo, the two largest cities in Syria, escalated dramatically.[69] Violence crept closer to the heart of the regime.

Then a bomb exploded at national security headquarters in Damascus, killing three of the country's leading military figures, the Defence minister, the Deputy Chief of the army and President Assad's brother-in law. The regime responded by shelling neighbourhoods in the city known to be supportive of the opposition. The Free Syrian Army expressed the fear that the regime's militia, the *shabbiha*, may be sent in to areas of the city to commit massacres similar to those in Houla and Tremseh. The bombing, emboldened the rebels and gave them unprecedented momentum. New evidence was emerging, however, that the rebel forces were committing atrocities of their own.

64 Syrian arrests are said to have snared thousands (2012).
65 Assad denies regime role in massacre (2012).
66 Arming of Syrian rebels gains momentum (2012).
67 Tremseh reports pile pressure on UN (2012).
68 Syria says UN wrong about Tremseh clashes (2012).
69 Syrian fighting rages in Damascus (2012).

The Russian foreign minister, Sergei Lavrov acknowledged that a decisive battle had commenced in Syria but said that to support the opposition was a 'dead end policy ... Assad will not go on his own and our Western partners have no idea what to do about that'. In response to the revelation that Western powers were in the process of drafting a new Security Council resolution, the Russian deputy foreign minister declared that: 'if our western partners could explain how they intend to use the reference to Chapter VII (of the UN Charter) against those who undertake terrorist attacks, we would be grateful to clear that up'. The Annan plan, together with several thousand more Syrians, had died.

Meeting urgently one day later, on 19 July 2012 the Security Council debated a third draft resolution on Syria proposed by France, Germany, Portugal, UK and the USA.[70] The resolution expressed grave concern at the escalation of violence in Syria and called upon all the parties to commit immediately to the six-point plan. It reiterated the prior demands made of the Syrian authorities to cease all troop movements towards population centres, end the use of heavy weapons near such centres and withdraw its troops to their barracks. It demanded that all parties commence work, together with the Joint Envoy, to implement a new transition plan that had been proposed by the Action Group on Syria three weeks earlier.[71] Finally, the draft resolution determined that if Syrian authorities had not fully complied with these demands within ten days, the Council would immediately impose measures under Article 41 of the UN Charter. In a concession to the Russian and Chinese side, the resolution did not go further to foreshadow Article 42 military intervention. Eleven members of the Council voted in favour, Pakistan and South Africa abstained, and Russia and China once again exercised their veto.

Mr Araud, the Permanent Representative of France, summarised the situation from the Western perspective:

> I had hoped not to have to go through this ghastly list. By 4 October 2011, repression in Syria had already claimed 3000 lives and Russia and China had vetoed the Council's actions for the first time. By 4 February, 6000 Syrians had been cut down by the regime, and Russia and China exercised their second veto on the Council's action. Today, 19 July, we now count 17,000 men, women and children dead. We mourn their memory alongside the Syrian people, and Russia and China have just exercised their veto for the third time.[72]

The Russian response was blunt. Mr Churkin said that:

> ... the Western members of the Council, which today made unacceptable statements, could have done something, anything, to promote dialogue between the Syrian parties and prevent the further militarisation of the conflict, rather

70 UNSC (2012h).
71 Action Group. on Syria (2012).
72 UNSC (2012i).

> than fan the flames of extremists, including terrorist groups. These Pharisees have been pushing their own geopolitical intentions, which have nothing in common with the legitimate interests of the Syrian people ... The draft voted on was biased. The threat of sanctions was levelled exclusively at the Government of Syria ... (that) does not reflect the realities of the country today.[73]

The Security Council's paralysis was complete.

Kofi Annan resigned from his post on 2 August. In a departing article for the *Financial Times*, Mr Annan summarised the diplomatic situation:

> Military means alone will not end this crisis. Similarly, a political agenda that is neither inclusive nor comprehensive will fail. The distribution of force and the divisions in Syrian society are such that only a serious negotiated transition can hope to end the repressive rule of the past and avoid a future descent into vengeful sectarian war. For a challenge as great as this, only a united international community can compel both sides to engage in a peaceful political transition. But a political process is difficult, if not impossible, while all sides – within a without Syria – see an opportunity to advance their narrow agendas by military means. International division means support for proxy agendas and the fuelling of violent competition on the ground.[74]

Annan urged the US, the UK, France Turkey, Saudi Arabia and Qatar to press the opposition to enter negotiations with the government in order to avoid a chaotic collapse. At the same time, he demanded that Russia and China should engage in concerted diplomatic activity to persuade the government to change course and embrace a planned, political transition. It was clear, he declared, that for such negotiations to take place, President al-Assad had to stand aside. In the wake of Annan's resignation, the General Assembly passed a resolution deploring the Security Council's failure to act on Syria. The Assembly expressed its support for a Syrian led political transition. More by way of aspiration than reality, it demanded the establishment of a consensus transitional governing body, a review of the Constitution on the basis of an inclusive national dialogue, and free and fair elections held within the framework of the new constitutional order.[75]

Finally, on 16 August, the long awaited report of the independent international commission of inquiry on the Syrian Arab republic was tabled before the UN Human Rights Council.[76] The Commission determined that government forces and the *shabbiha* had committed crimes against humanity, war crimes and violations of international human rights law and international humanitarian law. It also found that anti-Government armed groups had committed war crimes and

---

73 UNSC (2012i).

74 Annan (2012).

75 UN General Assembly (2012).

76 UN Human Rights Council (2012).

abuses of international law. Both parties had violated the rights of children. It concluded that the large-scale operations in which the most serious violations had been committed had been conducted with the knowledge and upon the order of the highest levels of government. Ultimate responsibility therefore rested with those in government who planned and implemented the acts and those who had failed to prevent or punish the perpetrators.

The preconditions for a Pillar 3 responsibility to protect intervention had clearly been fulfilled. Despite this, no intervention to protect the innocent Syrian civilians still caught up in the reciprocal criminal actions of the Government and opposition was anywhere in prospect.

III Libya/Syria

The preceding account of the Libyan and Syrian rebellions and repressions suggests many different reasons why the Security Council may have chosen to act differently in response to the two crises. Plainly the two situations were not the same and differences of approach might quite reasonably have been expected. Yet the political arguments presented by the principal Council antagonists go only partly to explain why rapid international military intervention was endorsed in Libya while paralysis as to approach found the Council in complete stalemate over Syria. Beneath the surface, powerful and competing interests of principle and strategy were at play.

Principle

A key principle at stake in Security Council negotiations and debates was that of respect for the sovereignty, territorial integrity, and independence of nations. This principle, and its related commitment to non-intervention in the domestic affairs of states, stands in stark contrast to the interventionist character of Pillar 3, R2P interventions by the international community. The tension between the two may be reconciled legally when R2P interventions are endorsed by the Security Council acting in accordance with Chapter VII of the UN Charter. At the Council, however, it can always be expected that arguments concerning the relative weight to be given to the preservation of state sovereignty, and the desirability of ending governmental atrocity, will play a critical role in determining what action, if any, the Council will endorse.

Both Security Council resolutions 1970 and 1973 in relation to Libya reflected the desire of the Council to balance the two considerations appropriately. Resolution 1970 sought an intervention in the Libyan crisis only indirectly, through the imposition of an arms embargo, asset freeze, travel ban and referral of the leadership to the Prosecutor of the International Criminal Court. In the first instance, therefore, external intervention constituting direct interference with national sovereignty was eschewed. As the situation deteriorated, however, the Council was forced to consider more forceful intervention to stop violence against

Libyan citizens. The no-fly zone was set in place and the Council endorsed 'all necessary measures' to protect civilian populated areas under attack. Despite the resolution having been adopted, dissent was plainly in evidence. The Permanent Representative of India remarked that:

> The Council has today adopted a resolution that authorizes far-reaching measures under Chapter VII of the United Nations Charter, with relatively little credible information on the situation on the ground in Libya. We also do not have clarity about details of enforcement measures, including who will participate, and with what assets, and how these measures will exactly be carried out. It is of course very important that there be full respect for the sovereignty, unity and territorial integrity of Libya.[77]

In this debate, the strength of feeling on the Council in favour of intervention to protect Libyan civilians outweighed the profound reservations of members who remained committed to the principle of non-intervention in Libya's sovereign affairs. The gravity of the situation was sufficiently severe to persuade potential veto-wielders to abstain rather than oppose the resolution.

In contrast, by the time the Council addressed the Syrian crisis for the first time in August 2011, sentiment amongst potential opponents had substantially altered. This was primarily because in Libya NATO had pushed the boundaries of resolution 1973 far beyond its primary objective. This had been to protect the civilian population from attacks by government forces.[78] China, Russia and the IBSA countries could swallow that objective. But committed as firmly as they were to the sovereignty principle, they could not abide a transformation to regime change.[79]

Thus, despite the fact that many thousands of deaths had already been recorded in Syria, China and Russia twice vetoed a draft resolution that would have imposed UN sanctions. The two countries, together with influential abstainers such as India, were not willing to countenance support for a resolution that they believed may once again be altered illegitimately to embrace the overthrow of the Al-Assad government. They argued instead that the government should stay in place and intense diplomatic pressure should be exerted to bring the warring parties to the negotiating table.

The Libyan experience revealed another in-principle point of departure. At the time at which resolution 1973 was adopted, it was generally assumed that the protection of civilians in Libya would situate NATO forces in a position of relative neutrality as between the warring parties. The stated objective was to ensure.[80] They took sides with the rebels against the regime. The adoption of this position could well be understood if and when a strategic military decision had

77 See Mr Hardeep Singh Puri (India), UNSC (2011g).

78 Evans (2012b).

79 Permanent Mission of Brazil to the United Nations (2011), Annex 1 [10]; Bellamy (2011b).

80 Welsh (2011), p. 258.

been taken that the only way to secure the Libyan population was by the removal of the Gaddafi government and the dismantling of its forces. Whether that point had been reached at the time NATO sided with the opposition, however, remains an open question. Russia and China clearly did not believe that it had been.

The debates on Syria at the Security Council disclosed another neglected issue of principle relevant to its approach to R2P intervention. The Council was seemingly bereft of reasoned criteria on the basis of which to judge the appropriateness and form of a Pillar 3 intervention.[81] Adherence to sovereignty was on one side. Prevention of atrocity was on the other. Nothing but circumstance was left in between. Crises, seemingly, would be judged case by case, political configuration by political configuration. It would be preferable if consistent criteria could be applied across cases, criteria that placed the necessity to protect citizens from genocide and crimes against humanity at their core. One senior diplomat put the matter to me like this:

> How are we to judge the level of massacre required before the Council intervenes? When do we cross the mental Rubicon – at the point at which the number dead in Syria exceeds those tens of thousands killed by Al-Assad's father? We have to do better than that. We have to give much more thought to how to determine the ethics and justification for intervention or non-intervention.[82]

The Council's adoption of such criteria was recommended by the ICISS and High-Level Panel reports as they elaborated R2P. The proposal should be put back on the table.[83]

Strategy

Next, it is clear that strategic concerns played an enormously important part in shaping the Libyan and Syrian Security Council debates. A fundamental question that Council members must address is whether or not a direct intervention of the kind undertaken in Libya and contemplated in Syria is likely to achieve its protective objective without causing more harm to the civilian population than might otherwise have occurred. The likely answer to that question will have been 'yes' in the Libyan case and 'no' in the Syrian.

Strategically and militarily, the Libyan regime was in a considerably weaker position than its Syrian counterpart. It had relatively few military resources; its army was divided, thus opening up the prospect of large-scale defections. Gaddafi himself was haemorrhaging political support and opposition forces had already made significant gains particularly in the east. Because the regime was effectively isolated, there was no likelihood that neighbouring states would enter the fray to

81 Evans (2012b), p. 9.

82 Personal Interview (New York) (2011); Pattison (2011), p. 273.

83 ICISS (2011); UN High-Level Panel on Threats Challenges and Change HLP. (2004).

defend an erratic and discredited dictatorship. Nor was it likely that the Libyan conflict would destabilise the immediate North African region.

None of these favourable conditions existed in Syria. It has substantial military resources; its military command and security intelligence services were relatively cohesive and loyal to the government; the President still retained the confidence of a substantial proportion of the population, particularly in Damascus and Aleppo. Recruits from Palestine, Lebanon and Iraq bolstered government forces. A steady flow of weapons arrived from Russia and Iran.

At the same time, the Syrian rebellion had substantially strengthened. The opposition counted many thousands of fighters amongst its number. Rebel forces crystallised into provincial commands. Swathes of the west and north-west became no-go areas for regime combatants. Homs and Hama remained hostile to Assad. Al-Qaeda and other assorted jihadist militia began to fight on the opposition side. The rebels launched wave after wave of attacks upon suburban areas of Aleppo. Government troops and *shabbiha* militia responded in kind with aerial bombing, shelling and indiscriminate killing. Atrocities were being committed on all sides.[84]

August 2012 was the bloodiest month of the conflict to date. As many as 4000 people may have died, 3000 of them civilians and rebels. The death toll has reached almost 250 a day. The conflict had been transformed into a sectarian civil war, with a Sunni led rebel movement pitted against the Alawite/Shia establishment. This was savage territory upon which, for good reason, no Western alliance was keen to tread.

Additionally and crucially, external military intervention on Libyan lines could have had severe, adverse effects on the stability of the entire Middle East. That likely consequence arose principally from Syria's geographical position, bordering five other nations almost all of which are volatile. Western intervention would be likely to incite Hezbollah in Lebanon, many of whose members might cross the border to fight. It could inflame sectarian tensions in Lebanon itself, risking the downfall of the already very fragile Lebanese government.

Syria's relations with Turkey worsened as a result of huge cross-border refugee flows from Syria's north. Ankara's relations with Damascus would plunge further should it be seen, as is likely, to engage in direct action against Syria through the imposition of sanctions. Meanwhile the Syrian government stirred trouble amongst its northern border Kurds who, together with the PKK in Turkey, were bent on independence from Ankara. The aim appeared to be to distract and deter Turkish authorities from facilitating incursions into Syrian territory for the purpose of creating safe-havens for refugees and an associated no-fly zone.

Syria is home to more than a million Iraqi refugees. An internationalisation of the fighting in Syria would complicate the refugee situation substantially with Iraqi refugees trapped between a conflict in Syria and the possibility of persecution upon return to Iraq. A rebel victory in Syria could embolden Iraq's Sunni minority and exacerbate tensions with Iraq's Shia majority. An increase in refugee flows from Syria to Jordan would similarly worsen relations between the two. Jordan is already home to

84 Glass (2012).

almost three million Palestinian and Iraqi refugees and was stretched by the arrival of more than 200,000 Syrians. This has the potential to create further political instability in Jordan, whose ruling, royal family is widely criticised and increasingly unpopular.[85]

Should there be a Western led military intervention, the probability that Iran may engage, whether indirectly through its Lebanese and Palestinian allies, or directly would be high. Iran has much at stake in Syria. Should the Assad government fall, the Iranians will have lost their principal ally in the Middle East Its likely replacement by a Sunni-led government would mean that the country could move closer to Tehran's Arab adversaries in the Gulf. It would also endanger the power of Hezbollah, Iran's most valuable regional asset.

The risk was, therefore, that the Syrian conflict could metamorphose into a highly dangerous proxy war on Syrian soil between Iran and its principal regional antagonists, Saudi Arabia, Qatar and Turkey. The two sides were already heavily involved in he Syrian uprising, principally through their extensive provision of intelligence, weaponry, funding and medical supplies to government and rebel forces respectively. It was in no nation's interest to exacerbate their antagonism.

Then there is Israel. The Golan Heights remained contested as between Israel and Syria and resentments between the two run deep arising from-long term competition for influence in Lebanon. Should a Western led intervention be perceived within Syria as providing a strategic advantage to Israel, strikes by Syrian forces against Israeli positions in the Golan Heights would be a distinct possibility. Israel, meanwhile, had become extremely concerned about Syria's arsenal of chemical weapons, particularly since Al-Qaeda and other extremist militants joined the war against President al-Assad.

A Western-led military intervention, therefore, could have had adverse effects upon many countries and governments in the Middle East in a way that was not, and was never likely to be replicated in the Libyan situation. Intervention there was an altogether less perilous enterprise.

Finally, the self-interest of nations has also played its part in discouraging Security Council endorsed intervention in Syria. No member of the Council on either side of the debate neglected its strategic interests entirely in order to assume a purely humanitarian stance. This is not the way the game of international politics is played. To state the obvious, the closer a Security Council member's ties with the Al-Assad regime have been, the less likely it was that that the state would favour an external intervention into the country's domestic affairs. The clearest example in this instance was Russia, although it is somewhat unfair to pick it out above some others.

Russia had been the principal opponent of any direct international action against Syria. Most often its arguments against an R2P intervention were delivered at the level of principle. It is not difficult, however, to discern the country's significant political, economic and strategic investment in Syria. It is a heavy investment that would not be yielded lightly.[86]

85 Pelham (2011b).

86 Barry (2012), p. 8.

Syria is a major purchaser of exports of Russian arms and defence equipment. The Syrian market is worth 6 per cent of the overall arms export industry. Future contracts for the sale of fighter jets and advanced missiles have been estimated to be worth some $US 4 billion. Syria hosts a strategically positioned Russian naval base at Tartus on the west coast, its only one outside the former Soviet Union. This facility provides it with the capacity to maintain and repair Russian ships that cross the Mediterranean. Russia intends to upgrade the base for its nuclear-armed warships. It has continued to send weapons to Syria throughout the period of the recent crisis. It has major economic investments in Syria, principally in the business of natural gas extraction. These include a pipeline and a liquefied natural gas processing facility 200 kilometres east of Homs. It is unsurprising given these important connections that the Russians did not wish to see them disturbed by the replacement of the Al-Assad regime. Its veto at the Security Council provided it with political power it needs to forestall any such possibility. A senior UN diplomat expressed the matter in this way:

> The question we ask in dealing with Russia is whether a matter is a Medvedev issue or a Putin issue. Syria is a Putin issue. It has, therefore, to be approached with considerable caution.[87]

Russia's, of course, is not the only national self-interest at play. The USA's substantial economic, political and strategic interests in Israel provide the most obvious counter-instance. It is clearly in the USA's interests to ensure the stability and viability of the Israeli state and take such actions as may be opportune to alter the political configuration of the region so as best to ensure that that objective is achieved. The removal of the Al-Assad regime would play into that agenda. The fall of Al-Assad would also constitute a huge setback for Iranian influence in the region and also remove a significant barrier to more concerted attempts by Israel and the USA to deprive Iran of nuclear capability.[88]

The underlying point is the same. In the Middle East, Syria is of enormous strategic significance. Libya was not. The way was clearer and surer, then, for steps to be taken by the West to displace Gaddafi in a way that would be far more fraught and dangerous in the case of Al-Assad.[89] 'Syria is a complex and diverse society in which outside 'do-gooders' risk destroying all they claim to support'.[90]

The Responsibility to Protect after Syria

The Security Council's paralysis with respect to Syria has clouded R2P's future considerably. This is not to say that R2P interventions will not occur. They may

87 Personal Interview (New York) (2011).
88 See Welsh (2011).
89 Shanahan (2011).
90 Glass (2011).

do. It is to say, however, that that the doctrine's implementation, particularly when coercive interventions are in contemplation, is likely to be more selective and circumstantially founded than might have been thought in the wake of the Libyan action. Judgments as to whether and when to intervene are likely in the foreseeable future to be made case by case rather than in accordance with sequential steps and pre-determined prudential criteria.

That having been, some useful generalisations about the nature and standing of R2P in Syria's wake can be made. Following from the encapsulation of R2P's standing after Libya proposed earlier, I suggest that the following propositions may be reasonably be advanced in relation to future Pillar 3 interventions.[91]

- Prior to approving a coercive Pillar 3 intervention, in the interests of national sovereignty and independence the Security Council will need to be satisfied that every possible diplomatic solution to a crisis has been exhausted. Pillar 3 intervention will occur only as the last resort.
- Prior to approving a coercive Pillar 3 intervention, the Security Council is likely in future to insist that its objectives be made clear and that its mandate be spelt out with precision.
- It is highly unlikely that the Security Council will approve a Pillar 3 intervention if its explicit or implicit objective is regime change.
- Given that a Security Council mandate for a Pillar 3 intervention is likely to have as its principal objective the protection of civilians, it is probable that the Security Council will require that the position of an intervening force be one of strict neutrality as between the contending parties.
- Before approving a Pillar 3 intervention, the Security Council will clearly need to be clearly satisfied first, that the intervention is likely to achieve its protective objective within the country concerned and, secondly, that it will not result in any wider regional destabilisation.
- A Pillar 3 intervention should, in all aspects, conform to the dictates of international law and in particular international humanitarian law.
- Where a contemplated coercive intervention runs contrary to the core political or strategic interests of a member of the P-5, it highly unlikely to proceed. This is unless the crimes against humanity committed are so extensive and so grave that no reasoned member could resist the demand that the crimes be fought. Even so, the failure of Russia and China to endorse even a very weak Security Council resolution against Syria in the face of clear evidence of the commission of mass atrocities has dispiritingly cast doubt even on that seemingly obvious proposition.
- However inadequate, engagement in Pillar 3 intervention that excludes action pursuant to Chapter VII of the UN Charter may still be preferable

91 By way of comparison see a comparable list of propositions set forth by the Permanent Mission of Brazil to the United Nations at: Permanent Mission of Brazil to the United Nations (2011). See also the perceptive discussion in Evans (2012a).

to provoking Security Council gridlock. This is because, as in Syria, the outcome of gridlock may be seen by antagonists to a conflict as an international licence for the commission of further crime.

- Alternatively, in response to mass atrocities, coalitions of the willing may decide to take action outside the legal framework of the UN Charter. Should this become common, R2P may wither to the great detriment of the international rule of law.

The Libyan and Syrian cases provided the international community with substantial challenges. However optimistic some may have been about R2P heralding a new dawn in international affairs in which crimes against humanity might be stilled, these conflicts demonstrated clearly and inevitably that the politics of international intervention would be far messier and contentious than the doctrine's founders may have hoped and intended.

The exercise has not been wasted. R2P will play its role in the resolution of forthcoming conflicts in far away places. The closer hostilities come to affecting the interests of major global powers, however, the more complex will questions relating to coercive intervention become. This is the reality. The ideal, as ever, remains impossibly elusive.

References

Action Group on Syria (2012) *Final Communique*, 30 June 2012.

A. Bellamy (2011a) 'Libya and the Responsibility to Protect: The Exception and the Norm' 25 *Ethics and International Affairs* 263.

A. Bellamy (2011b) *The Responsibility to Protect and the Problem of Regime Change*, The Responsibility to Protect: Challenges and Opportunities Following the Libyan Intervention e-International Relations available at http://www.e-ir.info/wp-content/uploads/R2P.pdf (accessed 15 July 2013).

A. Fordham (2011) 'Arab League Team Goes to Syria' *The Washington Post* 23 December 2011, A12.

'Arming of Syrian rebels gains momentum' (2012) *Financial Times* 8 June 2012.

'Assad denies regime role in massacre' (2012) *Financial Times* 3 June 2012.

B. Mroue (2011) 'Syrian President Orders Release of Some Protesters: Cabinet is Named' *The Washington Post* 15 April 2011, A13.

B. Gwertzman (2011) *Will Syria Follow Libya?*, Council on Foreign Relations available at http://www.cfr.org/syria-follow-libya/p25745 (accessed 18 July 2012).

J.F. Burns (2011a) 'Qaddafi and Zuma Meet But Reach No Agreement' *New York Times* 31 May 2011.

J.F. Burns (2011b) 'NATO Resumes Air Strikes After Qaddafi Vows to Fight On' *New York Times* 1 June 2011.

C. Glass (2011) 'Leave Syria to the Syrians' *Taki's Magazine* 2 May 2011.

C. Glass (2012) 'Aleppo betrayed by attacks that are foreign to its nature' *The National* 13 February 2012.

C.J. Chivers and D.D. Kirkpatrick (2011) 'Libyan Rebels Complain of Deadly Delays Under NATO's Command' *New York Times* 5 April 2011.

E. Barry (2012) 'As Nations Line Up against Syrian Government, Russia Sides Firmly with Assad' *The New York Times* 28 January 2012.

'Europeans on UN council offer Syria resolution' (2011) *Agence France Presse* 26 May 2011.

F. Deng and E. Luck (2011) 'Special Advisers of the United Nations Secretary-General on the Prevention of Genocide, Francis Deng, and on the Responsibility to Protect, Edward Luck, on the situation in Syria' *Press Release* 21 July 2011.

G. Evans (2011) *End of the Argument*, Foreign Policyavailable at http://www.foreignpolicy.com/articles/2011/11/28/gareth_evans_end_of_the_argument (accessed 15 July 2013).

G. Evans (2012a) *R2P and RWP after Libya and Syria*, The Responsibility while Protecting: What Next? Global Centre for the Responsibility to Protect and the Stanley Foundation.

G. Evans (2012b) 'Disquiet Over Libyan 'Win' Syria's Loss' *The Australian* 31 January 2012, 9.

ICISS (2011) *Report of the International Commission on Intervention and State Sovereignty*, IDRC.

K. Ali (2011) 'Woman and child among up to 26 bodies 'found in mass graves' outside city' *The Independent (London)* 18 May 2011, 24-25.

K. Annan (2012) 'My departing advice on how to save Syria' *Financial Times* 2 August 2012.

L. Stack (2011) 'In Syria, An Attempt To Placate Protesters' *The New York Times* 17 April 2011, 10.

'Libya Bitten, Syria Shy' (2012) *The Economist* 31 January 2012.

'Muammar Gaddafi son killed by NATO air strike – Libyan government' (2011) *The Guardian (United Kingdom)* 1 May 2011.

NATO (2011) *Statement on Libya*, Press Release, 8 June 2011.

N. Blanford (2011) 'Repeal of Hated Emergency Law is 'To Little To Late'' *The Times (London)* 22 April 2011, 21.

R. Nordland (2011) 'Many Libyan Rebels, Blaming NATO, Flee City in the East' *New York Times* 18 April 2011.

Office of the High Commissioner for Human Rights (2011) 'Syria: Pillay calls for urgent action to halt violence' *Press Release* 12 December 2011.

Organisation of Islamic Conference (2011) *OIC General Secretariat Condemns Strongly the Excessive Use of Force against Civilians in the Libyan Jamahiriya*, (Press release, 22 Feb 2011).

J. Pattison (2011) 'The Ethics of Humanitarian Intervention in Libya' 25 *Ethics and International Affairs* 271.

N. Pelham (2011a) 'The Libyan Deadlock' *The New York Review of Books* 12-25 May.

N. Pelham (2011b) 'Jordan Starts to Shake' *The New York Review of Books* 8 December 2011.

Permanent Mission of Brazil to the United Nations (2011) *Letter dated 9 November 2011 from the Permanent Representative of Brazil to the United Nations addressed to the Secretary-General*, UN Doc A/66/551-S/2011/701 (11 November 2011), Annex 1 [10].

Personal Interview (New York), (2011).

R. Thakur (2011) *R2P, Libya and International Poitics as the Struggle for Competing Normative Architectures*, The Responsibility to Protect: Challenges and Opportunities Following the Libyan Intervention e-International Relations available at http://www.e-ir.info/wp-content/uploads/R2P.pdf (accessed 15 July 2013).

R. Shanahan (2011) *R2P; Seeking Perfection in an Imperfect World*, The Responsibility to Protect: Challenges and Opportunities Following the Libyan Intervention e-International Relations available at http://www.e-ir.info/wp-content/uploads/R2P.pdf (accessed 15 July 2013).

'Syria says UN wrong about Tremseh clashes' (2012) *Financial Times* 15 July 2012.

'Syria: a Soviet hangover turned headache' (2012) *The Guardian, (London)* 1 February 2012.

'Syrian arrests are said to have snared thousands' (2012) *The New York Times* 27 June 2012.

'Syrian fighting rages in Damascus' (2012) *Financial Times* 16 July 2012.

T.S. Eliot (1925) *The Hollow Men* available at http://poetry.poetryx.com/poems/784/ (accessed 16 July 2013).

'Tremseh reports pile pressure on UN' (2012) *Financial Times* 16 July 2012.

UN draft resolution on Syria, (2012) The Guardian available at http://www.guardian.co.uk/world/2012/jan/31/un-security-council-draft-resolution-syria (accessed 15 July 2013).

UN General Assembly (2012) *Resolution adopted by the General Assembly [without reference to a Main Committee (A/66/L.36 and Add.1) The situation in the Syrian Arab Republic* A/RES/66/253 (15 February 2012).

UN High-Level Panel on Threats Challenges and Change HLP (2004) *A more secure world: Our shared responsibility*, UN Doc A/59/565 (2 December 2004).

UN Human Rights Council (2011a) *Res. S-15/1*, Doc A/HRC/RES/S-15/1 (25 February 2011).

UN Human Rights Council (2011b) *Report of the Human Rights Council on its fifteenth special session*, UN Doc A/HRC/S-15/1 (25 February 2011).

UN Human Rights Council (2011c) *Report of the Human Rights Council on its fifteenth special session*, A/HRC/S-15/1 (25 February 2011).

UN Human Rights Council (2011d) *Report of the independent international commission of inquiry on the Syrian Arab Republic*, UN Doc A/HRC/S-17/2/Add.1 (23 November 2011).

UN Human Rights Council (2012) *Report of the Independent International Commission of Inquiry on the Syrian Arab Republic*, UN General Assembly A/HRC/21/50, 16 August 2012.

United Nations Department of Public Information (2011) *Security Council Fails to Adopt Draft resolution Condemning Syria's Crackdown on Anti-Government Protestors, Owing to Veto by Russian Federation, China*, SC/10403, 4 October 2011.

UNSC (2006) *Res. 1674 (Protection of civilians in armed conflict)*, United Nations S/RES/1674 (28 April 2006).

UNSC (2009) *Res. 1894 (Protection of civilians in armed conflict)*, United Nations S/RES/1894 (11 November 2009).

UNSC (2011a) *Res. 1970 (Peace and security in Africa)*, United Nations S/RES/1970 (26 February 2011).

UNSC (2011b) *Res. 1973 (Libya)*, United Nations S/RES/1973 (17 March 2011).

UNSC (2011c) *Res. 1975 (Côte d'Ivoire)*, United Nations S/RES/1975 (30 March 2011).

UNSC (2011d) *Security Council Press Statement on Libya*, SC10180 (22 Feb 2011).

UNSC (2011e) *6528th Meeting*, UN Doc S/PV.6528 (4 May 2011).

UNSC (2011f) *Res. 2009 (Libya)*, United Nations UN Doc S/RES/2009 (16 September 2011).

UNSC (2011g) *6498th Meeting*, UN Doc S/PV.6498 (17 March 2011).

UNSC (2011h) *6566th Meeting*, S/PV. 6566 (27 June 2011).

UNSC (2011i) *6524th Meeting*, UN Doc S/PV. 6524 (27 April 2011).

UNSC (2011j) *Security Council Draft Resolution* UN Doc. S/2011/612 (4 October 2011).

UNSC (2011k) *6627th Meeting*, UN Doc S/PV.6627 (4 October 2011).

UNSC (2012a) *Res. 2040 (Libya)*, United Nations S/RES/2040 (12 March 2012).

UNSC (2012b) *Res. 2085*, United Nations S/RES/2085 (19 December 2012).

UNSC (2012c) *Security Council Draft Resolution*, UN Doc. S/2012/77 (4 February 2012).

UNSC (2012d) *Res. 2043 (Syria)*, United Nations SC Res. 2043 (20 April 2012).

UNSC (2012e) *6711th Meeting*, UN Doc S/PV.6711 (4 February 2012)

UNSC (2012f) *Statement by the President of the Council*, S/PRST/2012/6 (March 21 2012).

UNSC (2012g) *Resolution 2042 Adopted by the Security Council at its 6751st meeting*, S/RES/2042 (14 April 2012).

UNSC (2012h) *Draft Resolution*, S/2012/538 (19 July 2012).

UNSC (2012i) *Mr Araud (Permanent Representative of France) UN Security Council Meeting 6810*, 19 July 2012.

J. Welsh (2011) 'Civilian Protection in Libya: Putting Coercion and Controversy Back into RtoP' 25 *Ethics and International Affairs* 255.

P. Williams (2011) 'Briefing: The Road to Humanitarian War in Libya' 3 *Global Responsibility to Protect* 248.

Chapter 3

R2P + POC (+ IHRL) = R2PC: The United Nations Security Council and the Hybridisation of International Protection Principles

Hugh Breakey

For keen followers of the United Nations (UN) Security Council's ongoing engagement with the *Protection of Civilians in Armed Conflict* (POC), a subtle but intriguing occurrence unfolded in the Council's November 2011 open debate.[1] Ten of the 15 Council members invoked the claim – referred to as *R2PC* – that it is *the primary responsibility of the state to protect its civilians*. Also, of the five Member-States who did not assert R2PC in the November debate, three had recently asserted it in previous debates. Council members – and Council resolutions – often affirm that states have the primary responsibility for protecting their populations, or citizens, or individuals, or those within their territory or for ensuring the security or human rights of these groups. Why then should the increasing substitution of these catch-all terms with the term 'civilians' be worthy of remark, or portend anything more than a perhaps clumsy conflation of the Council's POC and *Responsibility to Protect* (R2P) agendas? It is clear that the secretary-general of the UN is concerned by exactly such a possibility; in his most recent report on POC, he sharply censures 'the continuing and unaccurate conflation' of the two concepts. In response (inter alia) to the secretary-general's censure, the most recent open debate – in July 2012 – saw a marked decline in assertions of R2PC.

This chapter develops the view that, when Council members speak of R2PC, they have in mind an inventive amalgamation of several different normative structures of international protection. It suggests, *pace* the secretary-general, that we should be cautious about assuming that countries amalgamating POC and R2P are guilty of inaccurate conflations. In its final section, the chapter reflects on R2PC as one instance of a broader aspect of international legal and political discourse – the increasing use of the concept of 'civilian' outside armed conflict *sensu stricto*.

1 UNSC (2011e). Meeting of Civilians in Armed Conflict, S/PV 6650 (9 November 2011).

Why is R2PC Important?

R2PC may seem a natural expression, but this section will explain why the phrase is important.

When Council members affirm R2PC, they are not simply rehearsing a precept of international humanitarian law (IHL) – centrally, the Geneva Conventions of 1949 and the Additional Protocols of 1977. IHL is intimately related to POC, and since states are the only signatories to IHL treaties, they are the first-instance duty-bearers of IHL's duties. Hence, in this context, it is correct to say that states have primary responsibility for POC.[2] However, R2PC is not merely rehearsing this truism of IHL, for two reasons. First, R2PC connotes that states have a special responsibility to protect *their* civilians. This is not a fundamental tenet of IHL; rather, it is international human rights law (IHRL) that makes central the state's special relation to its own population. IHL is primarily concerned with laying out, in the context of armed conflict, one state's obligations to *another state's* civilians – typically the civilians of an enemy or occupied state. Certainly, many parts of IHL protect local populations; for example, the restrictions on the placement of military objects, the constraints on the use of human shields, and the core requirements of Common Articles 1 and 3. But these duties apply equally to all parties to the conflict who hold territory; states have no especial responsibility to their own population. To the contrary, even in cases where IHL does grant protection to a state's own citizens, their protection rarely amounts to the wide scope and substance of the legal protection the Conventions afford to 'protected persons'; that is, the nationals of the *enemy* state.[3]

The second reason R2PC is not recapitulating IHL is that, as will be described below, R2PC is taken to apply *outside* as well as *inside* situations of armed conflict (as defined by IHL); hence, the responsibility invoked goes beyond the confines of IHL. As such, to say that a state has a primary responsibility to protect its civilians goes further than a simple acknowledgement of the legal requirements of IHL.

Turning to human rights law, R2PC is not a perspicuous way of expressing the central theme of IHRL. Most obviously, IHRL does not make the fundamental distinction between combatant and civilian (that is, between the armed and the unarmed), that shapes and defines IHL.[4] Rather, IHRL speaks of human beings, individuals and peoples; it explicitly applies to everyone, just by dint of their being human. It is not difficult to express this point of difference between IHRL (applying to *states* protecting *their citizens*) and IHL (applying to *parties to an armed conflict* being prohibited from harming *all civilians*). Numerous Council

---

2 Office of the High Commissioner for Human Rights OHCHR (2011), pp. 21 and 72. Indeed, this is the case even for non-treaty-based customary IHL. How exactly IHL (especially Com. Art. 3 and Add. Protocol II) applies to non-state actors in civil wars, presuming that it does, is a subject of some controversy. See Sassòli et al. (2011), paras 12.25 and 12.26.

3 Sassòli et al. (2011), para. 2.32.

4 This is often the first point of distinction made between IHL and IHRL. For example, Office of the High Commissioner for Human Rights OHCHR (2011), pp. 20 and 21.

resolutions avoid R2PC, and correctly separate the distinct demands of each legal regime. For example, the preamble of SC Res. 1888 (2009) sees the Council:[5]

> *Recognising* that states bear the primary responsibility to respect and ensure the human rights of their citizens, as well as all individuals within their territory as provided for by relevant international law.
>
> *Reaffirming* that parties to armed conflict bear the primary responsibility to take all feasible steps to ensure the protection of affected civilians.

Additionally, as was the case with IHL, the scope of R2PC is somewhat removed from the scope of the full applicability of IHRL. As will be seen below, R2PC protects a more limited set of rights than IHRL, but its full application applies across different contexts.

As well as departing from IHL and IHRL, R2PC is not an assertion of R2P. Affirmed by the General Assembly in the World Summit Outcome Document of 2005,[6] and by the Security Council in Resolution 1674 of 2006,[7] R2P sets up a threefold structural assignation of responsibilities to protect populations from atrocity crimes.[8] In the secretary-general's formulation,[9] R2P comprises the following three pillars:

> *Pillar 1*: The primary responsibility of the state to protect its population from atrocity crimes.
>
> *Pillar 2*: The responsibility of the international community to use diplomatic, humanitarian and other peaceful means to assist states in meeting their Pillar 1 responsibilities.
>
> *Pillar 3*: The responsibility of the international community, acting through the authority of the Security Council, in cases where peaceful means are inadequate and national authorities are manifestly failing to protect their population, to take collective action (including military measures, if necessary) to protect the population.

While R2PC parallels certain features of R2P, the latter has a much narrower scope, applying only to the four atrocity crimes of *genocide*, *war crimes*, *ethnic cleansing* and *crimes against humanity*. Such crimes have a *substantiality requirement* that they occur on a massive scale, and involve the deliberate and systematic targeting

---

5 UNSC (2009a).

6 UN General-Assembly (2005).

7 UNSC (2006).

8 The initial concept of R2P was developed in International Commission on Intervention and State Sovereignty ICISS (2001).

9 UN Secretary-General (2009).

of populations.[10] When used in Council open debates, however, R2PC includes myriad much lesser harms to individual civilians, which do not necessarily reach the pitch of atrocity crimes. Reflecting this, R2P refers to crimes against *populations*, whereas R2PC concerns itself with *civilians*.

In summary, then, R2PC is not a mere recapitulation of other international protection regimes such as IHL, IHRL or R2P. As we will see below, however, it draws on features from each of these.

The Evolution of R2PC

Claims by the Council invoking R2PC are in one sense not new. Since the 1990s, such claims (or their close analogues) can be found in Security Council resolutions mandating peacekeeping operations (PKOs) with POC objectives. The first such was Resolution 1270, which established the UN Mission in Sierra Leone (UNAMSIL) in 1999, wherein the Council charged UNAMSIL to protect civilians under imminent threat of physical violence, *taking into account the responsibilities of the Government of Sierra Leone*.[11] Almost all subsequent POC directives to PKOs have contained this qualification regarding the host state, with its clear imputation that the state *does* have the primary responsibility to protect civilians under threat. Nevertheless, nothing in the context in which this principle was asserted implied that a novel international protection principle was being invoked. In such cases, the Council is doing little more than acknowledging the presumptive primacy of the state in internal security arrangements generally. Pragmatically, this qualification serves to assuage somewhat any qualms host states might have about threats to their monopoly on the use of force. More positively, it affirms that best practice should have the PKO facilitating, rather than usurping, any protection responsibilities that are present or developing in the host state.

However, this implicit, and increasingly explicit, invocation of R2PC in peacekeeping contexts is not without significance.[12] As well as familiarising Council members and states with the idea that states have protective responsibilities for

10 Scheffer (2009).

11 UNSC (1999b), para. 14.

12 For example, UNSC (2011c). This resolution expressly affirmed 'the primary responsibility of each State to protect civilians' at 2 (Preamble). This resolution is of particular import because it set the stage for the secretary-general to authorize the use of French helicopters to destroy the heavy weapons of (ex-) President Gbagbo, precipitating de facto regime change. UN Secretary-General (2011). Explicit invocations of R2PC, in the context of peacekeeping, also can be found outside Council resolutions. The General Assembly's *Special Committee on Peacekeeping* (the 'C34 Committee') reports on peacekeeping have, since POC first appeared on its agenda in 2009, regularly included acknowledgements that, 'The Special Committee recognizes that protection of civilians is the primary responsibility of the host country …' For example, Special Committee on Peacekeeping Operations (C34) (2009), para. 127 and 176. See similarly DPKO/DFS (2010), para. 7.

vulnerable civilians, developments in peacekeeping doctrine began to concretise more exactly what POC required for peacekeepers.[13] In this way, this initial invocation of R2PC helped to delineate the principle's scope. Furthermore, something approaching a genuine responsibility has emerged in recent peacekeeping cases. In its 2010 resolution on Chad and the Central American Republic, the Council declared 'the primary responsibility of each State to protect civilians'; it also made the drawdown of its PKO (MINURCAT) contingent on commitments from the relevant governments to protect civilians and, for the first time, to achieve specific benchmarks with this regard to this objective.[14] No longer a toothless genuflection to state security interests, R2PC became, in this context, a genuine task imposed on a sovereign state.

Since 1999, alongside the progression of R2PC in peacekeeping contexts, the Council has developed its more general thematic engagement with POC.[15] In 2005 and 2006, the Council's POC agenda was augmented by the affirmation of R2P,[16] and its concomitant ideas of 'sovereignty as responsibility', and of primary state responsibilities backed up by remedial international responses. However, even in the open debate of 2005 – occurring just after the General Assembly's historic affirmation of R2P – invocations of R2PC were rare, with only one Council member using the phrase.[17] Less than six years later, at the May 2011 debate, seven members spoke of R2PC.[18] By November 2011, most Council members were able to speak the language of R2PC, with the expectation (apparently justified) that all other members accepted the principle: 'The responsibility to protect civilians belongs first, *we all know*, to national governments'.[19] Even in a debate otherwise riven by post-Libya schisms, no member state raised any objection to the R2PC term or the manner of its usage.

What Does R2PC Mean?

Council resolutions and presidential statements notoriously use creative ambiguities to paper over deep-seated disagreements among Council members;

13 Holt et al. (2009). See also DPKO/DFS (2010), para. 7.

14 UNSC (2010a), preamble paras 2 and 3. The subsequent secretary-general report's Section IV was entitled, 'Responsibility of the Government of Chad for the protection of civilians and United Nations and humanitarian organization personnel and assets'.

15 Beginning with: UNSC (1999a). As early as 2001, the Secretary-General's POC report had declared that, 'the primary responsibility for the protection of civilians rests with governments'. UN Secretary-General (2001), paras 7 and 47+. However, the Secretary-General grounded this claim on the guiding principles on humanitarian assistance set out in: UN General-Assembly (1999). Since this resolution only speaks of a state responsibility to take care of the victims of natural disasters (Annex, para. 4), it is unlikely the Secretary-General had anything as specific (see §3 below) as R2PC in mind.

16 See International Commission on Intervention and State Sovereignty ICISS (2001).

17 Tanzania: UNSC (2005), p. 25.

18 UNSC (2011d).

19 Representative of France, UNSC (2011e), p. 19 [emphasis added].

thus, circumspection is always required in the interpretation of such language. However, such ambiguities are less prevalent in Council members' statements in open debates, where sharp disagreement among members is not only possible but is common.

The content of the open debates suggests that Council members in fact have a fairly specific shared understanding of R2PC, viz.:

> Each state has the *primary responsibility* to protect its unarmed citizens from the *types of violence and harm clearly outlawed by IHL*, in *armed conflict broadly construed* (and – all the more – not to themselves perform such acts of violence).

Each italicised phrase here requires explanation and defense. First, 'primary responsibility' comes from both IHRL and R2P. From IHRL comes the *special legal* responsibility the state bears towards each of its citizens, considered one by one as individual bearers of rights. From R2P comes the idea of *primary* state responsibilities, with the implicit connotation that there are back-up international responsibilities.[20] Several Council members linked R2PC with the structural assignation of responsibilities familiar from R2P. For example, Bosnia and Herzegovina asserted:

> Although the primary responsibility for the protection of civilians lies with States and parties to armed conflicts, the United Nations, with its systematic approach to the protection of civilians, must be and is at the helm of the global effort.[21]

The second phrase requiring explanation is, 'the types of violence and harm clearly outlawed by IHL'. While the exact scope of R2PC in terms of outlawed acts is not settled, the phrase 'clearly outlawed by IHL' refers, at a minimum, to the basic standards set down in Common Article 3 of the 1949 Geneva Conventions, and in Article 4 of Additional Protocol II of 1977.[22] On a more expansive interpretation, states may have in mind all the harms prohibited by customary IHL.[23] The major harms involved are summary violence (especially murder, assault and rape) against the unarmed, and the harms that arise through the use of human shields, from forced displacement or from violence that prevents a person having the necessities of life (for example, the destruction of harvests and homes, or the forceful obstruction of humanitarian relief). Concern about such harms and the explicit links drawn between invocations of R2PC and IHL permeate the Council's open debates.[24] These minimum standards of IHL parallel closely the other source

20 Key aspects of this structural assignation of responsibility are also familiar from the nature and functioning of the ICC. Benzing (2008).

21 UNSC (2011e), p. 14. Re other states, see: UNSC (2011e), pp. 19 and 28.

22 ICRC (1949). See also ICRC (1977).

23 Henckaerts and Doswald-Becks (2005).

24 In the November debate, see especially: UNSC (2011e). Refer pp. 11–12, 24–5.

the Council draws upon in its discussion of R2PC – namely, the Council's use of the term in peacekeeping contexts. When the Council asserts that states have a responsibility to protect civilians, they have in mind much the same task they impose, within their means and areas of operation, upon PKOs. Again, several states linked their assertions of R2PC with POC in a peacekeeping context. For example, the United Kingdom asserted that:

> The primary responsibility to protect civilians lies with States. The concept of protection of civilians is firmly embedded in modern military doctrine in many countries and in the thoughts of policymakers around the world. It is now central to most United Nations peacekeeping operations and to military operations authorised by the Security Council.[25]

While respect for the full compass of IHL guarantees is an ideal, pursued by PKOs through both preventive and capacity-building activities, 'in its simplest form, the Council intends the instruction to "protect civilians" to ensure that peacekeepers help prevent and halt acts of extreme violence'.[26] When Council members assert R2PC, in drawing on both IHL and peacekeeping doctrine they are concerned with the prevention – through both direct and structural means – of widespread summary violence against civilians.

The final phrase requiring explanation is 'armed conflict broadly construed'. POC in *law* (that is, IHL) is, by definition, constrained to armed conflicts *sensu stricto*. However, POC as a *practice* and as a *policy agenda* – in the hands of humanitarians, peacekeepers and the UN Secretariat and Security Council – applies to armed conflict and other situations of mass, lawless violence. This scope includes situations of civil strife such as serious internal disturbances. Such disturbances, as defined by the International Committee of the Red Cross (ICRC) commentary, involve:

> … situations in which there is no non-international armed conflict as such, but there exists a confrontation within the country, which is characterised by a certain seriousness or duration and which involves acts of violence. These latter can assume various forms, all the way from the spontaneous generation of acts of revolt to the struggle between more or less organised groups and the authorities in power. In these situations, which do not necessarily degenerate into open struggle, the authorities in power call upon extensive police forces, or even armed forces, to restore internal order. The high number of victims has made necessary the application of a minimum of humanitarian rules.[27]

25 UNSC (2011e), p. 11. Other links asserted between R2PC and PKOs occur at pp. 18, 23, 29.

26 Holt et al. (2009), p. 6.

27 Sandoz et al. (1987), para. 4475.

Internal disturbances, therefore, involve grave and open violence, with a substantial number of interconnected acts across distance and time, and the violence occurring outside the normal use of police powers and domestic law. Distinct from institutionalised state repression, this violence disrupts the normal functioning of law and order, and marks an open confrontation between disputants. However, the confrontation has not reached the pitch of armed conflict in the sense of IHL; either because the fighting lacks the required intensity or because at least one of the sides lacks a command structure and organised military capability.[28] Internal disturbances can thus include low-level, minimally organised insurgencies; extreme state responses (using widespread lethal open violence outside normal police powers) to demonstrations or riots; and high-level internecine violence by un-organised militia against other militia or civilians.

Council concern, robust peacekeeping protective actions and humanitarian succor can all occur in such situations of violent civil strife, as well as in armed conflict proper.[29] R2PC invocations follow this larger purview. As Gabon asserted – echoing similar statements by Brazil and India – 'We believe that responsibility for the protection of civilians, both *in peacetime* and in armed conflict, falls primarily to States themselves'.[30] Hence, states could speak without contradiction of a population's 'violent and systematic repression by their own authorities' as a POC concern;[31] they could also hold Syria in November 2011 as a POC situation, despite the acknowledged lack of any armed conflict as such at that point.[32] Thus, POC as a practice and policy agenda applies outside 'armed conflict' narrowly construed, and R2PC follows this expanded ambit.

In sum, R2PC takes the responsibility assignation structure from IHRL and R2P, the focus on summary violence and basic needs from IHL and the scope of application from POC as a practice and policy agenda. Thus, formulated in terms of R2P's three pillars, R2PC comprises the following:

> *Pillar 1*: In situations of armed conflict broadly construed, states have the primary responsibility to protect their civilians from summary violence, forced displacement, deliberate starvation strategies and being used as human shields (and a fortiori not to perform these acts themselves).

28 These two conditions are the basic markers separating non-international armed conflict (in the sense of Common Article 3 of the Geneva Conventions) from internal disturbances and tensions. See International Committee of the Red Cross ICRC (2008). See also Vite (2009).

29 For defense of this claim, see Breakey (2012), p. 69.

30 UNSC (2011e), p. 25. See also pp. 15–17 [emphasis added].

31 Columbia; UNSC (2011e), p. 14.

32 There was, of course, disagreement on whether the Council should adopt a resolution on Syria. However, no state argued that Syria could not be a POC concern on the grounds that it was not an armed conflict in the sense of IHL. (Syria as a whole was not legally designated as an armed conflict by the ICRC until June 2012, though some discrete conflicts within it attained that status in the month earlier.)

> *Pillar 2*: The international community has the responsibility, with respect to states that are willing but unable to so protect their civilians, to – with the consent of the host state – help them build capacities to do so, including through the use of peacekeeping, conflict resolution, mediation, good offices and human rights monitoring missions.
> *Pillar 3*: When a state is manifestly failing to protect its civilians from widespread summary violence, the international community has a responsibility to condemn the violence against civilians, and to use all the peaceful diplomatic, mediation and political avenues open to it to convince the state to quell such violence and/or consent to monitors or peacekeepers. In extreme cases, the Security Council can consider the use of targeted sanctions and travel bans against state authorities, arms embargoes and/or referral of the situation to the International Criminal Court.

Can R2PC Pillar 3 justify 'humanitarian intervention' – the use of military force for protective purposes in a territory without state consent? While some Council members may have this in mind (treating R2P as effectively the limit case of R2PC),[33] it is safer to say that, in the extreme cases of atrocity crimes and direct threats to international peace, the principle of R2PC passes the baton to R2P and the Security Council's responsibilities under Chapter VII of the Charter. In this way, R2PC can be roundly affirmed by Council members without commitments to military interventions authorised by the Security Council. This would give R2PC an arsenal of responses similar to, for example, the Council's concern with 'women, peace and security' and 'children and armed conflict'. In these rubrics, the Council observes in principle that large-scale violence against women or children can threaten international peace and security (and thus is a rightful object of Council action under Ch. VII of the Charter), but in terms of direct action notes only that acts of violence against women or children will be a factor in establishing and renewing state-specific sanctions regimes.[34]

This article argues that the above definition accords with the use of R2PC in the recent Council open debates. The definition aligns with the positive claims that Council members make about R2PC, and no Council member asserted any claim that amounts to a denial of any one of these three features of R2PC. That is, no Council member put forward a contrary claim about the responsibility structure being invoked by R2PC, about the general types of crimes it targets, or (prior to 2012 at least, see below) about the scope of application of R2PC. If the definition does indeed accord with the use of R2PC then, contrary to the secretary-general's implication (at least with respect to invocations of R2PC), the Council members were not guilty of a conceptual confusion, but rather were fashioning a fairly sophisticated and potentially workable amalgamation of several distinct protection regimes.

33 For example, France, UNSC (2011e), p. 19.

34 UNSC (2000), para. 9; UNSC (2008), para. 5; UNSC (2010b), p. 3. With respect to its use of sanctions for POC more broadly, see Security Council Report SCR (2012), p. 12.

Why Has R2PC Arisen?

Since the early 1990s, various actors have formulated, concretised and refined POC roles for themselves. Such actors include humanitarians, the UN Secretariat, the UN Security Council, peacekeepers and regional organisations. Strikingly absent from the international POC movement, however, was the actor that forms the fundamental building block of international relations – the *state*. Just as theorists might speak of the different perspectives of *combatant POC*, *peacekeeping POC* and *humanitarian POC*,[35] R2PC is the first major step in formulating a distinct POC role for states.

In 2011, Thomas Weiss noted that R2P's success should not be ascribed solely to its normative entrepreneurs, but also to its 'demand-driven character';[36] that is, the fact that international actors had a genuine need for R2P's inventive refiguring of international law, state sovereignty and humanitarian necessity. However, some principles have even less 'supply-side' character than R2P, arising directly from the requirements and objectives of key actors, and taking shape in their negotiations, compromises, practices and statements. So it was for R2PC, which was created out of the crucible – the political realities and humanitarian exigencies – of the contemporary international milieu. Three particular forces drove its emergence.

First, from the beginning of its engagement with POC, the Council accepted that large-scale and summary violence against civilians was wrongful and illegal, whether in the context of armed conflicts *sensu stricto* or other situations of mass violence. The Council deemed such violence as worthy of international condemnation, and foresaw that such abuses – if not nipped in the bud – could lead to atrocities and threats to international peace.[37] The catastrophes in Rwanda and Srebrenica, and the UN and independent reports on these published in 1999 and 2000, framed from the outset the Council's treatment of POC.[38] While states disagreed on questions of intervention, no state was willing to assert that such assaults on civilians were not a rightful object of international concern and condemnation. From this point of departure it was but a short step to the principle that states bear primary responsibility for protecting their civilians, and that the international community bears back-up responsibilities for helping them to do so, or trying to pressure them to do so.

Second, there was a need to find a protection principle that would sit somewhere between R2P and IHRL. Although R2P's atrocity crimes provided an acceptable threshold for considerations of military intervention, it seemed widely accepted (or at least impossible to deny) that states had stronger humanitarian duties to their populations than merely to protect them from full-blown atrocities.[39] Conversely, however, the full application of IHRL possible in times of peace can

35 Breakey (2012), p. 40.

36 Weiss (2011), p. 288.

37 UNSC (1999a).

38 International-Panel (2000); UN (1999); UN Secretary-General (1999).

39 As implied in International Commission on Intervention and State Sovereignty ICISS (2001), p. 14ff.

seem ill-suited to situations of violence and lawlessness (and states can formally derogate from important provisions in emergencies).[40] Also, the required standard of treatment under the POC rubric is generally much lower than that required by IHRL. This means that states signing up to R2PC are not accepting that each and every infringement of a human right is a rightful subject of international attention. Instead, the focus is confined to the large-scale harms that can occur in situations of widespread lawless violence. In this respect, the minimum guarantees of POC, reserved for civilians rather than armed actors, present both a concrete and achievable standard. After all, if the guarantees of POC are legally required of state actors in their treatment of enemy civilians in war, there is a certain normative logic in thinking that they can be reasonably required of state actors in their treatment of their own civilians in situations of internal violence. As such, the minimum guarantees of POC provided a workable standard of appropriate conduct for states, developed precisely for situations of mass violence.

Third, advocating *primary* responsibility to the state, while admitting the possibility of international concern and action, also established an avenue for states to defend their sovereignty against intrusion. As was noted with respect to the atrocities in Darfur in 2004–05, the Government of Sudan shrewdly used R2P as a shield against external action, claiming that the responsibility to protect their population was, in the first instance, their own responsibility, and not that of the international community.[41] This factor probably explains why Council members ordinarily so resistant to humanitarian impositions on their sovereign authority have been willing to expound R2PC. China, for instance, is the single most consistent proponent of R2PC in the open debates. It was one of the very first users of the R2PC phrase, and is the only Council member to have invoked R2PC in every meeting since the beginning of 2007. If POC violations are *inevitably* going to be the subject of international attention – as the last dozen years of Council decision-making strongly suggest – then the best option discursively open to states nervous about infractions on their sovereignty is not to deny the moral significance of POC's minimum guarantees, but rather to emphatically declare that the state must be the primary agent for securing them.[42] Equally, it is sometimes observed that states' reasons for resisting the application of IHL to an internal situation stem less from a wish to avoid the basic legal constraints on action themselves than from the political consequences of recognising the existence of an internal armed conflict and the resultant quasi-legal (at least) status granted to the insurgents.[43] In this

40 UN General-Assembly (1966). See, Art. 4; Even so, 'disappearances' and summary extrajudicial violence remain prohibited. See UN Commission on Human Rights (UNCHR) (1984), paras 58 and 59. See also para. 70.

41 Bellamy (2005).

42 It should perhaps be observed that the allocation of responsibility to the *central* state may also be attractive to the authorities in China, who have arguably had some successes through centralising protection.

43 See the arguments and references in Abresch (2005), p. 756.

respect, R2PC's mandating of civilian protection outside armed conflict proper (or, at least, with no objective determination either way regarding the existence of such conflict) allows states to accept basic restraints on their targeting and harming civilians, without thereby elevating the legal status of insurgents or terrorists, or admitting the extent of these actors' operations and control of territory.

R2PC's Pillar 3 also reflects a prioritisation of sovereignty, in the sense that the fundamental Pillar 3 duty of the international community is to bring the situation back to a Pillar 2 scenario through concerted pressure and negotiation. That is, the international community is obliged to attempt to impel a state that is unwilling to protect its civilians to do so, rather than seeking to take over direct protection responsibilities itself. There is no clear consensus about the precise threshold at which the unwillingness of states to protect their civilians reaches the point that coercive measures (for example, targeted sanctions, travel bans, arms embargoes and International Criminal Court [ICC] referral) are justified. It is reasonable to presume that states have quite divergent positions on this matter – and indeed, that their positions in any given case reflect both their general principles and their specific relationships with the state in question; this is implied by the divergent responses of, for example, the United States vis-à-vis Libya and Israel, and of Russia vis-à-vis Libya and Syria.

Current Status and Future Prospects

The November 2011 open debate currently stands as the high-water mark for assertions of R2PC. As noted earlier, the most recent open debate – in June 2012 – saw a decided swing away from use of R2PC. There were at least two reasons for this shift. The first is the normative pushback against POC in the Security Council since late 2011, arising from both fall-out from the Libyan intervention, and new members rotating onto the Council. The arrival of Pakistan in 2012, in particular, changed the dynamic, because of the country's apparent unwillingness to be constrained by the robust POC practices that had occurred previously, when Pakistan was not a member of the Council.[44] In the June 2012 open debate, Pakistan raised concerns about the relationship of POC with the Security Council's role and mandate; for the first time in the history of the open debates, the country pursued a strictly legal understanding of the concept. This allowed Pakistan to criticise the Secretary-General's recent reports, which extended to situations (including Pakistan's own) 'that cannot be described as armed conflict'.[45] Alongside Pakistan's vocal stance against previous understandings of POC (and so, derivatively, against R2PC), and against the back-drop of the crisis in Syria, Russia also stood firmly

44 This was evident well before the 2012 open debate. See Security Council Report SCR (2012), p. 21.

45 UNSC (2012), p. 16. While Pakistan's claim targeted the last three reports, in fact the accusation would hold true back to the very first report in 1999.

against wider versions of POC. In the 2012 debate, Russia decried any need 'to dream up any new international legal or political concepts to bridge the supposed gaps in the protection regime of the Geneva conventions'.[46] R2PC could be seen as just such a concept.

The second factor pushing back against assertions of the broad POC agenda – and derivatively against R2PC – was the secretary-general's aforementioned censure in his 2012 POC report of the 'continuing and inaccurate conflation of the concepts of the protection of civilians and the responsibility to protect'.[47] The brevity that surrounds statements in the open debate makes conceptual discussion (of the sort presented here) difficult, and some states may have felt it easier to simply eschew use of the R2PC phrase rather than to consider the reasons it had been adopted in the first place. Indeed, the way the secretary-general posed the distinction between R2P and POC gave credence to Pakistan's position, although this was presumably not the intention. The secretary-general asserted – in language never used before or since in his POC or R2P Reports – that POC was a 'legal concept' and R2P a 'political concept'. In so doing, he laid the ground for a Council member such as Pakistan to try to force a retreat from the robust practical and policy POC concept that had informed recent Council (and, more gradually, peacekeeping) practice, and instead move it towards a narrow legal version.

With such sustained fire coming from both sides, is the nascent concept of R2PC likely to disappear entirely? In the wake of the 2012 open debate, R2PC's future is unclear. However, presuming that the Security Council's more general engagement with POC survives the current tumult, the three main reasons that prompted its existence will still stand. First, the continued practical significance of R2PC in the context of peacekeeping operations is to be expected, where the principle's division of responsibility represents a workable negotiated position between the responsibilities of PKOs and the states that host them. The PKO – and the Council authorising it – will not want the mission to be dismantled if it is still playing a vital role in protecting local civilians. The long shadow of the precipitous withdrawal of key Belgian contingents from Rwanda still looms over UN peacekeeping. Similarly, a state that has been engaged on a consensual basis with the PKO over a long period usually has strong incentives to part company cordially, and to demonstrate objectively its increasing control over local security – and, by implication, its legitimacy as the state authority. Thus, it is likely that constraints on PKO withdrawal – such as those in Resolution 1923 – will be used in the future.

A second reason is that the principle of R2PC will still offer a discursive route – especially in Council open debates and statements of representatives – for the international community to describe the minimum appropriate standards of conduct when states respond to internal unrest (R2PC Pillar 1). The idea of R2PC Pillars 2 and 3 will be invoked to justify the view that a state's failure to meet

46 UNSC (2012), p. 21.
47 UNSC (2012), p. 21.

those standards is a proper object of international concern, consensual aid and – potentially – sanction. However, states will deploy R2PC Pillar 1 to emphasise that they have primary responsibility to protect their own civilians. Even in the face of the secretary-general's complaint against conflation of the two concepts, both China and South Africa continued to use R2PC, perhaps because these states are attracted by the fundamental way R2PC shifts the sovereign state into the very centre of POC's international policy framework.

Of course, even if R2PC language helps to frame the debate in future cases, Council members will continue to have divergent perspectives on issues such as: (a) at what threshold the international community can rightly begin to consider condemnation and sanction; (b) what the actual state of affairs on the ground is in any particular case; and (c) what strategic interests are at stake for individual Council members, and how far they take those interests as decisive in voting and vetoing. At time of writing, in late 2012, Syria is a case in point.

The final advantage of R2PC is that, although (as argued here) there *is* a shared sense of meaning for R2PC, the principle departs from IHL, IHRL and R2P in not having an explicit and authoritative formulation.[48] This informality makes R2PC useful as a general way of drawing attention to and discussing particular situations, without needing to take a particular stand on issues such as whether there is an armed conflict in the sense of IHL, or a determinate risk of atrocity crimes in the sense of R2P. Additionally, without an explicit procedure (for example, that of R2P) being invoked, states can more easily speak about humanitarian concerns arising in other countries without being perceived as opening the possibility of military intervention or calling into question the legitimacy of a state regime. A breach of R2PC means only that a state is failing in some respect to fulfil a humanitarian obligation, often in a challenging situation of civil strife or insurrection. In contrast, a breach of R2P almost certainly implies that a state is committing or is complicit in a serious international crime of the sort that raises the question of its very legitimacy.

From a humanitarian perspective, are there dangers in the concept of R2PC? One concern is that, rather than augmenting other established norms, some international actors may treat R2PC as *replacing* such norms – leading these states to downplay the specific legal requirements of IHL, IHRL, the Rome Statute and the Genocide Convention. Another concern is that R2PC may lose the distinct meaning this article has argued it currently connotes, and become an amorphous catch-all term for international humanitarian concerns, which may in turn contribute to the conflation of R2P and the various POC perspectives.[49] This would be an unfortunate

48 In this sense, R2PC might be more accurately referred to as a protection *concept*, with the more precisely formulated R2P attaining the status of a protection *principle*, and the longstanding legal substance of IHL and IHRL furnishing them with the status of protection *norms*. See Bellamy (2009), p. 5ff., though it bears noting that different aspects of R2P have different statuses in international law. See Stahn (2007).

49 This is the view of R2PC critiqued in Lie (2008), p. 31ff. See also de Carvalho and Lie (2009), p. 4.

result, because the neutrality, impartiality and respect for sovereignty required by POC agents such as humanitarian actors and peacekeepers would become tainted by association with the controversial aspects of R2P's Pillar 3. Avoidance of such a result was the likely motivation for the secretary-general's novel claims about the bright-line 'legal–political' distinction between R2P and POC.

A final issue regarding R2PC (and cognate principles) that warrants reflection is its seeming introduction of IHL's combatant–civilian distinction into situations outside armed conflict (as defined by IHL).

The Concept of 'Civilian' in Situations of Civil Strife

Because it applies to situations whether or not they have legal status as 'armed conflict', R2PC invokes IHL's principle of distinction *outside* the context of armed *conflict sensu* IHL. This article is not the place for a comprehensive analysis of the legal notions of 'civilians' and 'combatants' as they might apply outside situations of armed conflict *sensu stricto*. Such an analysis would need to confront vexing questions about, for instance, what in these situations constitutes the role of military necessity, what amounts to direct participation in hostilities, when and for whom forfeiture of protection occurs and how equivalent duties can be imposed on all parties to the dispute.[50] These questions would embroil the discussion in issues that are somewhat removed from R2PC. However, it is perhaps worth noting that legally significant notions of 'civilians' and 'hostilities' outside of armed conflict *sensu stricto* are not as odd as they might at first appear.[51] In the context of the Security Council actions and resolutions, references to

50 Essentially, such an analysis would require careful investigation of the important differences between internal disturbances and internal armed conflicts, in the same way the differences between internal and international armed conflicts can guide the international law of internal armed conflict. See Sivakumaran (2011). The idea here is not that IHL functions as the *lex specialis* to IHRL in situations of intense civil strife. Rather, it is that some of the concepts, rules and distinctions familiar to IHL (for example, 'civilians' and 'direct participation in hostilities' may have a role in crafting specific objective rules from subjective rights in those situations).

51 First, Article 7 of the ICC (1 July 2002). It defines 'crimes against humanity', applies outside armed conflict and yet adverts to 'civilian populations'. Second, appeals to prior notions of 'civilians' have been used by Trial Chambers as one factor in judgments of the existence of 'armed conflict' (which would be logically impossible if 'civilians' could not legally exist outside 'armed conflict'): *Prosecutor v Ramush Haradinaj* et. al., case No. IT-04-84-T, Judgement of 3 April 2008, para. 49. Third, in *Isayeva, Yusupova and Bazayeva v Russia*, ECtHR, App Nos 57947–49/00 (24 February 2005) and *Isayeva v Russia*, ECtHR, App No 57950/00 (24 February 2005), the European Court of Human Rights eschewed any determination of whether an 'armed conflict' proper occurred (indeed, the phrase more generally is barely mentioned throughout the judgment). The concept of 'civilian', however, permeated the judgment.

civilians often appear outside determinations of 'armed conflict'. For example, the Council's declarations on the recruitment of child soldiers do not wait on a determination of armed conflict *sensu stricto*,[52] and the Council regularly invokes 'civilians', 'civilian populations' and 'civilian facilities' without making any reference to the existence of an 'armed conflict'.[53]

For present purposes, this article will consider just one potential concern that might arise with R2PC's injection of 'civilians' into contexts outside the armed conflict of IHL namely, the worry that IHRL is the presumptive body of law applicable in such 'grey zones', and it (as a most basic feature) contains no such distinction.[54] IHRL does not distinguish between different categories of persons in this manner; in particular, it does not authorise combatants to use deadly force in the same manner as IHL, nor does it allow combatants to have deadly force used on them.[55] Any such authorisation outside contexts where it is absolutely necessary – for example, in genuine armed conflicts – must be a concern for those promoting human rights and human security.

Two inter-related responses can be made to allay this concern. First, it is not clear that human rights must entirely eschew this type of distinction. After all, the links between human rights and the minimum guarantees of Common Article 3 of the Geneva Conventions (and, relatedly, of Article 4 of Additional Protocol II) are widely observed. Many have noted the congruence between these guarantees and the non-derogable human rights.[56] The International Court of Justice (ICJ), in its *Advisory Opinion* on the *Legality of the Threat or Use of Nuclear Weapons*, held that the right to life guaranteed in Article 6(1) of the *International Covenant on Civil and Political Rights*[57] did apply in situations of armed conflict, but that the test of what is an 'arbitrary deprivation of life' must be determined by the applicable *lex specialis*; viz., the rules, distinctions and principles of IHL.[58] Similarly, in *Juan Carlos Abella v Argentina*, the Inter-American Commission on Human Rights used IHL on the basis that the, 'provisions of common article 3 are pure human rights law … Article 3 basically requires the state to do, in large measure, what it is already legally obliged to do under the American Convention'.[59] But, of course,

52 See UN Secretary-General (2012), para. 6. See also UNSC (2009b), preambular para. 11 and operative para. 5.

53 For instance, in the February 2011 resolution on Libya: UNSC (2011a), premambular and operative para. 22(a). Note that by the time of UNSC (2011b), the Council did speak about the Libyan situation as one of armed conflict.

54 Office of the High Commissioner for Human Rights OHCHR (2011), pp. 20ff.

55 Office of the High Commissioner for Human Rights OHCHR (2011), pp. 66ff.

56 IRRC (1988), p. 4; ICRC (2003).

57 UN General-Assembly (1966).

58 Legality of the Threat or Use of Nuclear Weapons, Advisory Opinion, 1996 ICJ Rep. 226, 240 (8 July).

59 *Juan Carlos Abella v Argentina*, Report No. 55/97, Case 11.137, 18 November 1997, OEA/Ser.L/V/II.98 at fn. 19.

Common Article 3's minimum guarantees apply only to *civilians*; that is, 'persons taking no active part in the hostilities'.

R2PC can also be seen as one way of helping to specify a minimum core of fundamental protections that are due to those who are caught in both civil strife and armed conflict, and are victims rather than agents of that violence. In other words, to the extent that IHRL in situations of traditional armed conflict can make use of IHL principles, concepts and distinctions, so too can IHRL, in situations of mass violence and internal strife, make use – where appropriate – of those same IHL elements. As such, R2PC could be seen as the Council setting down what it perceives as the minimum standards required by respect for human rights – standards whose breach is a proper subject of international concern. R2PC's appeal to notions of 'civilians' – and the implicit requirement to distinguish between treatment of civilians and of those taking a direct part in hostilities – need not require a wholesale replacement of IHRL with IHL (which in some situations may provide less demanding or less specific constraints).[60]

The second response is that the civilian–combatant distinction in IHL has both an enabling and a prohibiting function. It licenses special actions taken to and by combatants that would otherwise be presumptively unlawful, and it prohibits those special actions being taken to and by civilians. The use of the term 'civilians' in R2PC, it is submitted, has the prohibiting function without the enabling one. That is, two categories are being created, and R2PC is setting down the proper standard for treatment and protection of one of them: civilians. However, R2PC is not in the same conceptual breath authorising all actions taken to and by combatants (a comparison may be drawn with the Geneva Convention's Common Article 3 and with Additional Protocol II, which likewise fail to recognise combatants).[61] Rather, it is best understood as altogether refraining from making any determinate prescriptions regarding that category of persons. R2PC is declaring that *whatever may be the status and necessary treatment of those participating in hostilities*, civilians – at the least – must retain their basic protections. For this reason, the concept of civilians in R2PC should perhaps be understood restrictively.[62] The concept is referring to people for whom there is no epistemological difficulty in establishing their unarmed status, and no tenable legal argument made that they

60 This point that, in situations of internal disturbance, IHRL may offer more protection than IHL (or, at least, of Com. Art. 3 of the Geneva Conventions) is made in ICRC (2003), p. 5. The point about specificity is made in Abresch (2005), pp. 747ff.

61 As Albresch says: 'This omission is due to the great reluctance of states to accept that domestic insurgents ever have any *right* to attack government forces'. See Abresch (2005), p. 757.

62 And, conversely, what counts as 'participation in hostilities' interpreted broadly. While R2PC is not a legal norm, it is nevertheless a standard by which states accept they may be judged and even sanctioned, and it is plausible to think that state's presumptive concerns about military necessity will loom large, especially given the application to internal conflicts. See Schmitt (2010), pp. 832ff.

pose any substantial danger to the legitimate objectives of armed groups or the state. It may be that, legally speaking, in situations of civil strife, someone who is an insurgent or terrorist by day but is at home in his or her bed at night should be treated by state military and police forces as a civilian (albeit a criminal) when they descend upon the person. But it is plausible to think that R2PC does not pronounce either way on such matters. The reasons canvassed above explain why R2PC must have the prohibitive aspect without the enabling one. For humanitarian reasons, such licensing may contribute to the removal of legal protections that would otherwise pertain; for state-based reasons, the licensing of combatants to use deadly force threatens to place insurgents – guilty of criminal violence (from the state's perspective) – on an equal plane with state forces. In this fashion, R2PC parallels other draft instruments and declarations on civil strife that aim to reaffirm,

> … an irreducible core of humanitarian norms and human rights that must be respected in all situations and at all times, a safety net independent of any assertions that a particular conflict is below the threshold of applicability of international humanitarian law and is not addressed by existing international law.[63]

Like these instruments, R2PC uses the civilian–combatant distinction (or cognate phrases, such as 'not taking part in acts of violence') to lay down guarantees of treatment for the protected class that reflect their entitlements in armed conflict proper, *without* thereby pronouncing that the contrary of that class has the same suite of entitlements and liabilities it possesses in armed conflict proper.

To sum up, any potential injection of the civilian–combatant distinction into situations outside armed conflict is a cause for reflection. However, insofar as it is understood in a purely restrictive register, R2PC aims to capture the protections due unarmed non-violent persons in armed conflicts and other situations of mass violence, without clashing with IHRL by licensing violence in those situations.

Conclusion

In conclusion, over the past six years the UN Security Council has developed in nascent form an informal international protection principle – R2PC – which inventively hybridises the three major international normative structures of protection: IHL, IHRL and R2P. Although its future is at present unclear, the principle allows widespread assaults on civilians to be a proper object of international attention, while at the same time making the state the primary agent for effecting the protection of those civilians. As a rough and ready compromise between the desires of humanitarian actors and sovereign states, R2PC may continue to be found useful in the approaching years.

63 Eide et al. (1995), p. 216. See also Meron (1988).

References

W. Abresch (2005) 'A Human Rights Law of Internal Armed Conflict: The European Court of Human Rights in Chechnya', 16, *European Journal of International Law* 741.

A. Bellamy (2005) 'Responsibility to Protect or Trojan Horse? The Crisis in Darfur and Humanitarian Intervention after Iraq', 19, *Ethics and International Affairs* 31.

A. Bellamy (2009) *Responsibility to Protect: The Global Effort to End Mass Atrocities*, Polity.

M. Benzing (2008) 'Sovereignty and the Responsibility to Protect in International Criminal Law', in Doris Konig et al. (eds) *International law today: new challenges and the need for reform?*, Springer 17.

H. Breakey (2012) 'The Protection of Civilians in Armed Conflict: Four Perspectives', in Charles Sampford, Angus Francis and Vesselin Popovski (eds) *Norms of Protection: Responsibility to Protect, Protection of Civilians and their Interaction*, United Nations University 40.

B. de Carvalho and J.H.S. Lie (2009) *Challenges to Implementing the Protection of Civilians Agenda*, Norwegian Institute of Public Affairs (NUPI).

DPKO/DFS (2010) *Draft Operational Concept on the Protection of Civilians in United Nations Peacekeeping Operations*, United Nations.

A. Eide et al. (1995) 'Combating Lawlessness in Gray Zone Conflicts Through Minimum Humanitarian Standards', 89, *The American Journal of International Law* 215.

J.-M. Henckaerts and L. Doswald-Becks (2005) *International Committee of the Red Cross: Customary International Humanitarian Law*, CUP.

V. Holt et al. (2009) *Protecting Civilians in the Context of UN Peacekeeping Operations: Successes, Setbacks and Remaining Challenges*, DPKO, OCHA.

ICC (1st July 2002) *Rome Statute of the International Criminal Court.*

ICRC (1949) *Convention (IV) relative to the Protection of Civilian Persons in Time of War.*

ICRC (1977) *Protocol Additional to the Geneva Conventions of 12 August 1949, and relating to the Protection of Victims of Non-International Armed Conflicts (Protocol II)*, International Committee of the Red Cross.

ICRC (2003) *International Humanitarian Law and Other Legal Regimes: Interplay in Situations of Violence*, ICRC.

International-Panel (2000) *Rwanda: The Preventable Genocide: Special Report of the International Panel of Eminent Personalities to Investigate the 1994 Genocide in Rwanda and the Surrounding Events.*

International Commission on Intervention and State Sovereignty ICISS (2001) *The Responsibility to Protect*, IDRC.

International Committee of the Red Cross ICRC (2008) *How is the Term "Armed Conflict" Defined in International Humanitarian Law?*, ICRC.

IRRC (1988) 'Internal Disturbances and Tensions: A New Humanitarian Approach?', 262, *International Review of the Red Cross* 3.

J.H.S. Lie (2008) *Protection of Civilians, the Responsibility to Protect and Peace Operations*, Norwegian Institute of Public Affairs (NUPI) available at http://www.nupi.no/Publications/Books-and-reports/2008/Protection-of-Civilians-the-Responsibility-to-Protect-and-Peace-Operations# (accessed 15 November 2012).

T. Meron (1988) 'Draft Model Declaration on Internal Strife', 262, *International Review of the Red Cross* 59.

Office of the High Commissioner for Human Rights OHCHR (2011) *International legal protection of human rights in armed conflict*, United Nations.

Y. Sandoz et al. (eds) (1987) *Commentary on the Additional Protocols of 8 June 1977 to the Geneva Conventions of 12 August 1949*, ICRC.

M. Sassòli et al. (2011) *How Does Law Protect in War? Cases, Documents and Teaching Materials on Contemporary Practice in International Humanitarian Law*, ICRC.

D. Scheffer (2009) 'Atrocity Crimes: Framing the Responsibility to Protect', in R.H. Cooper and J.V. Kohler (eds) *Responsibility to Protect: The Global Moral Compact for the 21st Century*, Palgrave MacMillan 77.

Michael N. Schmitt (2010) 'Military Necessity and Humanity in International Humanitarian Law: Preserving the Delicate Balance', 50, *Virginia Journal of International Law* 795.

Security Council Report SCR (2012) *Cross-Cutting Report on Protection of Civilians in Armed Conflict.*

Sandesh Sivakumaran (2011) 'Re-envisaging the International Law of Internal Armed Conflict', 22, *European Journal of International Law* 219.

Special Committee on Peacekeeping Operations (C34) (2009) *2009 Report*, UN General Assembly.

Carsten Stahn (2007) 'Responsibility to Protect: Political Rhetoric or Emerging Legal Norm?', 101, *American Journal of International Law* 99.

UN (1999) *Report of the Independent Inquiry into the Actions of the United Nations during the 1994 Genocide in Rwanda*, UN.

UN Commission on Human Rights (UNCHR) (1984) *The Siracusa Principles on the Limitation and Derogation Provisions in the International Covenant on Civil and Political Rights*, UN Commission on Human Rights available at http://www.unhcr.org/refworld/docid/4672bc122.html (accessed 15 November 2012).

UN General-Assembly (1966) *International Covenant on Civil and Political Rights (ICCPR)*, United Nations available at http://www2.ohchr.org/english/law/pdf/ccpr.pdf (accessed 15 November 2012).

UN General-Assembly (1999) *Strengthening of the Coordination of Humanitarian Emergency Assistance of the United Nations*, United Nations General Assembly.

UN General-Assembly (2005) *Res. 60/1: World Summit Outcome Document.*

UN Secretary-General (1999) *Report of the Secretary General pursuant to General Assembly Resolution 53/55: The Fall of Srebrenica*, UN General Assembly.
UN Secretary-General (2001) *Report of the Secretary-General to the Security Council on the Protection of Civilians in Armed Conflict*, United Nations.
UN Secretary-General (2009) *Implementing the Responsibility to Protect*, A/63/677 UN General Assembly.
UN Secretary-General (2011) 'Statement by the Secretary-General on the situation in Côte d'Ivoire', 4th April, 2011.
UN Secretary-General (2012) *Report of the Secretary-General: Children and Armed Conflict*, United Nations.
UNSC (1999a) *Res. 1265 (Protection of civilians in armed conflict)*, United Nations.
UNSC (1999b) *Res. 1270 (Sierra Leone)*, UN Security Council.
UNSC (2000) *Res. 1314 (Children and armed conflict)*, United Nations.
UNSC (2005) *Meeting: Protection of Civilians in Armed Conflict*, UN Security Council.
UNSC (2006) *Res. 1674 (Protection of civilians in armed conflict)*, United Nations.
UNSC (2008) *Res. 1820 (Women and Peace and Security)*, United Nations.
UNSC (2009a) *Res. 1888 (Women and Peace and Security)*, United Nations.
UNSC (2009b) *Res. 1882 (Children and armed conflict)*, United Nations.
UNSC (2010a) *Res. 1923 (Chad, Central African Republic)*, UN Security Council.
UNSC (2010b) *Statement by the President of the Security Council: Children and Armed Conflict*, UNSC.
UNSC (2011a) *Res. 1970 (Peace and security in Africa)*, United Nations.
UNSC (2011b) *Res. 1973 (Libya)*, United Nations.
UNSC (2011c) *Res. 1975 (Côte d'Ivoire)*, United Nations.
UNSC (2011d) *Meeting: Protection of Civilians in Armed Conflict*, UN Security Council.
UNSC (2011e) *Meeting: Protection of Civilians in Armed Conflict*, UN Security Council.
UNSC (2012) *Meeting: Protection of Civilians in Armed Conflict*, UN Security Council.
S. Vite (2009) 'Typology of armed conflicts in international humanitarian law: legal concepts and actual situations', 91, *International Review of the Red Cross* 69.
T.G. Weiss (2011) 'RtoP Alive and Well after Libya', 25, *Ethics and International Affairs* 287.

Chapter 4

R2P and the East Timor Intervention

Clinton Fernandes

In 1975, Indonesia illegally invaded East Timor, a Portuguese colony that had been declared a non-self-governing territory within the meaning of Chapter XI of the United Nations Charter. During the 24-year occupation, there were widespread occurrences of war crimes, killing, famine, torture, rape, violations of the rights of children and other crimes against humanity. The people of East Timor suffered perhaps the largest loss of life relative to total population since the Holocaust.[1]

The question of East Timor remained on the UN's agenda for the duration, with the UN General Assembly reaffirming the people's right to self-determination. A ballot on self-determination was held on 30 August 1999: with 98 per cent of registered voters participating, only 21.5 per cent favoured special autonomy while 78.5 per cent chose independence. The Indonesian authorities immediately carried out a forced displacement campaign in East Timor, deporting approximately 250,000 people across the border into Indonesian West Timor. Approximately 70 per cent of the buildings in East Timor were destroyed, vital infrastructure was crippled, and there were more than 1,400 killings, as well as acts of rape, looting and arson. Indonesia's first civilian defence minister, Juwono Sudarsono, unwittingly conceded that his country had committed state-sponsored terror, saying that senior military personnel 'were just carrying out state policy'.[2] Under mounting international pressure, the UN Security Council established a multinational force, the International Force – East Timor (INTERFET), with the power to restore security by force. Led by Australia, this force entered East Timor on 20 September 1999. The liberation of East Timor has since been described as a remarkable success of the so-called 'Responsibility to Protect' (R2P) doctrine.

This chapter is a critical evaluation of what is often portrayed as a noble moment in Australia's history of overseas interventions. Looking beyond the state-centric lenses of conventional analysis, it argues that Australian policymakers were forced to send in a peacekeeping force under the pressure of a tidal wave of public outrage. This outrage did not arise spontaneously; rather, it was the result of a conscious process of grassroots activism by an international coalition of activists who were committed to an independent East Timor. Mainstream accounts of East

1 For details of the death tolls and the robust methods used to determine them, see CAVR (2005), vol. 6.

2 Tedjasukmana (2000).

Timor's path to independence[3] have very little to say about the crucial role played by activists in forcing the Australian Government to do the exact opposite of that which it had long argued was in its national interest. This chapter will outline their role in opposing government policy and, ultimately, in overturning it. Accordingly, it will show that it was activists who upheld the R2P principle in the case of East Timor in the teeth of longstanding, ferocious opposition from many states.

The Australian Government's role in opposing an independent East Timor during Gough Whitlam's time as Prime Minister has been discussed elsewhere.[4] The government acted to neutralise domestic public opinion by issuing perfunctory statements supporting East Timor's right to self-determination. These statements were no more than routine representations, with the understanding by both Australia and Indonesia that no meaningful action would be taken to prevent the invasion. The government did identify opportunities that would give the East Timorese some diplomatic support – in order to ensure that no support would be given. An example is the Labor government's hostility to the Labor Party's own proposal to organise a parliamentary delegation to East Timor:

> On the return of the delegation to Australia we could expect public statements which could reflect the anti-Indonesian impressions members might have gained in Portuguese Timor. These will make the conduct of our relations with Indonesia more difficult than the problem of Portuguese Timor in itself might otherwise make them … A visit by a joint Parliamentary delegation would be the most substantial external incursion … in recent years. Would it not encourage others?[5]

Had there been a desire to keep what Article 73 of the UN Charter calls a 'sacred trust' to uphold 'the well-being of the inhabitants' of East Timor, there were several alternatives available. Australia could have lobbied internationally for an UN-supervised referendum at any time. It could have ensured a de-colonisation process under the auspices of the UN, thereby internationalising the issue and obstructing the Indonesian invasion. Australia could have recognised the major political parties in East Timor and insisted on their legitimacy as representatives of the East Timorese in any de-colonisation process. Australia could also have informed Indonesia, the US and other states that it wanted to see an independent East Timor, even if under heavy Australian influence. None of these steps were taken, and Indonesia invaded on 7 December 1975.

Just before the invasion, Australian activists took decisive steps to protect some East Timorese leaders who would play an important role in the independence struggle. David Scott, a 50-year old father of two who was Founding Director and Chairman of Community Aid Abroad, was in East Timor before the invasion. His

3 See, for example, Kelly (2009); Goldsworthy (2003); Greenlees and Garran (2002) and others.

4 See, for example, Dunn (2003); Taylor (1999).

5 Way (2000), p. 144.

personal links with East Timor went back to his father-in-law, Lieutenant Colonel Bill Leggatt. Leggatt had commanded the 2nd/40th Battalion at Kupang (West Timor), and had gone to Portuguese Timor where he organised the landing of Australian commandoes in December 1941. Scott was evacuated to Darwin just before Indonesia invaded East Timor. Once in Darwin, Scott realised that Jose Ramos-Horta, Rogerio Lobato and Mari Alkatiri were still trapped in Dili. As key members of the East Timorese leadership, they would certainly be singled out for a swift death. He and other activists applied every available means of pressure to ensure the evacuation of these men. A frantic round of lobbying began, culminating in one final evacuation flight for the three men being personally ordered by the new Foreign Minister, Andrew Peacock. Scott flew back to Melbourne, and – although he did not realise it at the time – would work for the independence of East Timor until he was 74 years old.

In Melbourne, Scott addressed 300 people at a meeting, called at very short notice, at the Brotherhood of St Lawrence hall in the Melbourne inner-city suburb of Fitzroy.[6] The Australia-East Timor Association (AETA) was formed that afternoon – the day of the invasion. Below are a few examples from the AETA archives of letters and donations sent in by members of the public:

> Just a small donation [$2] … It would be larger but that I am a pensioner (Eva R. Barnett, Helens Road, Mount Dandenong). P.S. No receipt please.
>
> On behalf of the Congregation of the Highett Presbyterian Church … $25 to be used in connection with the United Nations Delegation to East Timor. (Mr D.J. Smith, 23 Jan. 1976).
>
> Please find enclosed a donation for $37.31, for use by your Association in its work for the independence of East Timor. Members of our family raised this money by not buying family Christmas presents, and it was our wish that the work of your Association be supported. (Marg and John Bottomley, 8 Jan. 1976).

Those who portray the East Timor intervention in 1999 as an example of R2P have very little to say about the role of David Scott or the other so-called 'ordinary Australians' who opposed Australian foreign policy from the very beginning and continued to do so for the next 24 years.

Australian activists first tried to send shiploads of aid to various ports of East Timor. Groups planning to send ships ranged from the Catholic Bishops to a few trade unions.[7] In September 1976, four activists – Cliff Morris, Robert Wesley-

6 Except where otherwise indicated, this section relies on original research of the Australia East Timor Association, whose papers and other documents of the period are archived at the University of Melbourne (henceforth known as 'AETA Archives'). Australia East Timor Association (n.d.).

7 Australia East Timor Association (n.d.), Box 1.

Smith, James Zantis and Manolis 'Manny' Mavromatis – were arrested while trying to sail to East Timor with medical supplies provided by Community Aid Abroad. Their vessel (*Dawn*) had large supplies of medicines, some food, radio equipment and six firearms for personal protection. They were charged with attempting to smuggle drugs (viz. the medicines) and guns (the six firearms) to East Timor. On 14 February 1977, after ten days in court, they were convicted and placed on small bonds. The Northern Territory Supreme Court later overturned their convictions on appeal, but the attempt cost Wesley-Smith his life-savings.

He persisted, despite the financial blow. In response to reports that Indonesia had used napalm in its aerial bombing campaign, Wesley-Smith advertised that he was going to burn a dog on a public oval in Darwin.[8] This action attracted considerable publicity. On the appointed day, 14 July 1978, Wesley-Smith arrived at the oval with a dog hidden under his shirt. Also present were a large crowd of curious onlookers, animal rights activists, members of the media, police and fire brigade. The police had earlier warned Wesley-Smith that he would be arrested if he attempted to carry out his plan. When he pulled the dog out from inside his shirt, it turned out to be a fluffy toy dog. He then declared that people were prepared to be outraged at the burning of a dog, but not of the burning of humans in East Timor by napalm. While there was relief from the animal rights activists and disappointment from some of the onlookers, who had brought their cameras along to record the occasion, the goal of the publicity stunt had been accomplished: Wesley-Smith had raised awareness of Indonesia's actions.

Perhaps, the most elaborate project undertaken by Australian activists in this period was the construction of an illegal radio link between the Northern Territory and East Timor.[9] Warwick Neilley, the organiser of the North Australian Workers Union (later the Miscellaneous Workers Union), purchased several Single Side Band (SSB) radios from a store in Darwin and sent them to East Timor before the invasion. Once the Indonesian invasion began, the East Timorese resistance used an SSB radio mounted on the back of a donkey to communicate with Australian activists, who broadcast from Outpost Radio, VJY Darwin. The Australian Government banned these transmissions, making it unlawful to transmit from Australian territory without a license – although simply listening to broadcasts from East Timor remained lawful. Australian activists therefore set up an alternative, illegal communications network. They outfitted a Toyota Coaster to look just like a tourist vehicle, complete with a small boat on the roof and a trail bike in the back. An activist would broadcast from it while travelling around the Top End of Australia as a tourist.

The game of cat and mouse between activists and the police continued for several years. Sometimes the broadcaster would be caught and the radio confiscated, other times he would evade capture by stealth and deception. Activists

8 Australia East Timor Association (n.d.), Box 3.

9 This section is based on an examination of the AETA archives, interviews with activists in the illegal radio project; see Manning (2003); Wesley-Smith (1998), pp. 83–102.

adopted even more covert tactics, seeking volunteers who were reliable, unknown in the Northern Territory and able to operate autonomously. Each volunteer would work in isolation for six months before handing over to the next volunteer. They obtained four such volunteers from the southern states of Australia. The illegal radio operation continued to operate until the end of 1978 as the only link between the external solidarity movement and the Timorese resistance. According to an Indonesian journalist who accompanied the military on their operations, a battle on 23 September 1978 was soon followed by the capture of Alarico Fernandes and the Fretilin radio.[10] The military leader of the armed resistance, Nicolau Lobato, was killed on 31 December 1978. With the loss of the radio and Lobato's death, Australian activists could not receive any more news from the territory.

The US solidarity movement for East Timor began just before Christmas 1975, when Arnold Kohen, a journalist at a radio station called WVBR in Ithaca, New York, heard that East Timor had been invaded. He tried to find out more about the issue, and looked around for academics in the field of Asian Studies. By coincidence, Ithaca was the home of Cornell University, whose Modern Indonesia Project was the most influential Indonesian studies program in the US. He was therefore immediately in touch with the leading Indonesia scholars of the era. Kohen became extremely well-informed about East Timor while continuing to work as a journalist. He began an energetic and highly effective campaign of raising public awareness with the help of a very small group of scholars, including Professor Benedict Anderson, Richard Franke, Sue Nichterlein, Roberta Quance, Michael Chamberlin, Jeremy Mark and Noam Chomsky. Whatever public knowledge of East Timor existed in the US during the 1970s can be traced to the activities of these individuals.

Chomsky's testimony was read to the UN's Special Committee on Decolonisation (also known as the Fourth Committee) in 1978, at a time when the Indonesian military launched an 'encirclement and annihilation' campaign to crush the resistance. Famine conditions began to emerge at this time. According to East Timor's Commission for Reception, Truth and Reconciliation (known by its Portuguese initials of CAVR), the population was interned in camps which:

> ... became the sites for a fully-fledged famine in which unknown numbers died. Already in a weakened state when they entered the camps, internees endured extended periods without access to food gardens or emergency humanitarian aid ... [I]n exchange for food the military and their auxiliaries extorted money, family heirlooms and other valuables (for example gold and traditional beads), and sexual favours.[11]

When the US media were refusing to interview East Timorese refugees, claiming that they had no access to them, Chomsky personally paid for the airfares of

10 Subroto (1997).

11 CAVR (2005), p. 81.

several refugees, bringing them from Lisbon to the US, where he tried to get them into the editorial offices of the *New York Times* and other outlets. Most of his financial commitment to such causes has – because of his own reticence – gone unnoticed. Kohen and Chomsky's efforts enabled the refugees' plight to reach the editorial page of the *New York Times*, where Karl Meyer, David Unger and Tina Rosenberg editorialised against the Carter administration's policies. An East Timorese activist said, 'we learnt that the Chomsky factor and East Timor were a deadly combination' and 'proved to be too powerful for those who tried to defeat us'.[12]

At this time, the Liberal-National coalition was in power in Australia under Prime Minister Malcolm Fraser and Foreign Minister Andrew Peacock. As the death toll rose in East Timor, the Fraser government moved to legitimise the Indonesian presence by extending de facto recognition of Indonesia's sovereignty in January 1978, followed by de jure recognition with the opening of negotiations with Indonesia on the seabed boundary in the Timor Gap in February 1979. The Australian Labor Party was in opposition while all this was occurring. It adopted a series of strong National Conference resolutions on the subject of East Timor. The 1979 Resolution declared:

> The ALP condemns, in the strongest terms, the Australian government's recognition of Indonesia's annexation of East Timor and undertakes, on becoming the Government of Australia, to reverse the decision.[13]

Three years later, Labor's official position was unchanged. The 1982 Resolution read:

> The ALP recognises the inalienable right of the East Timorese to self-determination and independence and rejects the Australian government's recognition of the Indonesian annexation of East Timor.[14]

Labor's spokesman on foreign affairs at the time, Lionel Bowen, is said to have 'accept[ed] the policy to placate the Left on the foreign affairs and defence policy committee'. If Labor won the election, he would 'have no trouble diluting it to avert problems'.[15] When Labor *did* win the election, of course, it reversed these policies very quickly. Former Defence Minister Bill Morrison led an Australian parliamentary delegation on a so-called 'fact-finding tour' of East Timor. On this tour, Fretilin representatives tried to make contact with Morrison on the road between Baucau and Los Palos but were rebuffed. They were later captured and killed by the Indonesian military. Morrison's report concluded that the

12 Pereira (1996), p. viii.
13 ALP (1979).
14 ALP (1982).
15 Hayden (1996), p. 396.

'administrative authority … of the Indonesian government [was] firmly in place' and that the Indonesian Government was acting in good faith in the territory.[16] While there was a dissenting statement by Senator Gordon McIntosh, the Chairman of the Senate Foreign Affairs Committee, the Official Report found no evidence of human rights abuses and no real insecurity in East Timor.[17] The Official Report was no more than a public relations exercise to defend the Labor government's policy.

It had the desired effect: the Hawke Labor government used the report to reverse ALP policy, which had previously called for the suspension of all defence aid to Indonesia. Foreign Minister Bill Hayden sought to justify this policy reversal in his memoirs. He argued that the earlier policy was 'retributive' and 'unambiguously confrontationist',[18] and asserted that there were many positive aspects to the Indonesian invasion and occupation:

> East Timor has benefited from more social and economic development in the past twenty years under Indonesian administration than it received through four centuries under the dead hand of Portuguese colonialism. In fact much of the dissidence occurring in East Timor today is a product of exaggerated expectations of what the new economic order could provide and not of sympathetic responses to Fretilin's sporadic and limited insurgency activity.[19]

The real problem was the free flow of information, which might alert the public to the real nature of Australian foreign policy – in other words, the same problem that had confronted the Whitlam and Fraser governments. Hayden accused elements of the media of being 'the cause of the greatest strains in bilateral relations'.[20] In his view, the media had a responsibility to avoid 'unnecessary damage to our national interests with other countries'.[21]

According to Hayden, human rights advocates were 'noisy groups in the community who, unlike government, can afford to behave with indifference to the broader national interest'. Instead, it was important to be 'a constructive partner not a strident public, carping critic'.[22] He argued that:

> … the notion of universal human rights is relatively new and it is not universally endorsed … Much of what has been defined as morality over the centuries has been Eurocentric in its values and origins … there are, relatively, only a few democracies in the world … [Democracy] is a complex and difficult system …

16 Taylor (1999), pp. 140–142.
17 Australian Parliament (APH) (1983).
18 Hayden (1996), p. 395.
19 Hayden (1996), pp. 397–8.
20 Hayden (1996), p. 399.
21 Hayden (1996), p. 398.
22 Hayden (1996), p. 400.

> culturally a great many nations are incapable of embracing it successfully at this stage, or may not want to at any stage, of their development.[23]

Yet the Hawke government was able to solemnly reaffirm Australia's revocation of the de jure recognition of the incorporation of the Baltic countries into the USSR, saying that it 'demonstrated our continuing commitment to the purposes and principles of the United Nations Charter and to the cause of democracy and freedom in the world'.[24]

Under Hawke, the Australian Government continued negotiations with Indonesia on the sea-bed boundary in the Timor Gap, signing the Timor Gap Treaty in December 1989. This treaty ensured that Australia and Indonesia would rob East Timor's oil, while the Indonesian army continued to occupy East Timor. Gareth Evans – today a prominent advocate of the 'Responsibility to Protect' – was Foreign Minister when he signed the Timor Gap Treaty with Indonesia's foreign minister, Ali Alatas. When asked what he would say to 'those who would point to Australia's international obligations that we shouldn't be recognising territory acquired by anyone by force', Evans replied, 'Well, we don't accept that there's any international legal obligation not to recognise acquisitions of that kind'. He added, 'I want to make it clear that we don't recognise, as I say, any such legal obligation'.[25] While Evans was foreign minister, he did his best to provide diplomatic cover for the Indonesian occupation of East Timor. In 1990, he dismissed concerns about Indonesia's invasion and occupation of East Timor, saying:

> What I can say is simply that the world is a pretty unfair place, that it's littered over the course of the decades and the centuries with examples of acquisitions by force which have proved to be, for whatever reason, irreversible.[26]

On 12 November 1991, a peaceful procession of mourners left the Motael church in Dili for the Santa Cruz cemetery. Some 1,500 people began the procession, but they were joined en route by many more people, including schoolchildren on their way to classes. When the mourners arrived at the cemetery, Indonesian troops cut them off from the rear. They opened fire, killing 271 people. No other single event did more to harm Indonesia's diplomatic initiatives since the invasion than this one, which would be known henceforth as the 'Santa Cruz Massacre'. The massacre was a major setback for Indonesian diplomacy. Larry Dinger, a political officer at US Embassy in Jakarta from 1987–90 and the Indonesia Desk Officer at the US State Department when the massacre occurred recalls its impact on US foreign policy towards Indonesia:

---

23 Hayden (1996), pp. 419–20.

24 Hayden (1996), p. 419.

25 Domm and Aarons (28–30 October 1990).

26 Domm and Aarons (28–30 October 1990).

> In 1990–92, when I manned the State Department's Indonesia Desk, Principals and Deputies Committees never met about Indonesia, and even Assistant Secretaries and their Deputies were seldom seized with the issues. An exception was Defense Under Secretary Wolfowitz, a former Ambassador to Jakarta, who retained a keen interest. Policy – in effect to maintain the status quo – was mostly affirmed via working levels which consulted frequently and harmoniously, always within the context that the 'realist' approach was appropriate.
>
> That working-level coalition could rebuff Portuguese and human-rights lobbyists' efforts, in part because the few in Congress who took the topic seriously couldn't energise broad interest in their views. That low-key environment changed dramatically on 12 November 1991.[27]

The Santa Cruz massacre was indeed a watershed event. Yet the massacre would never have been filmed or broadcast were it not for the international solidarity movement. Australian activist Shirley Shackleton, widow of the murdered journalist Greg Shackleton, had been invited by the Oxford University academic Peter Carey to Oxford's inaugural seminar on East Timor. While in England, she briefed Peter Gordon, a producer at Yorkshire Television, about conditions in the territory. As a result of this briefing and assistance provided by British solidarity activists, Peter Gordon visited East Timor with a Yorkshire Television crew in 1991. He hired British freelance cameraman Max Stahl, who filmed the massacre. Stahl was able to have his footage smuggled out by Saskia Kouwenberg, a Dutch-born solidarity activist for East Timor.

When news of the massacre broke, Gareth Evans was unconcerned about any 'Responsibility to Protect'. He tried to absolve the institutional role of the Indonesian military, describing the massacre as 'an aberration, not an act of state policy'.[28] Evans and Keating continued to pursue closer military-to-military ties with the Suharto regime. As Prime Minister, Paul Keating visited Ireland in September 1993. The visit was supposed to be part pilgrimage, part triumphant homecoming.[29] But he had not taken into account one of the most effective groups in the international solidarity movement – the East Timor Ireland Solidarity Campaign (ETISC). This group flew Shirley Shackleton to Ireland two weeks before Keating's visit. The activists organised a constant stream of interviews for her on radio and TV, ensuring that the Irish press and public were aware of Keating's policy towards Indonesia and East Timor. As a consequence, Keating was badgered about East Timor throughout his visit. Although guest of honour at the All-Ireland Gaelic football final – the highest profile event in the country's sporting calendar – Keating was heckled throughout the game by several spectators about his record on East Timor. A state dinner in his honour at Dublin Castle that

27 Dinger (2000), p. 3.
28 Aarons and Domm (1992).
29 Keating is of Irish heritage.

evening was picketed by hundreds of protestors who held up candles as the official convoy entered the gates. Several guests at the dinner wore badges with signs saying 'Hands off East Timor's oil' and 'Australia: Where is your conscience?' At Keating's speech to the combined houses of the Irish Assembly, several members from all parties wore white carnations in support of the East Timor. Although he did not mention East Timor even once during his speech, his press conference a few minutes later was almost completely taken up with questions about the subject. Throughout his visit, Keating was left in no doubt about the extent of Irish opposition to his government's policy. ETISC found that its membership increased rapidly as a result of the publicity. It is worth noting that Paul Keating's speechwriter, Don Watson, makes no mention at this entire highly embarrassing episode in *Recollections of a Bleeding Heart*, his paean to the Keating years.[30]

ETISC also acted as a policy transmission line between local activists, the Irish Government and the European Union. Previously, the Irish Government had largely ignored the 1975 invasion and the subsequent occupation. After the formation of ETISC, Ireland's position on East Timor evolved from non-involvement to active participation. Eilis Ward's examination of *Oireachtas* (Houses of Parliament) debates shows that between 1992 and 1996, a total of 65 questions were tabled in the Dáil (lower house), four motions were passed in the Senate, three detailed statements on East Timor were also delivered in the Senate by the minister for foreign affairs or his representative, and in the Oireachtas Committee for Foreign Affairs (established in 1993), East Timor was debated in detail four times.[31]

For Gareth Evans and Paul Keating, the pressure continued back home in Australia. In 1995, there were 1,360 East Timorese who were seeking asylum in Australia.[32] The Keating government was opposing them on the grounds that they had Portuguese citizenship – while also maintaining that Portugal had no claims preventing Australia and Indonesia from extracting oil from the Timor Sea. Activists formed the Sanctuary Network – a citizen-based attempt to oppose the Keating government's policy. It consisted of more than 8,000 individuals, as well as a large number of organisations, all of whom pledged to defy Australian law by hiding these asylum seekers if their bids were rejected. As Christian activist Ciaron O'Reilly put it, 'We basically said to the government that you should offer these people sanctuary and if you fail to do so then we will break the law and hide these people out'.[33] A secret list of safe houses and other support services was prepared. Members of the network were fully aware of the legal implications – a penalty of six months imprisonment for obstructing immigration procedures. Nevertheless, they took the view that if there were a large enough network, it would be politically harder for the government to arrest everyone. The sanctuary network was explicit about its aim – to raise the political cost of the government's policy. The Sanctuary Network 'gained support from many other

30 Watson (2002), pp. 420–423.

31 Ward (2000), pp. 155–6.

32 Smythe (2004), p. 116.

33 O'Reilly (1996).

religious congregations (predominantly those of women), and then from as many as ten thousand Catholic laity'.[34] The government was forced to back down.

On 29 January 1996, three women entered the British Aerospace military base at Warton, Lancashire armed with household hammers. They smashed the radar nose and control panel of a Hawk ground-attack aircraft, which was part of an order of 24 aircraft destined for Indonesia. They called their act a Ploughshares Action, which was inspired by the biblical injunction 'to beat swords into ploughshares'.[35] A British activist named Chris Cole had performed a Ploughshares action on British Aerospace three years earlier.[36] The three women – borough counsellor Joanna Wilson, gardener Lotta Kronlid and nurse Andrea Needham – were charged with illegal entry and criminal damage. The fourth member of the group was environmental campaigner Angie Zelter,[37] who had supported them and publicly announced her intention to carry out another Ploughshares Action. Zelter was arrested the next year while on her way to a public meeting. Their trial by jury began on 23 July 1997. Solidarity activists organised blockades, sit-ins, teach-ins and other vigils, all of which combined to generate enormous negative publicity for the Indonesian occupation. Sensationally, they were all acquitted after the jury accepted their defence – they claimed they had acted lawfully because they were using 'reasonable force' to prevent the much greater crime of genocide.[38] The entire episode served to highlight Indonesia's human rights abuses, and the equally crucial factor of Western support for Indonesia's actions.[39]

Meanwhile, the independence campaign achieved perhaps its most significant victory of the 1990s – the awarding of the Nobel Peace Prize to Jose Ramos-Horta and Bishop Carlos Belo. This victory occurred as a direct result of actions taken by a few activists in the international solidarity movement. Yiannis Tavridis, a student at the University of Bergen in Norway, had set up a local community group in Bergen in 1991 and proposed East Timor as a candidate for a human rights prize awarded by the Rafto Foundation of Bergen, Norway. This foundation memorialises the economist Professor Thorolf Rafto, who was a champion of spiritual, political and economic freedoms. The Rafto Prize is sometimes regarded as a precursor to the Nobel Peace Prize. Tavridis and two other Oslo-based activists (media researcher Elisabeth Eide and linguistics professor Lars Vikoer) were the 'permanent core' of the Norwegian solidarity movement,[40] channelling information about East Timor to the Norwegian media. The three activists built good relations with the Norwegian Labour Party, the Christian Peoples' Party and the Socialist Party. Soon, the moderate Right-wing party also became informal allies of the East Timor cause.

34 Smythe (2004), p. 116.
35 Isaiah 2:4 and Micah 4:3
36 Baird (1994), p. 21.
37 Zelter (1996).
38 Zelter (1996).
39 Martin et al. (2001), p. 153.
40 Tavridis (15 January 2009).

In 1993, the Rafto Foundation awarded its Rafto Prize to 'The People of East Timor represented by Jose Ramos-Horta'. This legitimized East Timorese independence within conservative Scandinavian circles. Tavridis, Federer, Ramos-Horta and Arnold Kohen decided to make a determined bid for the Nobel Peace Prize. Kohen had ensured that good personal relations were built between Bishop Belo and Gunnar Stalsett, a clergyman, theologian and Rector at Oslo University. Help came from an unexpected source: Sigurjon Einarsson, the manager of Morten Harket of the world-famous pop group *A-Ha!*, convinced three Icelandic women parliamentarians (Kristín Ástgeirsdóttir, Anna Ólafsdóttir Björnsson and Kristín Einarsdóttir of the *Samtök um kvennalista*, or Women's Alliance, a feminist political party) to endorse Ramos-Horta as a possible candidate. Jochen Schilde, a German living in Norway, helped a lot in the lobbying process. All these actions secured more momentum for East Timor amongst the Scandinavian political class. Einarsson and Harket's pop music profile ensured that the wider Scandinavian public heard a lot about East Timor in 1996. Einarsson produced a film with Max Stahl about Bishop Belo in 1996. Entitled, *Sometimes I Must Speak Out Strongly*, it used footage shot by Australian activist Dr Andrew McNaughtan during his 1994 visit to East Timor.[41] On 11 October 1996, Bishop Carlos Belo and Jose Ramos-Horta were named joint winners of the 1996 Nobel Peace Prize.

It was a huge victory for the independence campaign. As foreign minister Ali Alatas later said, 'It was as if we had been besieged. The 1996 Nobel Peace Prize showed how seriously we had been besieged'.[42] According to Horta's long-term adviser Dr Juan Federer, the Nobel Peace Prize 'was probably *the* turning point. The Santa Cruz massacre was a turning point, of course, but for the international work, for achieving respectability, the Nobel Prize was it'.[43] Prior to the Nobel Prize, he says,

> Nobody really wanted to see us. We were received by foreign ministries but in their Human Rights Sections. It was undeniable that East Timor was a human rights issue. But nobody was really terribly interested or committed to it. They had to receive us but it was clear that they wished we went away.[44]

After the Nobel Peace Prize,

> All of a sudden all sorts of invitations appeared. Everybody wanted to be associated with Horta. Everybody wanted to have a Nobel Laureate decorating

41 Einarsson (4 November 2009).

42 Santa Cruz incident a turning point in our diplomacy: Interview with Ali Alatas (2000).

43 Santa Cruz incident a turning point in our diplomacy: Interview with Ali Alatas (2000).

44 Santa Cruz incident a turning point in our diplomacy: Interview with Ali Alatas (2000).

> their tables, their dinners, their meetings, their conferences and their events because it gave them prestige. This is particularly the case in the US, where he was a celebrity. And Horta knew masterfully how to use that to the advantage of the cause.[45]

By this time, John Howard was Prime Minister of Australia, and his government did its best to ignore the award even though Ramos-Horta was a resident of Sydney. It joined Indonesia in boycotting the ceremony in Oslo. That year, however, an expatriate Australian, Professor Peter Doherty, was awarded the Nobel Prize for Physiology/Medicine. He was flown at government expense from the US to official receptions in Melbourne and Canberra. Howard was so sensitive to questions about Ramos-Horta's victory that he made an embarrassing 'slip of the tongue': at the official reception in Parliament House, Canberra, he publicly congratulated Professor Doherty for having won the Nobel Prize for Peace [sic].[46] There was an audible gasp among the audience as an unwelcome guest had metaphorically been ushered in by the very man who had sought to bar him.

The Howard government's record on East Timor's quest for independence was one of steadfast opposition. Recently, however, a leading Australian journalist, Paul Kelly, has claimed that Howard and Foreign Minister Alexander Downer were secretly working to bring about an independent East Timor, even though nearly everyone else – including the Defence Department – believed that the plan was to keep East Timor within Indonesia. Kelly's book, *The March of Patriots*,[47] was launched with great fanfare and received with reverence and ecstasy. Alan Kohler, chairman of the book's publisher, Melbourne University Publishing, praised Kelly and his 'intellectual journalism'. 'For journalists', Kohler said, 'Paul is a benchmark and an inspiration'.[48] Prime Minister Rudd said the book was 'a stupendous piece of work … a monumental account that will become a benchmark for future research on this period of Australian history'.[49] Les Carlyon wrote, 'This is how political history should be written but seldom is'.[50] Not to be outdone, Laurie Oakes called it 'brilliant – ambitious in scope and forensic in detail'.[51] I will therefore assess this book in order to see whether it provides evidence that the Howard government did, in fact, exercise its 'Responsibility to Protect' the people of East Timor.

It is useful to begin by examining Kelly's methodology. History is a reconstruction of past events. The credibility of the reconstruction depends in large part on the sources of evidence used by the historian, as well as the emphasis given

45 Federer (18 January 2008).
46 P. Doherty and P. Doherty (3 January 2009).
47 Kelly (2009).
48 Kerr (2009).
49 Rudd (7 September 2009).
50 Carlyon (2009).
51 Oakes (2009).

to various aspects of the narrative. Richard Evans, the distinguished Cambridge University historian, once provided an expert report as a witness in a trial between Holocaust-denier David Irving and Penguin Books. Evans wrote that historians:

> … distinguish between primary sources, which were produced at the time of the events to which they relate, and secondary sources, which were produced afterwards and rely on memory or on the work of other historians. Clearly, primary sources are prima facie regarded as more reliable, although they must of course be assessed critically as to their authenticity, their authorship and their purpose.[52]

It is important, wrote Evans, to ask 'what were the motives behind a particular document coming into existence' so as to 'control it for possible bias, tendentiousness, or downright intention to mislead'. However, 'perhaps the most problematical kind of evidence' is 'interviews conducted with participants after the event by the historian'. For obvious reasons, decision-makers will tend to provide the most self-serving explanations, justifications and excuses. Historians must therefore 'probe the motives and purposes of those whom they are interviewing; and they must not take everything they are told at face value'.[53]

Turning now to Kelly's chapter on East Timor, we find that it runs for 35 pages with an additional 140 references. An astounding 97 of these are nothing more than interviews with the participants. In addition, Kelly relies heavily on *East Timor in Transition 1998–2000: An Australian Policy Challenge*.[54] This book was published by the Department of Foreign Affairs and Trade (DFAT) in 2001 and launched by Alexander Downer. Unlike other historical publications by DFAT, this one was not produced by DFAT's Historical Documents Project, but by a team of departmental officers who had worked on East Timor during the crisis. In other words, those who had implemented policy were assessing their own performances within the covers of a book they had themselves written, using material they had themselves selected. As one foreign affairs expert has noted, its discussion of East Timor's political awakening and the period of Indonesia's invasion is 'by far the weakest and might induce informed readers to proceed no further.' Its discussion of Australia's role is 'profoundly misleading'.[55] Kelly's reliance on this book casts further doubt on his methodology. The point is not that he should not quote participants, of course; it is that he should not take everything he is told at face value. He should verify claims against available documentary evidence, and compare the participants' actions with their subsequent claims.

Under Howard, Australian policy towards Indonesia was operating within a long-established bi-partisan framework; he maintained his predecessor's support

52 Evans (2000).
53 Evans (2000).
54 Department of Foreign Affairs and Trade (DFAT) (2001).
55 Cotton (2001).

of the Suharto regime and of Indonesian rule over East Timor. When the regime cracked down on pro-democracy demonstrators in July 1996, there had been no official expressions of criticism or even disapproval from the new Foreign Minister, Alexander Downer. Deputy Prime Minister Tim Fischer said that Suharto was 'perhaps the world's greatest figure in the latter half of the twentieth century'.[56]

However, a hugely significant event had occurred in 1997: the Australian Labor Party's spokesperson on foreign relations, Laurie Brereton, had fractured the longstanding bi-partisan consensus towards Indonesian rule over East Timor, calling for the first time for a 'right of self-determination'.[57] This right of self-determination was, he argued, the only real solution to the problem of East Timor. The bi-partisanship that had been an enduring feature of Australia's position on East Timor had allowed successive governments to contain the problem of public opinion. By maintaining bi-partisanship, parliamentary oppositions provided governments with a margin of comfort necessary to neutralise public opinion. By the time Howard had come to power, no foreign minister or shadow foreign minister had visited East Timor in more than 20 years. Brereton's move opened up political space that had previously been closed to civil society groups that campaigned for democracy in Indonesia and self-determination for East Timor. The constant pressure he would apply in Parliament and in the media meant that the government would have no comfort zone. Particularly in 1999, it was always on the back foot, forced to defend its stance to an increasingly agitated public.

Also in October 1998, another development unnerved the Indonesian and Australian foreign policy establishments. Indonesia's new president, B.J. Habibie, had previously announced that many combat troops would be withdrawn from East Timor. Alexander Downer praised this decision, calling it 'a step in the right direction'.[58] However, Dr Andrew McNaughtan, a Sydney-based activist, smuggled out the entire Indonesian army personnel records for East Timor. The documents showed that Indonesia was merely rotating combat personnel, not withdrawing them, and that its claims of demilitarisation in East Timor were false. McNaughtan and his fellow activists maximised publicity by holding simultaneous press conferences in different cities around the world. The exposure of the personnel records led to a dramatic increase in the pressure on Habibie and the Indonesian foreign policy apparatus. These actions are missing from Kelly's perspective, with its heavy reliance on interviews with participants.

Meanwhile, the economic situation in Indonesia was plunging to new depths. In the second quarter of 1998, real GDP was 16.5 per cent below the same period in 1997. The exchange rate was at 11,000 Indonesian rupiah to one US dollar, more than four times lower than the previous year. Inflation was skyrocketing, the price of food was soaring and the purchasing power of the rupiah was plummeting. Wage-earners had lost more than a third of their real incomes. Domestic unrest was

56 Lague (1996), p. 15.

57 Greenlees (1997).

58 Stewart (1998).

threatening to get out of control. Oil prices – a key source of government revenues – were stagnating at $10–12 per barrel. In the midst of all this, Indonesia's foreign policy apparatus was proving unable to argue effectively for economic assistance because it was confronted constantly by questions about East Timor. It was a problem the new government did not need.

The Indonesian military's political and economic weaknesses were temporary; at some time in the future, it would once again be strong enough to crush East Timorese demands. Self-determination would have to be delayed until such a time. Howard therefore wrote to Habibie on 19 December 1998, suggesting that 'the East Timorese desire for an act of self-determination' could be addressed 'in a manner that avoids an early and final decision'. Howard approvingly cited the Matignon Accords, which 'enabled a compromise political solution to be implemented while deferring a referendum on the final status ... for many years'. Indonesia too could adopt the formula of 'a substantial period of autonomy' followed by 'an act of self-determination by the East Timorese at some future time'.[59]

The then-Secretary of the Defence Department, Paul Barratt, writes that Howard's letter:

> ... was a plan to find a fig-leaf behind which to put to bed once and for all the incorporation of East Timor into Indonesia. Rather than being a plan for East Timorese independence, this plan would have more in common with the Israeli approach to the Palestinian question before the first intifada – spend some money to make the material circumstances of the people a bit better, wean them away from the insurgency by talk of some sort of autonomy in the indeterminate future, and hope that with the passage of time the act of self-determination, if it ever comes to that, will produce a majority in favour of the status quo.[60]

As Senator Robert Hill put it, there had been no shift in policy: 'the Prime Minister has come to the conclusion that ... an autonomous East Timor within Indonesia, at least for the time being, would be the better option'.[61] The Deputy Secretary of DFAT explained later that 'a very important part of our thinking at the time that the Prime Minister dispatched his letter was that Indonesia had only one last chance to keep East Timor as part of Indonesia'.[62] Howard's letter was therefore an attempt to make the best of this 'one last chance' for the Indonesian military to contain the forces of East Timorese independence. None of this can find its way into Kelly's account, given his peculiar methodology.

When Habibie announced that he would allow the East Timorese to vote on whether they wanted to remain in Indonesia or be independent, the Indonesian authorities severely restricted the number of official ballot monitors. Neither

59 Department of Foreign Affairs and Trade (DFAT) (2001).

60 Barratt (2009).

61 Hill (11 February 1999), p. 205.

62 Dauth (9 September 1999).

the Australian nor the Indonesian Government expected that there would be an unprecedented level of international scrutiny despite these restrictions – nearly 2,300 international solidarity activists also converged on East Timor as election observers, to say nothing of the 1,700 Indonesian and East Timorese non-governmental observers. There were also approximately 600 journalists present.[63] It would be impossible to engineer a repeat of the fraudulent 1969 Act of Free Choice, in which 1,022 West Papuans out of a total population of 700,000 were coerced into joining the Indonesian republic. This action, too, is something that Kelly's account cannot deal with.

The Indonesian military commenced a campaign of militia-backed terror in order to coerce the East Timorese into voting to stay within Indonesia. Habibie's foreign affairs adviser, Dewi Fortuna Anwar, sounded a public warning about what was in store. Writing in the *International Herald Tribune*, she said that 'Indonesia's 500,000 strong military cannot be relied on to do the job [of providing security for the ballot] because it is not regarded as neutral'.[64] Alarmed, the US Assistant Secretary of State Stanley Roth met the Secretary of Australia's Department of Foreign Affairs and Trade (DFAT), Ashton Calvert five days later in Washington DC. According to the highly sensitive transcript of the conversation, Roth was of the view that:

> ... a full-scale peacekeeping operation would be an unavoidable aspect of the transition ... Australia's position of keeping peace keeping at arm's length was essentially defeatist, and that it was necessary to go forth and persuade Congress and UN member states that it simply had to be done.[65]

Stating the Australian Government's position, however, the head of DFAT, Ashton Calvert, made it clear that Australia would not support peacekeepers. It is important to understand that the transcript of the Calvert-Roth meeting was leaked to the media soon after. Had it not leaked, the Australian public would not have found out about the government's secret rejection of Roth's proposal until 2029, when the archives open up under the 30-year rule. By contrast, the real-time leak resulted in a swift escalation of political pressure. Try as they may, Calvert and Roth's subsequent interviews with Kelly cannot erase this glaring fact.

Alexander Downer continued to publicly reject the need for peacekeepers. Emerging from a meeting with the UN Secretary-General, Kofi Annan, he said:

> We hope that there won't be a need for a peacekeeping force because if you need a peacekeeping force, you need a peace to keep and peace first has to be negotiated and we hope that when the peace is negotiated it will be a peaceful peace that won't require a peacekeeping force.[66]

---

63 CAVR (2005), vol. 3, p. 136.

64 Anwar (1999).

65 Lyons (1999), pp. 25–9.

66 Downer (14 March 1999).

What we get from Kelly, however, verges on the comical – Downer and Calvert as heroes:

> 'I want to be a lot more active on East Timor', Downer told Calvert after the re-election. He was talking to the right man – Calvert had been waiting for this opportunity.[67]

In June 1999, the US military's Hawaii-based Pacific Command raised the possibility of attaching Australian military officers to a possible US peace enforcement operation in East Timor. The US request spoke of using 'overwhelming force to stop the killing' and was conveyed to the Commander Australian Theatre, Air Vice Marshal Treloar. Since Treloar commanded the headquarters that would oversee any deployment of troops to East Timor, the US military was deliberately addressing the Australian Defence Force (ADF) officer best placed to advise the government that the proposal was feasible.[68] Treloar undertook to refer the request to senior levels in the Australian Government. The request was declined 'after lengthy, top-level consideration'.[69]

When asked about such a request during Question Time in Parliament, Downer initially claimed that he had neither seen the cable nor knew of the request, although he was an addressee, as were the Prime Minister, the Minister for Defence and the heads of their respective departments. Downer assured the House that he was 'completely unaware of any proposal by the United States defence force to mount a peace enforcement exercise in East Timor'.[70] A diplomatic cable containing a copy of the request was leaked to members of the press. Late that night, the government learnt that early editions of the next day's *Age* were carrying detailed excerpts of the cable. Downer rushed back to Parliament at 11:32 pm. and made a 'clarification', saying that 'apparently' the issue 'was informally raised' by officials who 'asked hypothetically' about peace enforcement. But, he continued, this was not a 'formal United States Government request'.[71] It was Downer's third forced 'clarification' since becoming Foreign Minister.

The Australian Government refused a direct US request to hand over intelligence material detailing links between the Indonesian armed forces and pro-Jakarta militias. The requests were made on several occasions to Australia's Ambassador in Jakarta, John McCarthy, and to Australia's Ambassador to the US, Andrew Peacock. Both envoys refused to make the information available.[72] The Australian intelligence liaison officer to the US, Merv Jenkins, was required to exchange intelligence as part of his normal duties. The US intelligence community

67 Kelly (2009), p. 486.
68 Daley (1999).
69 Daley (1999).
70 Downer (9 August 1999).
71 Downer (9 August 1999b).
72 Wilkinson (1999).

was particularly interested in material that tied the Indonesian military to the militias. When Jenkins passed on such intelligence to his US counterparts, he was placed under heavy pressure by the Australian authorities, who flew to the US, interrogated him and threatened him with prosecution and imprisonment. Jenkins committed suicide following this treatment.[73] This information, too, is missing from Kelly's account.

The Australian National Audit Office later conducted a performance audit into the management of the deployment of the Australian-led force. It concluded that the Department of Defence:

> ... could not provide evidence that formal planning for [a multilateral operation] began until later in 1999 ... The nature and size of the ADF involvement in East Timor were not known until shortly before deployment.

This is because:

> ... there was no government strategic requirement for the ADF to be able to form or lead an international peace-keeping coalition force ... the actual nature and size of the military operations to be undertaken were not clear until shortly before deployment. The number, size and force capability to be provided, and the support required, by the non-Australian troop contributing nations were not known until after the deployment had started.[74]

The Australian Defence Force, not expecting to have to arrange for a peacekeeping force, had to borrow 4,000 flak jackets from the United States. The head of the military's support command, Major General Mueller, said that the demand for items that were not in its catalogue had 'been very, very significant' and led to a very significant surge in purchasing materials off-the-shelf in Darwin and Sydney.[75]

These and many other aspects of East Timor's independence go unexplained in Kelly's account, which also contains careless errors. For example: the Indonesian occupation of East Timor lasted for 24 years. Kelly says that it lasted for 30 years[76] and 35 years.[77] Prime Minister Rudd may have unintentionally put his finger on the problem when he said at the launch that 'it provides perspective that could only come about through Paul's proximity to those in power through this period'.[78]

To conclude, the deployment of troops to East Timor is often portrayed as a fine example of the 'Responsibility to Protect' in action. By contrast, the historical record shows that it was activists who upheld the R2P principle despite

---

73 ABC (14 February 2000).

74 Australian National Audit Office (ANAO) (2002).

75 Mueller (2 December 1999).

76 Kelly (2009), p. 485.

77 Kelly (2009), p. 504.

78 Rudd (7 September 2009).

longstanding, ferocious opposition from many states. Activists became the little wheel inside the bigger wheel of public opinion, turning it against the Australian Government's opposition to an independent East Timor. The East Timor case illustrates a point made recently by a scholar-activist:

> Even though states do not adhere to the UDHR, and some formally reject much of it (crucially including the world's most powerful state), nonetheless it serves as an ideal that activists can appeal to in educational and organizing efforts, often effectively. My suspicion is that a major contribution of the discussion of R2P may turn out to be rather similar, and with sufficient commitment, unfortunately not yet detectable among the powerful, it could be significant indeed.[79]

References

M. Aarons and R. Domm (1992) *East Timor: A Western-made Tragedy*, Left Book Club.

ABC (14 February 2000) *Four Corners*, ABC TV.

ALP (1979) *Australian Labor Party National Conference Resolution*, Mitchell Library.

ALP (1982) *Australian Labor Party National Conference Resolution*, Mitchell Library.

D.F. Anwar (1999) *International Herald Tribune* 17 February.

Australia East Timor Association (n.d.) *AETA Melbourne Archives*, University of Melbourne.

Australian National Audit Office (ANAO) (2002) *Management of Australian Defence Force Deployments to East Timor: Report No. 38*, ANAO.

Australian Parliament (APH) (1983) *Official Report of the Australian Parliamentary Delegation to East Timor*, Australian Government Publishing Service.

V. Baird (1994) 'Bringing the Blood back to British Aerospace', 253, *New Internationalist.*

P. Barratt (2009) 'Paul Kelly on East Timor', *Australian Observer* 14 September.

L. Carlyon (2009) *The March of Patriots (Promotional Advertising)*, MUP.

CAVR (2005) *Chega! – Final Report of the Commission for Reception, Truth and Reconciliation*, Commission for Reception, Truth and Reconciliation.

N. Chomsky (23 July 2009) *Statement to the United Nations General Assembly Thematic Dialogue on the Responsibility to Protect*, United Nations available at http://www.un.org/ga/president/63/interactive/protect/noam.pdf (accessed 30 July 2009).

J. Cotton (2001) 'Australia's commitment in East Timor: A review article', *Contemporary Southeast Asia* 1 December.

P. Daley (1999) 'US marines set for Dili', *The Age* 10 August.

79 Chomsky (23 July 2009).

P. Daley (1999) 'We snub offer to send in the Marines', *Sunday Age* 31 August.

J. Dauth (9 September 1999) *Foreign Affairs, Defence and Trade Senate Committee Hansard*, Australian Parliament.

Department of Foreign Affairs and Trade (DFAT) (2001) *East Timor in Transition: An Australian Policy Challenge*, Brown and Wilton.

L. Dinger (2000) *East Timor and US Foreign Policy: Making Sausage*, United States National War College, National Defense University.

P. Doherty and P. Doherty (3 January 2009) *Personal Communication.*

R. Domm and M. Aarons (28–30 October 1990) *Background Briefing*, ABC Radio National.

A. Downer (14 March 1999) *Press Conference*, Canberra.

A. Downer (9 August 1999b) *Clarification of Response to Question without Notice*, Australian Parliament.

J. Dunn (2003) *East Timor: A Rough Passage to Independence*, Longueville Books.

S. Einarsson (4 November 2009) *Interview with the author.*

R. Evans (2000) *Expert Report – David Irving, Hitler and Holocaust Denial* available at http://www.hdot.org/en/trial/defense/evans.

J. Federer (18 January 2008) *Interview with the author.*

D. Goldsworthy (2003) 'East Timor', in P. Edwards and D. Goldsworthy (eds) *Facing North: a Century of Australian Engagement with Asia:1970s to 2000*, Melbourne University Press.

D. Greenlees (1997) 'Labor policy ups ante for autonomy in East Timor', *The Australian* 18 October.

D. Greenlees and R. Garran (2002) *Deliverance*, Allen and Unwin.

W. Hayden (1996) *Hayden: An Autobiography*, Angus and Robertson.

R. Hill (11 February 1999) *Foreign Affairs, Defence and Trade Senate Committee Hansard*, Australian Parliament.

P. Kelly (2009) *The March of the Patriots: The Struggle for Modern Australia*, Melbourne University Press.

C. Kerr (2009) 'Rudd attacks John Howard's reform record at launch of Paul Kelly's The March of Patriots', *The Australian* 7 September.

D. Lague (1996) 'The looming crisis with Jakarta', *Sydney Morning Herald* 3 August, 15.

J. Lyons (1999) 'The secret Timor dossier', *The Bulletin* 12 October, 25.

B. Manning (2003) 'Charlie India Echo Tango calling East Timor', in H. Alexander and P. Griffiths (eds) *A Few Rough Reds: Stories of Rank and File Organising*, Australian Society for the Study of Labour History.

B. Martin et al. (2001) 'Political Jiu-Jitsu against Indonesian Repression: Studying Lower-Profile Nonviolent Resistance', 13 *Pacifica Review*.

D. Mueller (1999, 2 December) *Foreign Affairs, Defence and Trade Senate Committee Hansard*, Australian Parliament.

C. O'Reilly (1996) 'East Timor and Christian fighters for peace', *The Guardian* 14 February.

L. Oakes (2009) *The March of Patriots (Promotional Material)*, MUP.

A. Pereira (1996) 'Foreword', in N. Chomsky (ed.) *Powers and Prospects*, South End Press.

K. Rudd (7 September 2009) *Speech at the launch of The March of Patriots* available at http://www.theaustralian.news.com.au/story/0,25197,26038812-5013871,00.html (accessed 6 January 2010).

'Santa Cruz incident a turning point in our diplomacy: Interview with Ali Alatas' (2000) *Tempo* 18–24 September.

P. Smythe (2004) *The Heaviest Blow: the Catholic Church and the East Timor issue*, Lit Verlag.

I. Stewart (1998) 'Downer hails Timor troop withdrawal', *The Australian* 28 July.

H. Subroto (1997) *Eyewitness to the Integration of East Timor*, Pustaka Sinar Harapan.

Y. Tavridis (15 January 2009) *Telephone interview with the author.*

J. Taylor (1999) *East Timor: The Price of Freedom*, Pluto Press.

J. Tedjasukmana (2000) 'Interview with Juwono Sudarsono', 155 *Time Magazine.*

E. Ward (2000) 'The Local meets the Global: East Timor and Ireland's Presidency of the European Union', in Paul Hainsworth and Stephen McCloskey (eds) *The East Timor Question: The Struggle for Independence*, IB Taurus 151.

D. Watson (2002) *Recollections of a Bleeding Heart*, Knopf.

W. Way (ed.) (2000) *Indonesia and the Incorporation of Portuguese Timor*, Melbourne University Press.

R. Wesley-Smith (1998) 'Radio Maubere and Links to East Timor', in J. Aubrey (ed) *Free East Timor: Australia's culpability in East Timor's genocide*, Random House.

M. Wilkinson (1999) 'Why we kept Timor secrets from the US', *Sydney Morning Herald* 13 August.

A. Zelter (1996) *The International Law Defence*, The Greenhouse.

Chapter 5

When is There Sufficient Information to Decide if There is an R2P Situation or Not?: From the Intervention in Timor-Leste to the Crisis in Sri Lanka

Paul Harpur

Introduction

The Responsibility to Protect (R2P) doctrine reaffirms that genocide and ethnic cleansing are abhorrent acts and that the community of nations has a responsibility to intervene whenever such acts are pending or occurring. The R2P doctrine contains the process by which military humanitarian intervention can be authorised by the Security Council.[1]

This chapter will analyse the process by which the United Nations Security Council determines if there is an R2P situation. In particular, this chapter will critically analyse the ability of the Security Council to access reliable information and whether the United Nations should adopt new processes to ensure the Security Council has sufficient evidence to enable it to make the important judgment about whether or not genocidal activities or ethnic cleansing are occurring in a target State.

This chapter will firstly analyse the development of the R2P doctrine and then will analyse two case studies to illustrate the problems with the current operation of the R2P doctrine. The first case study concerns the United Nations intervention in Timor-Leste following the independence vote in 1999. While this intervention occurred prior to the adoption by the United Nations World Summit of the R2P doctrine in 2005, the case study in Timor-Leste provides an example of where the Security Council had reports that violence was pending but failed to act in a timely manner. This chapter will postulate that the Security Council simply lacked the political will to act and, accordingly, the world only acted when the violence reached an extreme level. This chapter will argue that the Security Council should have analysed what caused the delays in responding to the crisis in Timor-Leste and improved these processes when adopting the R2P doctrine. This chapter argues that one problem with the Security Council monitors in 1999 in Timor-Leste was that those monitors did not directly address the difficult issue of whether or not there was a risk of genocidal activities or ethnic cleansing occurring. The

1 Evans (2008a).

issuing of a report stating genocide or ethnic cleansing was occurring would have placed increased political pressure upon the Security Council to make an earlier decision to intervene.

The second case study demonstrates the problems that arise when accurate and reliable information is unavailable. The second case study concerns the final stages of the Sri Lankan Civil War in 2009. During this conflict, there were serious allegations made about the way in which the Sri Lankan Government prosecuted the war. In Timor-Leste, there were potential limitations with the flow of information about the situation on the ground. Unlike in Timor-Leste, in Sri Lanka there were no Security Council monitors or independent observers. As a consequence, the world had virtually no reliable information as to the nature of the conflict. Without such information, it was impossible for the Security Council to determine whether or not there was an R2P situation in Sri Lanka. As the Sri Lankan Government was largely responsible for the limited flow of information, the operation of the R2P situation during the Sri Lankan Civil War in 2009 sets the precedent that if a State prevents any official reporting of its conduct, that State may be able to avoid the Security Council deciding whether or not there are instances of genocidal activities or ethnic cleansing.

This chapter suggests that the Security Council should send inspectors into conflict zones to report directly to the Security Council on the nature of the conflict and whether an R2P situation has arisen or is likely to arise. If the Security Council has accurate information, this will increase the probability that the R2P doctrine can be used to utilise military and non-military interventions to prevent genocidal activities or ethnic cleansing.

The Development of R2P and the Need for Timely and Reliable Reporting

The respect for state sovereignty and the principle of non-intervention has a long history under international law.[2] A fundamental principle of sovereignty is the independence of one State from any outside authority or intervention.[3] The development of the R2P doctrine operates as an exception to this principle of non-intervention.

The R2P Doctrine requires other States to take coercive action against a rogue State, where that rogue State is perpetrating, or failing to prevent, the occurrence of genocide, if the following conditions are met:

1. Actual or anticipated mass loss of life with genocidal intent or wide spread ethnic cleansing;
2. The intervening State must take action with the intent to reduce human suffering and not for ulterior motives;

2 Halberstam (1995).

3 Hoffmann (1996), p. 12.

3. The nature of the intervention should be the minimum necessary to reduce human suffering;
4. Military intervention must be the last option, have reasonable prospects of success, be conducted with UN Security Council authorisation and be adopted after all non-military means have been explored.[4] These non-military interventions include political/diplomatic, economic and legal measure.[5]

The problems in gaining international consensus to establish the R2P doctrine have significantly reduced the effectiveness of possible humanitarian interventions. Bellamy (2006)[6] observes that the alteration of the doctrine to reach consensus has reduced the possibility that the R2P doctrine will avoid situations like Kosovo (where the Security Council was deadlocked in the face of a humanitarian crisis) and future disasters such as Rwanda (where States lacked the political will to intervene). Despite the limitations of this doctrine, this chapter will focus on a limitation of the R2P doctrine which could be remedied within the current system and without attracting significant political hostility.

This chapter argues that the Security Council should become more proactive in sending out inspectors who can report directly to the Security Council about what is occurring in conflicts where genocide or ethnic cleansing is possible. Increased information is necessary to ensure that the Security Council has sufficient information to judge correctly what is occurring on the ground. It is critical that the Security Council makes the correct decision. If the Security Council fails to act to prevent genocide or ethnic cleansing, then the R2P norm will not have achieved its potential. The R2P has the potential of preventing atrocities from being perpetrated, such as the killing fields of Cambodia, the machetes of Rwanda or the crisis in Darfur.[7]

If the Security Council incorrectly determines that genocidal activities or ethnic cleansing is occurring, this could have a devastating impact on the continuing operation of the R2P doctrine. If the Security Council incorrectly took action based upon humanitarian grounds it is likely that the intervention would appear politically motivated. This would provide fuel for the concerns of many States that humanitarian interventions will act as a pathway to unilateral, politically motivated interventions.[8] For example, one group of authors argues that the perception that the United States and its allies attempted to legitimatise their invasion of Iraq on humanitarian grounds has weakened the consensus around humanitarian military action generally.[9] The fear that R2P will be misused by powerful States to justify

4 International Commission on Intervention and State Sovereignty (2001), p. 32; Thakur (2007).

5 For discussion see, Bellamy (2009a); Bellamy and Williams (2006).

6 Bellamy (2006).

7 Evans (2008b).

8 Bellamy (2008).

9 Bellamy (2005); Visser (2007).

their invasion of other countries can be evinced from the recent United Nations debates on the R2P norm.[10]

In the United Nations General Assembly on 30 January 2009, Secretary-General Ban Ki-moon outlined a new three-pronged approach to implement the R2P doctrine.[11] The first pillar of Secretary-General Ki-moon's three pillar approach centres upon prevention and on an 'early and flexible response tailored to the specific circumstances of each case'. The second pillar focuses upon utilising confidential or public persuasion, education and training to avert conflict. The third pillar encourages States to take 'timely and decisive action', instead of focusing on arbitrary, sequential or graduated policy ladders that prize procedure over substance and process over results.

This chapter argues that Secretary-General Ki-moon's three pillars all hinge upon the Security Council having accurate and timely information on what is occurring on the ground. If the Security Council does not have timely and accurate information then it is extremely difficult to determine whether or not there is an R2P situation. Without such determination it is unlikely military interventions will be authorised.

If the Security Council fails to take action due to a lack of information, this could threaten the continued existence of the R2P norm. If the Security Council makes no determination about whether genocidal activities or ethnic cleansing is occurring, this could result in concerned States seeking alternative ways to authorise their interventions. If the Security Council fails to act, States could approach the UN Secretary-General and request the exercise of the power under Article 99 of the Charter of the United Nations to authorise the intervention. The State could also raise the matter before the General Assembly for their motion condemning the impugned conduct. If all these avenues fail, then the State could arguably take action at the regional level pursuant to Part VIII of the Charter of the United Nations. Any military action which does not have Security Council approval is potentially unlawful under international law.[12] Regardless of the legality of such action, if States continue to adopt approaches to subvert the R2P doctrine, this could result in the R2P doctrine becoming redundant in determining what is lawful humanitarian intervention.

Case Studies which Suggest a Security Council Investigation and Report may Defuse Conflict

Background to the 1999 Humanitarian Crisis in Timor-Leste

Timor-Leste (then called East Timor) formed part of the Portuguese empire from 1702 to 1975. In 1974, Portugal recognised the right of self-determination of the people of Timor-Leste and devised a plan of transition to democratic rule. Prior

10 Anderson (2009).

11 United Nations Press Office (2009b).

12 Bellamy and Williams (2006); Brown (2001).

to the transition plan being realised, Timor-Leste fell into civil war. In August 1975, Frente Revolucionaria de Timor-Leste Independente (Fretilin) declared East Timor an independent State.[13] A few months later, in December, the Indonesian military crossed the border from West Timor into Timor-Leste in an unlawful act of aggression. For the next 25 years, the people of Timor-Leste suffered under a violent occupation which was condemned by the international community. The Indonesian occupation involved disappearances, rape, murder and the deaths of about 800,000 East Timorese (or approximately one quarter of the population of Timor-Leste).[14] For example, in 1991 hundreds of Timor-Leste civilians were killed while attending the funeral of a student who had been murdered by the Indonesian military. This event became known as the Santa Cruz massacre (also known as the Dili massacre) and attracted international condemnation as this massacre was captured on television camera by a BBC crew.[15]

Indonesia was subjected to continuing international pressure over its occupation of Timor-Leste and, in 1999, growing internal unrest and international pressure motivated the Indonesian Government to offer the peoples of Timor-Leste the option of increased autonomy as part of Indonesia or secession from Indonesia with full independence. In 1999, the United Nations, Portugal and Indonesia concluded the Agreement between Indonesia and Portugal on the Question of East Timor; the Agreement between the United Nations and the Governments of Indonesia and Portugal Regarding the Modalities for the Popular Consultation through a Direct Ballot; and the Agreement between the United Nations and the Governments of Indonesia and Portugal Regarding Security Arrangements. These agreements essentially provided that the United Nations would conduct the ballot, Indonesia would ensure security and the United Nations Assistance Mission in East Timor would monitor the conduct of the Indonesian forces.

On 11 June 1999, the Security Council established the United Nations Mission in East Timor and deployed a small contingent of personnel to assist with the election and to provide an objective assessment of security. The lead-up to this vote witnessed sustained and systematic violence by Indonesian trained and controlled militias.[16] In the lead-up to the elections the United Nations had to twice delay the vote due to the violence perpetrated by the Indonesian-led militias.[17] Even though there were creditable signs that the Indonesian military would not ensure the security of Timor-Leste, the international community did not adopt any effective preventative measures.

Despite the violent intimidation on 30 August 1999, approximately 99 per cent of voters cast their vote, 78 per cent of which called for independence from Indonesia. Following the independence vote on 4 September 1999, the Indonesian military and militias engaged in a scorched-earth campaign of mass murder, rape and

13 Jolliffe (1978).
14 Frease (2006), p. 284; Gerlovin (1995).
15 McCloskey (2000).
16 United Nations High Commission for Human Rights (2000), pp. 47+.
17 Voon (2002), p. 55.

destruction. The violence before the election was reasonably targeted. Following the independence vote, the two-week rampage of destruction focused upon widespread vengeance.[18] The conduct of the Indonesian military and militia arguably constituted genocide and ethnic cleansing. Over 200,000 people were forced across the border into Indonesian-occupied West Timor, over 1,300 people were murdered and 80 per cent of the country's infrastructure was destroyed or stolen by the Indonesian forces.

After intense political and economic pressure, the Indonesian Government agreed to accept international assistance in restoring security. Shortly after, the Australian forces and the United Nations International Force in East Timor landed and stopped the violence. There has been strong criticism of the United Nations for leaving the security to Indonesia when there was strong evidence that there was a pending mass loss of life.[19]

Why the United Nations Reports Prior to the Violence in Timor-Leste Failed to Motivate Action

While R2P is an emerging norm, the R2P doctrine operates within the traditional United Nations framework and requires Security Council approval. Article 39 of the Charter of the United Nations authorises the Security Council to make the crucial threshold decision as to the existence of a 'threat to the peace, breach of the peace, or act of aggression' and to decide which of the responses enumerated in Articles 41 and 42 should be invoked to respond to the crisis.[20] While the Security Council has a powerful mandate to act to prevent genocide and ethnic cleansing, it can be very difficult, in practice, to obtain consensus that such conduct is occurring or about to occur.

In many cases, this disunity is caused by uncertainty about the nature of the conflict. In the 1999 Kosovo crisis, there was disunity in the Security Council about the nature of the conflict and whether it was a fundamentally internal dispute.[21] The Security Council members also have their own vested interest which guides their decision-making. For example, China and Russia in particular have internal disputes which are associated with serious human rights abuses. In addition Russia had strong historic and ethnic connections to the Serb forces. This meant any motion for a military intervention in the Kosovo crisis was likely to have confronted problems in the Security Council. Rather than taking the dispute to the Security Council, NATO States elected to authorise the intervention through NATO. United Nations approval for the NATO intervention came in the form of Resolution 1244 which was adopted at the end of a 78-day NATO bombing campaign.[22]

18 Voon (2002), p. 56; Frease (2006).
19 Katzensrein (2003); Thomashausen (2009).
20 Franck (2006), p. 598.
21 Walling (2008).
22 Sharp (1999).

The situation in Timor-Leste was markedly different from Kosovo due to the fact there was international recognition that Indonesia was illegally occupying Timor-Leste. In addition, there was no dispute that Indonesia was the military power and had the capacity to protect the people of Timor-Leste or to perpetrate atrocities. Why, then, did the world fail to protect the people of Timor-Leste? This chapter argues the main reasons the community of nations failed to protect the people of Timor-Leste from the Indonesian military and militias were a lack of political will and the quality of the information about the situation on the ground.

The problem in obtaining Security Council clearance is extremely difficult where there is an anticipated mass loss of life, rather than a genocidal conflict. Bellamy explains that '[t]he first part of a prevention system is its early warning mechanism'.[23] It is relatively easy to identify when States are at risk of political turmoil or humanitarian disaster but it is much more difficult to identify that a genocidal conflict is about to occur. Where there is uncertainty about what is occurring on the ground, it becomes even harder to justify any preventive military action.

In 1999, the community of nations argued that the Indonesian military would be able to control the militias and would be able to ensure the security of the elections. Australia is Timor-Leste's closest neighbour (but for Indonesia) and was in a good position to be aware of the pending violence. In February 1999, the Indonesian presidential foreign affairs adviser stated that the Indonesian military was not independent and could not be guaranteed to keep the peace in Timor-Leste.[24] Despite this, the Australian Government insisted the Indonesian military could ensure the peace in Timor-Leste. Australia had always been a strong ally of Indonesia and supported Indonesia's occupation by signing the Timor Gap Treaty which enabled Australia and Indonesia to exploit the oil gas reserves of Timor-Leste.[25] Other governments have also been accused of placing economic interests before the near genocide in Timor-Leste.[26]

Australia continued to support Indonesia, even when confronted with extreme violence perpetrated by Indonesian military personnel and militias. In March 1999, Indonesian military and militia went to Liquiça village. The local villagers were hiding in a church, seeking safety. The Indonesian forces removed the priests and then threw gas into the church to force the people to flee. The Indonesian militias then murdered 86 villagers. Following this massacre, the Australian Foreign Affairs Minister stated:

> Well, look, they [the Indonesian military] were present, I understand, at the incident but there again, there's a debate about what part they played. They clearly didn't themselves kill people, but there is an argument, about whether

23 Bellamy (2009a), p. 106.
24 D. Anwar Anwar (1999).
25 Pilger (2006); Watkins (1999).
26 For example, see Klaehn (2003).

> they did try to stop the fighting or they didn't do enough to try to stop the fighting, and the trouble is it's very hard given we ourselves had no eye witnesses there, to be able to prove the case either way.[27]

Rather than taking action based upon strong evidence of violence, the Australian Government continued to claim a lack of information or an inability to take action to stop the violence in Timor-Leste.

Finally, the community of nations placed substantial pressure upon Indonesia when the evidence of the widespread scorched-earth policy became overwhelming. Ultimately the political pressure was effective and Indonesia consented to a military intervention. Indonesia consented to the United Nations supporting a military mission in Timor-Leste when considerable political and economic pressure was levelled at Indonesia. In particular, if Indonesia did not agree to international intervention then IMF and World Bank loans would be withheld, military assistance would be terminated and the United States would continue to use political pressure against the regime.[28] While the non-military measures were very effective in gaining Indonesia's consent, this chapter argues that such measures should have been adopted earlier when evidence demonstrated widespread violence was pending.

The fact that Australia and other nations could claim a lack of information as a justification for not acting demonstrates that more needs to be done to ensure the Security Council and the community of nations has accurate and timely information to act upon. Rather than just sending in general United Nations personnel, the Security Council should give this task to military representatives from the armed forces of the nations that are members of the Security Council. These Security Council inspectors must be tasked with providing clear answers to whether a particular State was unable to prevent actual or pending genocidal activities or ethnic cleansing. In Timor-Leste, the reports demonstrated there was violence, but these reports were not written by military personnel and/or left sufficient uncertainty which enabled politicians, who did not have the political will to act, to claim a lack of information to justify their inaction. One of the lessons from the violence in Timor-Leste in 1999 was that the role of Security Council monitors needs to be improved to increase the flow of reliable information which clearly articulated whether or not a State was willing or able to prevent genocidal activities or ethnic cleansing.

Background to the 2009 Humanitarian Crisis in Sri Lanka

Sri Lanka is a small island of 66,000 square km (which is similar to the size of Tasmania or half the size of Alaska) which is separated from the southern tip

27 Downer (1999).

28 Wheeler (2008).

of India by the Palk Strait. In this least-developed State, 20 million people have endured a civil war between 1983 and 2009.

The Sri Lankan Civil War was fought between the two main ethnic groups, the Sinhalese and Tamils. The power relationship between these ethnic groups has altered over the centuries. In the thirteenth century, the Chola Empire was a Tamil empire based in Southern India which stretched across much of India, up to Burma and included control over the land mass now called Sri Lanka. During this time, the Tamil population was the dominant power group. The Chola Empire fell and centuries later, in 1505, the island was in civil war when the Portuguese landed. In 1507, Portugal founded Colombo and created a colony. The Dutch took control over Sri Lanka in 1660 and then lost control to the British in 1802.

Under the British Empire, the power relationship modified so that Tamils became an ethnic minority. This dynamic between the Tamils and the Singhalese continues to this date. The Singhalese ethnic group controlled the Sri Lankan military and the Tamils had a number of irregular forces. In 1983, these two groups became engaged in a civil war.

A power struggle took place in the Tamil community over which group would be dominant and the Liberation Tigers of Tamil Eelan, commonly known as the Tamil Tigers, emerged dominant. The Tamil Tigers became one of the world's most effective guerrilla groups and were recognised as a terrorist group by the United Nations Security Council Resolution 1373 of 28 September 2001.

The 26-year-long Sri Lankan Civil War has been marked by serious human rights abuses. For example, in September 1990, there was widespread ethnic violence where thousands of Tamils were shot, hacked to death with machetes or burnt alive by Singhalese radicals. During the so-called Black September, there were various massacres of Tamils, including the Eastern University massacre and the Sathurukondan massacre. Following Black September, the Sri Lankan Civil War continued. There were a number of unsuccessful attempts to reach a peaceful end to hostilities, and in early 2009, the civil war culminated in a violent end to the Tamil Tigers.

This chapter is concerned with the fighting in the latter stages of the Sri Lankan Civil War in 2009. During January to May 2009, the United Nations agencies have estimated that more than 7,500 Tamil civilians were killed and over 15,000 were wounded.[29]

The Sri Lankan military started an all-out offence against the Tamil Tigers in 2009. This proved an extremely successful military campaign, with the Tamil Tigers being forced into an ever-shrinking area of land. As the Tamil Tigers retreated, they reportedly forced thousands of civilians to retreat with them. This created a very dangerous situation where civilians were being forced to move away from their sources of food and shelter and into a small pocket of land about the size of Central Park in New York.[30]

---

29 International Crisis Group (2009a).

30 Templer (2009).

The use of human shields by the Tamil Tigers is unlawful under international law. Responding to human shields is a challenging military problem which has been addressed in other conflicts.[31] When confronted by human shields, a combatant must ensure that the use of force discriminates between combatants and human shields. Where a combatant cannot discriminate between combatants and human shields, the Geneva Conventions require the combatants to treat everyone as civilians and to hold their fire.[32]

In March 2009, an estimated 150,000 civilians were trapped behind Tamil Tiger lines and being used as human shields.[33] If these civilians attempted to leave the Tamil Tiger-held areas, they were unlawfully shot and killed by the Tamil Tigers. If they remained in the Tamil Tiger territory, they were reportedly subjected to indiscriminate shelling by the Sri Lankan military.[34] Human Rights Watch reported that a Sri Lankan military drone plane was seen flying over a Tamil hospital compound minutes before shells started landing around and in the hospital.[35]

The proximity of human shields created a problem for the Sri Lankan military. As Tamil Tigers were hiding around civilians, any attack was likely to kill civilians. To reduce the numbers of civilian deaths, the Sri Lankan military ordered tens of thousands of civilians to move into areas which were designated no-fire zones. These safe zones were not necessarily safe from attack. On 10 May 2009, the UK Guardian reported that at least 378 civilians were killed by a Sri Lankan attack on a no-fire zone.[36] The International Crisis Group estimates that between 500 and 5,000 Tamil civilians were killed between January 2009 and April 2009.[37]

In April 2009, the British opposition Liberal Democrat foreign affairs spokesman, Ed Davey, told the British Parliament that the situation in Sri Lanka could degenerate into Rwandan-style genocide.[38] In this address, Davey cited Professor Francis Boyle from Illinois University who claimed that the Sri Lankan Civil War could have descended into genocidal violence.

On 19 May 2009, the Sri Lankan Government declared an end to the civil war and confirmed the deaths of the Tamil Tiger leadership.[39] With the war over, this chapter will analyse the responses by the international community and ask: should the United Nations have done more to force the Sri Lankan and Tamil Tiger forces to permit independent observers to ensure an R2P situation did not arise?

---

31 See for example, Hussein in Iraq, Garamone (2003); Hezbollah in Lebanon, Hoyer (2007); Millosevic in Kosovo, Kozaryn (1999); Chechnya, Smith (2003); Sudan, United Nations Security Council (2008).

32 Bellamy (2009b).

33 Patten et al. (2009).

34 Brahimi (2009).

35 Human Rights Watch (2009a).

36 Chamberlain (2009).

37 Patten et al. (2009).

38 Sarkar (2008).

39 Weaver and Chamberlain (20009).

Why the R2P Question Could Not Be Answered in Sri Lanka?

The United Nations or a regional group of States cannot take action under the R2P norm until there is sufficient evidence of ethnic cleansing or genocide. It is rare that there is sufficient evidence and political will for the international community to take action to prevent genocide or ethnic cleansing.[40] Establishing this causal story is made even more difficult where independent observers are barred from accessing the war zone.

The problem of determining what is occurring on the ground is always difficult, but in Sri Lanka this problem was further complicated by the extremely dynamic nature of the conflict. The pending mass loss of life arose very quickly in Sri Lanka. For most of the civil war, both ethnic groups had effective combat forces. At the height of its power, the Tamil Tigers held a third of Sri Lanka. In October 2008, the Sri Lankan military claimed to have neutralised the Tamil Tiger air force but in February 2009, the Tamil Tigers launched an air raid on the Sri Lankan capital, Colombo. This created the impression that the Tamil Tiger forces continued to have effective operational capacity. Whether this impression was accurate appears doubtful. Within a few months of this air raid the Tamil Tigers were finished as an effective military force and were hiding behind human shields. It could be argued that the rapid, unexpected demise of the Tamil Tiger military and their tactic of using human shields created a humanitarian crisis with R2P potential that caught the world's media and political attention by surprise.

The uncertainty about the humanitarian crisis during early 2009 was partially caused by the conduct of the Sri Lankan Government. The Sri Lankan Government took steps to enhance the uncertainty about how the conflict was progressing by preventing any independent reporting on issues surrounding human rights abuses. During the final stages of the Sri Lankan military's assault on the Tamil Tigers, there was substantial confusion about the civilian population. Unless the world was certain genocide or ethnic cleansing was occurring, R2P could not be invoked. The restrictions on independent reporting meant the world community could not agree upon important facts and therefore could not decide on the appropriate humanitarian intervention.

The confusion about the civilian population was so great that the world was not even sure how many civilians were at risk. An article on the International Crisis Group's website explains that the Sri Lankan Government were claiming that 170,000 civilians had escaped the death zone and that over 100,000 civilians remained in the few remaining kilometres of Tamil Tiger-controlled territory.[41] These reports conflicted with earlier claims by the Sri Lankan Government that only 38,000 civilians were in Tamil Tiger territory. During the same time, the Red Cross estimated that there could be 50,000 civilians in the Tamil Tiger

40 Dastoor (2009).

41 Steinberg (2009).

territory while the United Nations estimated there were over 60,000 people.[42] This confusion meant that the world community could not even be certain of how many people were in the battle zone.

The lack of independent reporting resulted in the world relying upon conflicting reports from Sri Lankan and Tamil Tiger forces. The Tamil Tigers claimed that the Sri Lankan military's heavy shelling of civilians in no-fire zones had caused over 2,000 deaths, while the Sri Lankan Government claimed to have nothing to do with the shelling.[43] The Sri Lankan Government claimed that they were engaging in the world's largest hostage rescue mission and that the Tamil Tigers were killing their own people to gain international support.[44] It was extremely difficult for the world to confirm what was occurring on the ground as the United Nations observers were blocked from the fighting zone.[45]

The confusion about what was occurring during the final stages of the Sri Lankan Civil War was partially caused by a crackdown on independent reporting. Journalists were barred from getting anywhere near the battle or fleeing refugees.[46] For example, in May 2009, a British Channel 4 television team were detained by Sri Lankan forces after reporting on abuse and ill-treatment of Tamil refugees.[47]

Even after the Tamil Tigers were defeated, the Sri Lankan Government prevented independent reporting and went so far as to prevent two Canadian politicians from visiting Sri Lanka[48] and excluded independent observers from the process of screening refugees for Tamil combatants.[49]

By preventing independent reporting of their military campaign, the Sri Lankan military effectively prevented potentially shocking images from being broadcast around the world, which could have placed political pressure upon governments and prevented there being sufficient evidence to establish that there was or was not an R2P situation. Whether independent reporting would have witnessed shocking images is not the point. The Sri Lankan Government's claims about the Tamil Tigers and the Sri Lankan military activities could have been accurate. The point is that accurate information was denied to the Security Council. The power of the media and images can be demonstrated by the crisis in East Timor. During the Indonesian occupation of East Timor, massacres were reportedly common. The Dili Massacre was a turning point because a British television crew captured the Indonesian military killing unarmed civilians.[50] The images of this massacre were broadcast around the world, causing general outrage which resulted in increased

42 International Crisis Group (2009b).
43 Chamberlain (2009).
44 Sri Lankan Ministry of Defence (2009).
45 United Nations Press Office (2009).
46 Templer (2009).
47 CNN (2009).
48 Stuparyk (2009).
49 Oxfam America (2009).
50 Voon (2002).

political interest. Between 1991 and 1999, there was sufficient media attention and political pressure globally which resulted in comparatively greater political pressure in 1999 when a humanitarian crisis developed. In Sri Lanka, there was no similar build-up or sufficient information for the world to respond quickly to the humanitarian crisis.

Should the United Nations Have Responded Differently in the Sri Lankan Civil War in 2009?

In February 2009, Human Rights Watch[51] released 'War on the Displaced: Sri Lankan Army and LTTE Abuses against Civilians in the Vanni', wherein they accused the Sri Lankan Government of human rights abuses and attempting to prevent any independent reporting. As there was no independent reporting, it was difficult to verify if civilians were being killed and, importantly, how this was occurring. Were the deaths accidental or done with genocidal intent? Without this information, the world could not conclude whether or not there was an R2P situation.

The difficulty in establishing a causal story of an aggressor was substantially complicated in Sri Lanka by the fact both sides to the conflict were responsible for the potential mass loss of life. In Sri Lanka, the Tamil Tigers reportedly used the Tamil population as human shields.[52] By forcing civilians to live around jungle bases, the Tamil Tigers created a situation where any Sri Lankan attack would kill large numbers of civilians.

During the 2009 stage of the Sri Lankan Civil War, various States criticised the Sri Lankan Government but no substantive punitive action was proposed. Arguably, the United Nations could have placed increased economic and political pressure upon Sri Lanka to permit independent observers to ascertain whether or not any humanitarian response was required. The Sri Lankan Government claimed they were rescuing the Tamil human shields from the Tamil Tigers. The Sri Lankan Government should have been pressured to permit United Nations observers to check the accuracy of these assertions.

During the final stages of the Sri Lankan Civil War and after the conflict was complete, there have been a number of calls for war crimes investigations into the conduct of the Sri Lankan and Tamil Tiger forces.[53] In addition, a White House statement called upon both parties to cease hostilities and permit humanitarian aid to reach the thousands of Tamil hostages.[54] In the Sri Lankan situation, Bellamy claims, inter alia, the Sri Lankan Government should have ensured that 'its use of force discriminately targeted against combatants and military objects only, and where it cannot discriminate between combatants and non-combatants treat everyone in its

51 Human Rights Watch (2009a).

52 G8 Foreign Ministers (2009); Human Rights Watch (2009a); Stroehlein (2009).

53 For example, European Union, Anonymous (2009); Human Rights Watch (2009a); Human Rights Watch (2009b); International Crisis Group (2009a).

54 The White House (2009).

sights as civilians'.[55] The Sri Lankan Government elected not to suspend military operations and to continue hostilities until the Tamil Tiger leadership was dead.

The threat of war crimes charges can deter some breaches of humanitarian law.[56] This threat is weakened in a situation like Sri Lanka where the government asserted the Tamil Tigers were murdering their own people and that the Sri Lankan military was rescuing civilians. If the Sri Lankan Government's factual scenario is accepted, then charges of war crimes are difficult to prosecute. A key aspect of war crimes investigations is evidence. While evidence can be gathered after the fact, in terms of war crimes charges acting as a deterrent, if timely reports are emerging about war crimes in progress, then this enables the world community to bring home to combatants the probability that their actions could result in war crimes. Accordingly, an increase in timely and reliable military reports would increase the ability of the community of nations to use the threat of war crimes prosecutions to alter conduct.

Working with Target States to Increase Information

During the latter stages of the Sri Lankan Civil War, various groups called for the Sri Lankan Government to call a cease-fire to enable civilians to escape.[57] On 24 April 2009, a White House press statement called on the Sri Lankan Government to 'stop shelling the "safe zone" and blocking international aid groups and media from accessing those civilians who have managed to escape. International aid workers should have access to all sites where internally displaced persons are being registered and sheltered'.[58] The Sri Lankan Government ignored these calls and continued to press their offensive against the Tamil Tigers. Considering the Sri Lankan Government had been engaged in an extremely bitter and violent civil war against the Tamil Tigers for over two decades, it was unlikely that the Sri Lankan Government was going to call a cease-fire. A cease-fire would have enabled the Tamil Tigers to regroup and may not have freed the human shield hostages. Calling upon a State to refrain from prosecuting a war against enemy combatants is unlikely to result in any improvements on the ground.

The R2P norm permits the Security Council to work with a target State with the deployment of inspectors or military forces.[59] If a State is requested to permit Security Council inspectors into the combat zone, then a target State is far more likely to acquiesce to such a request. Unlike a call for a cease-fire, if the Security Council sends observers into a war zone, the encumbrance upon a target State's sovereignty is considerably reduced. Permitting Security Council inspectors into a conflict will not reduce the capacity of that army to engage in lawful military

55 Bellamy (2009b).

56 Bassiouni (2008).

57 Bellamy (2009b); Egeland et al. (2009).

58 The White House (2009).

59 Matthews (2008).

activities. This means there are reduced grounds for target States to refuse to permit inspectors to monitor the conflict.

If Security Council military inspectors are able to monitor the activities of the target State, this would provide the international community with a reliable source of information. If a target State is engaging in a scorched-earth policy or shelling civilians indiscriminately, then Security Council inspectors can provide the Security Council the information it needs to determine what action to take. Hypothetically, if Security Council inspectors report genocidal activities or ethnic cleansing, there would be considerable political pressure upon the Security Council and the international community to do more than simply request a cease-fire.

Conclusion

This chapter has argued that the Security Council should significantly improve its access to timely and reliable information to improve the ability to determine whether or not an R2P situation exists in a target State. In 1999, the Security Council had monitors in Timor-Leste who reported on the violence perpetrated by the Indonesian military and militias, yet the world delayed before acting. One reason States did not act was that they argued they did not have enough information. This should have motivated the Security Council to improve the quality of its reporting mechanisms. The problems with accurate and reliable information again prevented the Security Council and the community of nations from determining whether or not an R2P situation existed during the final stages of the Sri Lankan Civil War in 2009. In the bloody end to the Sri Lankan Civil War, independent observers were barred from the conflict zone. Without reliable information it was impossible to judge whether or not there was genocidal activities or ethnic cleansing.

The Security Council should urgently consider increasing its access to accurate and reliable sources of information. If the Security Council sent inspectors into a target State with a brief to report whether or not the target State is able and willing to prevent genocidal activities or ethnic cleansing, such reports would reduce the ability of States to use a lack of information as an excuse for inaction.

The proposal in this chapter is not a silver bullet which will ensure the Security Council has access to accurate information nor a guarantee that the Security Council will put aside politics to act in the best interests of victims of genocide or ethnic cleansing. Politics continues to strongly influence the operation of the R2P doctrine.[60] The operation of the R2P norm is emerging and as United Nations Secretary-General Ban Ki-moon observes:

> Curbing mass atrocities will be neither easy nor quick. There is no certain blueprint for getting the job done. We are all novices in this field.[61]

60 Dastoor (2009); Evans (2006); Janssen (2008).

61 Ki-Moon (2008).

References

A. Acharya (2011) 'Norm Subsidiarity and Regional Orders: Sovereignty, Regionalism, and Rule-Making in the Third World', 55, *International Studies Quarterly* 95.

G. Anderson (2009) 'R2P articles file – The State's Duty to Protect: Enforcement in Question', 8, *America* 201.

Anonymous (2009) 'British Journalists Held in Sri Lanka after News Report)', *CNN* 9 May 2009.

C. Bassiouni (2008) 'Advancing the "responsibility to protect" through international criminal justice', in R. Cooper and J. Voïnov Kohler (eds) *The responsibility to protect: the global moral compact*, Palgrave Macmillan.

A. Bellamy (2006) 'Whither the Responsibility to Protect? Humanitarian Intervention and the 2005 World Summit', 20, *Ethics and International Affairs* 143.

A. Bellamy (2008) 'The Responsibility to Protect and the Problem of Military Intervention', 84, *International Affairs* 615.

A. Bellamy (2009a) *A Responsibility to Protect*, John Wiley and Sons.

A. Bellamy (2009b) *The Conflict in Sri Lanka and the Responsibility to Protect* e-International Relations available at http://www.e-ir.info/?p=1053 9 (accessed 21 October 2009).

A. Bellamy (2005) 'Responsibility to Protect or Trojan Horse? The Crisis in Darfur and Humanitarian Intervention after Iraq', 19, *Ethics & International Affairs* 31.

A. Bellamy and P. Williams (2006) 'The UN Security Council and the Question of Humanitarian Intervention in Darfu', 5, *Journal of Military Ethics* 144.

L. Brahimi (2009) *Sri Lanka: A Slaughter Waiting to Happen*, International Herald Tribuneavailable at http://www.crisisgroup.org/home/index.cfm?id=6013&l=1 (accessed 21 October 2009).

C. Brown (2001) 'Moral Agency and International Society', 15, *Ethics and International Affairs* 87.

G. Chamberlain (2009) 'Hundreds dead on bloodiest day of Sri Lankan battle to destroy Tamil Tigers', *Guardian* 10 May 2009.

CNN (2009) 'EU Demands Sri Lanka War Crimes Investigation: International News', *News of the World* 18 May 2009.

D. Anwar Anwar (1999) *International Herald Tribune* 17 February 1999.

N. Dastoor (2009) 'The Responsibility to Refine: The Need for a Security Council Committee on the Responsibility to Protect', 25–74, *Harvard Human Rights Journal* 25.

A. Downer (1999) *Interview with Glen Milne*, Channel Seven.

J. Egeland et al. (2009) *Open Letter to the Security Council on the Situation in Sri Lanka*,available at http://www.globalr2p.org/pdf/OpenLetterSriLanka.pdf (accessed 21 October 2009).

G. Evans (2006) 'R2P articles file- Crimes against Humanity: Overcoming Indifference', 8, *Journal of Genocide Research* 325.

G. Evans (2008a) 'The responsibility to protect: roots and rationale – The responsibility to protect: from an idea to an international norm', in R. Cooper and J. Voïnov Kohler (eds) *The responsibility to protect: the global moral compact*, Palgrave Macmillan.

G. Evans (2008b) *The Responsibility to Protect: Ending Mass Atrocity Crimes Once and for All*, Brookings Institution Press.

T. Franck (2006) 'Symposium: UN Reform: Collective Security and UN Reforms: Between the Necessary and the Possible', 6, *Chicago Journal of Internaitonal Law* 597.

T. Frease (2006) 'Playing Hide and Seek with international Justice: What went wrong in Indionesia and East Timor', 10, *ILSA Journal of International Comparative Law* 283.

G8 Foreign Ministers (2009) *Statement by G8 Foreign Ministers on Sri Lanka*, Press Statement Foreign and Commonwealth Office available at http://www.fco.gov.uk/en/newsroom/latest-news/?view=PressS&id=16878471 (accessed 21 October 2009).

J. Garamone (2003) 'Myers Warns Iraq Against Using Human Shields', *American Forces Press Service* 15 January 2003.

L. Gerlovin (1995) 'The Forgotten War: Conflict and Coercion in East Timor', 18, *Harvard International Review* 58.

M. Halberstam (1995) 'The Legality of Humanitarian Intervention', 3, *Cardozo Journal of International Comparative Law* 1.

S. Hoffmann (1996) *The Ethics and Politics of Humanitarian Intervention*, University of Notre Dame Press.

S. Hoyer (2007) 'Hoyer Condemns Use of Human Shields in Armed Conflict', *Press Release* 25 April 2007.

Human Rights Watch (2009a) 'Sri Lanka: Repeated Shelling of Hospitals Evidence of War Crimes', available at http://www.hrw.org/en/news/2009/05/08/sri-lanka-repeated-shelling-hospitals-evidence-war-crimes (accessed 21 October 2009).

Human Rights Watch (2009a) 'Sri Lanka: Repeated Shelling of Hospitals Evidence of War Crimes', available at http://www.hrw.org/en/news/2009/05/08/sri-lanka-repeated-shelling-hospitals-evidence-war-crimes (accessed 21 October 2009).

Human Rights Watch (2009b) 'War on the Displaced: Sri Lankan Army and LTTE Abuses against Civilians in the Vanni', available at http://www.hrw.org/en/node/80901 (accessed 21 October 2009).

International Commission on Intervention and State Sovereignty (2001) *The Responsibility to Protect: Report of the International Commission on Intervention and State Sovereignty*, International Development Research Centre.

International Crisis Group (2009a) 'Sri Lanka: Report', available at http://www.crisisgroup.org/home/index.cfm?id=4459 (accessed 21 October 2009).

International Crisis Group (2009b) 'Sri Lanka: After the War', available at http://www.crisisgroup.org/home/index.cfm?id=6070&l=1 (accessed 21 October 2009).

D. Janssen (2008) 'Humanitarian intervention and the prevention of genocide', 10, *Journal of Genocide Research* 289.

J. Jolliffe (1978) *East Timor: Nationalism and Colonialism*, University of Queensland Press.

S. Katzensrein (2003) 'Hybrid Tribunals: Searching for Justice in East Timor', 16, *The Harvard Human Rights Journal* 245.

B. Ki-Moon (2008) *Address at event on "Responsible Sovereignty: International Cooperation for a Changed World":15 July 2008*, Ethics and International Affairs United Nations available at http://www.un.org/News/Press/docs/2008/sgsm11701.doc.htm (accessed 21 October 2009).

J. Klaehn (2003) 'Canadian Complicity in the East Timor Near-Genocide: A Case Study in the Sociology of Human Rights', 11, *Portuguese Studies Review* 49.

B. Kozaryn (1999) 'NATO, U.S. Claim Milosevic Uses Refugees as Human Shield', *American Forces Press Service* 18 May 1999.

M. Matthews (2008) 'Note: Tracking the Emergence of a New International Norm: The Responsibility To Protect and the Crisis In Darfur', 31, *Boston College International and Comparative Law Review* 137.

S. McCloskey (2000) 'Introduction: East Timor – From European to Third World Colonialism' in P. Hainsworth (ed.) *The East Timor Question: The Struggle for Independence from Indonesia*, Tauris.

Oxfam America (2009) *Sri Lanka: Grave concerns for civilians who escaped war zone*, Press Release, available at http://www.oxfamamerica.org/press/pressreleases/grave-concerns-over-conditions-for-civilians-who-escaped-sri-lankas-war-zone (accessed 21 October 2009).

C. Patten et al. (2009) *Statement by Crisis Group Board of Trustees: Crisis in Sri Lanka: 20 April 2009*, Crisis Group Board of Trustees available at http://www.crisisgroup.org/home/index.cfm?id=6063&l=1 (accessed 21 October 2009).

J. Pilger (2006) 'Australia builds its empire', 135, *New Statesman* 24.

S. Sarkar (2008) 'Civil Society and the Governed', 2, *Indian Journal of Human Devleopment* 449.

W. Sharp (1999) 'Operation Allied Force: Reviewing the Lawfulness of NATO's Use of Military Force to Defend Kosovo', 23, *Maryland Journal of International Law and Trade* 295.

C. Smith (2003) *Human Rights in Belarus and Chechnya*, Proceedings and Debates of the 108th Congress, 1st Session US Congress available at http://www.csce.gov/index.cfm?FuseAction=UserGroups.Home&ContentRecord (accessed 21 October 2009).

Sri Lankan Ministry of Defence (2009) 'Sri Lankan Pro-LTTE media once again misleads international community', available at http://www.defence.lk/new.asp?fname=20090510_08.

D. Steinberg (2009) *Sri Lanka's Death Zone*, Reuters available at http://www.crisisgroup.org/home/index.cfm?id=6074&l=1 (accessed 21 October 2009).

A. Stroehlein (2009) 'Sri Lanka's 50 000 Hostages', *The Guardian* 11 May 2009.

M. Stuparyk (2009) *Feds dismayed after Bob Rae deported from Sri Lanka*, 10 June 2009 edn, The Star available at http://www.thestar.com/news/canada/article/648432 (accessed 21 October 2009).

R. Templer (2009) *Day of Reckoning in Sri Lanka*, 20 April 2009 edn Foreign Policy Crisis Group available at http://www.crisisgroup.org/home/index.cfm?id=6069&l=1 (accessed 21 October 2009).

R. Thakur (2007) 'Humanitarian Intervention', in T. Weiss and S. Daws (eds) *Handbook of the United Nations*, OUP 397.

The White House (2009) *White House statement on the situation in Sri Lanka*, 24 April 2009 edn, Office of the Press Secretary available at http://www.reliefweb.int/rw/rwb.nsf/db900sid/SNAA-7RFBMD?OpenDocument&RSS20&RSS20=FS 9 (accessed 25 April 2009).

S. Thomashausen (2009) *Humanitarian Intervention in an Evolving World Order: The Cases of Iraq, Somalia, Kosovo and East Timor*, Africa Institute of South Africa.

United Nations High Commission for Human Rights (2000) *Report of the International Commission of Inquiry on East Timor to the Secretary General: 54th Sess U.N. Doc. S/2000/59 (2000)*, UNHCR.

United Nations Press Office (2009) *Sri Lanka coping with twin humanitarian crises, top UN official says on visit*, 28 April 2009 edn Press Release available at http://www.un.org/apps/news/story.asp?NewsID=30613&Cr=sri%20lanka&Cr1 (accessed 30 April 2009).

United Nations Press Office (2009b) 'Ban calls for three-pronged strategy to implement 'responsibility to protect', available at http://www.un.org/apps/news/story.asp?NewsID=29732&Cr=protect&Cr1=peace (accessed 21 October 2009).

United Nations Security Council (2008) *United Nations Security Council Resolution*, Resolution 1828 of 24 February 2009.

B. Visser (2007) 'Can the US-Led Invasion of Iraq be Justified as a Humanitarian Intervention?', 26, *Social Alternative* 53.

T. Voon (2002) 'Closing the Gap between Legitimacy and Legality of Humanitarian Intervention: Lessons From East Timor and Kosovo', 7, *UCLA Journal of International Law and Foreign Affairs* 31.

C. Walling (2008) *The United Nations Security Council and Humanitarian Intervention: Causal Stories about Human Rights and War*, University of Minnesota.

L. Watkins (1999) 'Timor Shame', *The New Zealand Truth* 17 September 1999, 7.

M. Weaver and G. Chamberlain (20009) 'Sri Lanka declares end to war with Tamil Tigers', *The Guardian* 19 May 2009.

N. Wheeler (2008) *Operationalising the Responsibility to Protect: The Continuing Debate over Where Authority Should Be*, NUPI.

Chapter 6

The Responsibility to Prevent: Could the UN Have Prevented the Atrocities in East Timor and Kosovo?

Hitoshi Nasu

Introduction

The responsibility to protect (R2P) is a multifaceted and evolving concept. Nevertheless, it is generally agreed that the concept encompasses a continuum of prevention, reaction and rebuilding, spanning from early warning to diplomatic pressure, to coercive measures and to peace-building efforts.[1] The 2005 World Summit Outcome, which sets out the consensus among the world leaders on the R2P concept, envisages prevention as an inseparable component.[2] Despite the significance of prevention in the entire R2P discourse, there has been a relative lack of attention to the preventive aspect of this concept,[3] particularly in terms of the international collective responsibility and the need for an early and flexible response in Pillars 2 and 3. In fact, the focus of academic commentary and policy debate has been given to the responsibility to react in Pillar 3, not least because it is this dimension where the international aspects of the concept are directly engaged.

The responsibility to prevent has consistently been framed as policy suggestions for domestic implementation in each state, rather than as legal obligations or criteria, or for international engagement. Those basic ideas are reflective of the policy debates on conflict prevention in general,[4] largely focusing on the strengthening of early warning systems and capacity-building. Little consideration has been made of the challenge that necessarily confronts any robust international engagement to state sovereignty.[5]

1 The 2009 UN Secretary-General's Report on Implementing the Responsibility to Protect recategorised different dimensions of the responsibility to protect into three pillars: Pillar 1 – the protection responsibilities of the state; Pillar 2 – international assistance and capacity-building; and Pillar 3 – timely and decisive response. See Ki-moon (12 January 2009).

2 UN General Assembly (24 October 2005). See also Evans (2008); International Commission on Intervention and State Sovereignty (2001), p. xi.

3 Cf. Rosenberg (2009), p. 442; Stamnes (2008).

4 See, for example, Hampson and Malone (2002); Jentleson (2000); Lund (1996); Miall et al. (1999).

5 An exception is represented by Sucharipa-Behrmann and Franck (1998), p. 485.

An early engagement by the international community is easier said than done. There are many questions that have been left unaddressed in relation to what the R2P concept indicates for the role of the international community in preventing mass atrocity crimes in the face of a strong assertion of state sovereignty. What exactly is it expected of the international community in discharging its responsibility when there is a lack of political will? To what extent should the international community assume the responsibility to protect potential victims of mass atrocity before the crimes are committed, especially when the claim of secession by the vulnerable group of population is involved? What is the legal consequence of the international community failing to discharge its responsibility to prevent mass atrocity crimes?

After reviewing the conceptual gulf between the responsibility to prevent and the responsibility to react, this chapter examines the situations of Kosovo and East Timor in 1999, posing the question as to whether the mass atrocities committed in those situations could have been prevented by robust international engagement had the R2P concept applied to those situations. A critical reflection of those situations will then provide a ground for discussion on three distinct issues relating to the clarification of the international responsibility to prevent as part of the R2P doctrine: (1) how international political will can be generated at an early stage; (2) how the issue of self-determination and secession can be addressed; and (3) what is the nature of the international responsibility to provide assistance or to take collective action for the purpose of prevention of mass atrocities.

The concept of the responsibility to protect, as agreed upon by world leaders in 2005, is narrowly confined and qualifies their commitment to the responsibility to prevent. It is dubious whether the intensity and the character of the violence in East Timor and Kosovo in 1999 would have been enough to shift the responsibility to protect to the international community. This chapter will address this conceptual gap, emphasising the need for finding a closer operational link between the responsibility to prevent and the responsibility to react as well as a normative link between the responsibility to protect and principles of international law.

Responsibility to Prevent

Despite the fact that the earlier reports envisaged a wider context where the R2P applies,[6] the text of the 2005 World Summit Outcome makes clear that world leaders agreed upon the narrower scope of responsibility and action confined to four types of mass atrocities: genocide, war crimes, ethnic cleansing and crimes against humanity.[7] Given the legal technicalities involved in proving the criminal nature of conducts, doubt would remain as to whether the R2P extends to civilians under

6 For example, the 2004 High-Level Panel Report encompasses mass murder and rape, deliberate starvation and exposure to disease as well. See Secretary-General's High-level Panel (2004), p. 65.

7 UN General Assembly (24 October 2005), para. 138.

imminent threat of physical violence when the intention of suspected perpetrators remains to be proven. As long as the responsibility to react is strictly separated from the responsibility to prevent, any move towards recognising the international responsibility for early and flexible engagements to protect populations from mass atrocity crimes will inevitably suffer a setback from the indeterminacy as to when mass atrocity crimes are being committed or imminently apprehended.

It is arguable that the inclusion of a preventive dimension in the concept is aimed at addressing such a concern.[8] The 2005 World Summit Outcome, in fact, acknowledges that the responsibility 'entails the prevention of such crimes, including their incitement',[9] including 'helping States build capacity to protect their populations … *before crises and conflicts break out*' (emphasis added).[10] Yet, the commitment to prevention was diluted by qualified expressions such as 'should, *as appropriate*, encourage and help States to exercise this responsibility', and '*intend to* commit ourselves, *as necessary and appropriate*, to helping States build capacity to protect their populations' (emphasis added). The responsibility to prevent has been framed too broadly to have any distinguishing meaning as a juridical principle.[11] The tone used to embrace prevention in the R2P discourse has been weak at best.

It is debatable that the narrowly confined scope of R2P as envisaged by world leaders has also expanded a conceptual gulf in relation to the wider protection agendas, especially if the responsibility to prevent extends to structural prevention as well as operational prevention as envisaged by the 2001 ICISS Report.[12] The consistency with the narrowly defined R2P concept will be better maintained by taking a narrow but deep approach, focusing only on the prevention of mass atrocity crimes.[13] This idea is shared by some states that urge a clear distinction between the R2P and more general protection of civilians during an armed conflict.[14] However, there is an inevitable difficulty as to how the responsibility to prevent as narrowly defined can be distinguished from more general conflict prevention, given that it is difficult to discern measures specifically directed at preventing mass atrocity crimes and those relating more broadly to the prevention of an immediate crisis in general, and human rights protection during armed conflict in particular.

The debate leading up to the adoption of the Summit Outcome shows that China and Russia vehemently rejected the suggestion that the Security Council be empowered to act in anticipation of a humanitarian crisis.[15] This position is clearly

8 Luck (August 2008).

9 UN General Assembly (24 October 2005), para. 138.

10 UN General Assembly (24 October 2005), para. 139.

11 Molier (2006), p. 48.

12 International Commission on Intervention and State Sovereignty (2001), pp. 22–7, paras 3.18–3.43.

13 See Bellamy (2009), p. 101. But see Ngugi wa Thiong'o (23 July 2009), p. 5.

14 See, for example, UN General Assembly (24 July 2009).

15 Bellamy (2006), p. 151. Cf. International Commission on Intervention and State Sovereignty (2001), p. 33, para. 4.21.

reflected in the text of the Summit Outcome which states that 'we are prepared to take collective action, in a timely and decisive manner, through the Security Council … *should peaceful means be inadequate*' (emphasis added).[16] It is therefore arguable that the Summit Outcome not only exacerbated the conceptual predicament in relation to the responsibility to prevent but also diluted the significance of the international community's commitment at an early stage of conflict.

Filling the conceptual gulf between the responsibility to prevent and the responsibility to react in the way that leads to timely and decisive international action against mass atrocity crimes is one of the challenges that confront the international community in embracing and operationalising the R2P concept. Difficulties involved in implementing the responsibility to prevent are well illustrated by the way in which the international community responded to the situations in Kosovo and East Timor in 1999. Although neither of the cases directly involved the R2P concept, an analysis of the international engagements in those cases demonstrates repercussions for the implementation of the responsibility to prevent by the international community.

Lessons from Kosovo and East Timor

Kosovo

NATO's bombing in Kosovo in 1999 has been often linked to the discussion of the R2P concept,[17] despite the recent efforts by some advocates to shift the focus from military intervention to a broad range of tools available to the United Nations.[18] Much of the tension over the concept revolves around whether it would simply be another form of justification for powerful states to use their powers to intervene into the affairs of weak states. In that context, it would be worthwhile asking whether the R2P, had it already emerged in 1999, would have justified or otherwise legitimated NATO's intervention in Kosovo and, more broadly, the way in which the international community responded to the situation. In other words, how should the event in Kosovo be re-evaluated to learn lessons for the purpose of examining how the responsibility to prevent should be operationalised?

Critics of the R2P concept argue that the situation in Kosovo before the commencement of NATO bombing campaign did not involve massive or widespread human rights violations.[19] The NATO bombing did not end the atrocities but rather precipitated almost all the crimes *committed* in the aftermath.[20] Furthermore, the massive number of civilian casualties and devastation resulted

16 UN General Assembly (24 October 2005), para. 139.

17 See especially, International Commission on Intervention and State Sovereignty (2001), pp. 53–4, paras 6.30, 6.34.

18 Evans (23 July 2009), p. 3; High Level Panel on Threats (2004), pp. 65–6, para. 201.

19 See Charney (1999), p. 839.

20 Chomsky (23 July 2009), p. 6.

from the NATO bombing campaign, which may have appeared, by contrast, to indicate a commission of mass atrocities as narrowly defined by world leaders. Yet, it is not clear whether the situation can be categorised as a R2P situation in cases where it is partly the intervening power's own making.[21] Nor is it clear whether the Serbian national authorities were manifestly failing to protect the population in Kosovo from the risk of mass atrocities to warrant international collective action.[22]

It may well be argued that the NATO bombing campaign was a preventive measure to avoid full-scale ethnic cleansing in Kosovo, as the alleged Serb massacre of civilians in the Kosovo town of Racak was widely perceived as a warning bell. There was reportedly a sense of urgency for action among Western nations reflecting upon their failure to prevent genocide in Bosnia and Rwanda.[23] However, given the technicalities involved in proving the criminal nature of conducts, be they genocide, war crimes, ethnic cleansing or crimes against humanity, it would have been difficult to establish at the stage NATO initiated the bombing campaign that the situation would have involved one of the four mass atrocity crimes to trigger the international responsibility to protect.

This does not necessarily suggest that the R2P concept should not have been extended to address the situation in Kosovo in 1999. Rather, it arguably suggests that the R2P situations should not be so narrowly or strictly confined to four mass atrocity crimes. This is especially so when the international community is to assume the responsibility to prevent violence from escalating into mass atrocities, as opposed to the responsibility to react when mass atrocity crimes have already been committed. In this respect, it is worth revisiting the question as to whether the R2P concept should extend to civilians under imminent danger of violence when the intention of suspected perpetrators remains to be proven.[24]

Even assuming that the R2P concept extended to the situation in Kosovo in 1999, the way in which the international community took steps to intervene into the Kosovo affairs was problematic. Peaceful measures described as the second pillar in the 2009 Report of the Secretary-General on R2P were proactively resorted to at the initiative of the Security Council.[25] However, the Security Council did so in the way that left the primary responsibility to achieve a political solution to the issue

---

21 Cf. Roberts (1999), p. 120.

22 The 2005 World Summit Outcome contemplates the recourse to collective action only if two conditions are met: (a) 'should peaceful means be inadequate'; and (b) 'national authorities are *manifestly* failing to protect their populations' (emphasis added). UN General Assembly (24 October 2005), para. 139. See also Bellamy (2006), p. 165.

23 Falk (1999), p. 849.

24 For discussion, see, for example, Nasu (2009), p. 209; Wills (2009).

25 After large-scale violence flared up in Kosovo in late 1997 to early 1998, the Security Council intervened to facilitate a peaceful settlement first by adopting Resolution 1160 on 31 March 1998 and then Resolution 1199 on 23 September 1998, in which it condemned both Serbian police for their excessive use of force and the Kosovo Liberation Army (KLA) for their acts of terrorism. See, UN Security Council Resolution S/RES/1160 (1998), para. 3; UN Security Council Resolution S/RES/1199 (1998), preamble.

of Kosovo in the hands of the Federal Republic of Yugoslavia (FRY) Government. Even when the UN Security Council adopted Resolution 1244 (1999) to conclude the hostilities, the international commitment to the issue of Kosovo's status was restricted to 'facilitating a political process designed to determine Kosovo's future status', whilst confirming the FRY's sovereignty and territorial integrity over Kosovo.[26] This arrangement imposed a restriction upon the way in which the political process should take place to determine Kosovo's future status.

There is no doubt that the Security Council's action in relation to Kosovo was guided by the policy tools of conflict prevention, as systematically compiled first by the former UN Secretary-General Boutros Boutros-Ghali in his 1992 Report – *An Agenda for Peace*.[27] However, its effort in facilitating the prevention of mass atrocity crimes in Kosovo was limited due to the opposition of Russia and China concerned about the implications of any stronger measures upon sovereignty and the principle of non-intervention. Although the Security Council demanded that the FRY withdraw its security units used for civilian repression,[28] it did not go far enough to deploy international security ground forces to fill in the vacuum that could have been created by the withdrawal. In contrast, the NATO bombing campaign, even though its legitimacy can be questioned on the legal basis, could well be seen as a more humane and effective preventive measure to achieve the protection agenda.[29] Therefore, it must be critically reviewed as to whether employing those traditional conflict prevention measures for a broader purpose of maintaining international peace and security is enough for the international community to discharge its part of responsibility to prevent mass atrocity crimes.

East Timor

In hindsight, it is obvious that the international community failed in both preventing and reacting to the occurrence of mass atrocity against East Timorese. The case of East Timor is anomalous in the sense that there was no legitimate and lawful authority that should have been given the primary responsibility to protect them. Therefore, when Indonesia invaded the East Timorese territory, trampling upon the East Timorese aspiration and political movements to achieve an independent status in 1975, the responsibility to protect would have been directly transferred to the international community, had it been the norm at that time.

Even looking at the situation in 1999 when the R2P concept is about to emerge, the international community's engagement with the protection of East Timorese people was at most minimal,[30] in contrast to its more active, albeit still cautious,

26 UN Security Council Resolution S/RES/1244 (1999), para. 11(e) and Annex 1.

27 Secretary-General (17 June 1992).

28 UN Security Council Resolution S/RES/1199 (1998), para. 4(a).

29 See International Commission on Intervention and State Sovereignty (2001), p. 21.

30 The Security Council adopted only two resolutions after the 1975 Indonesian invasion of East Timor: UN Security Council Resolution S/RES/384 (1975); UN Security

engagement with the Kosovo situation. In East Timor, the Security Council established the UN Mission in East Timor (UNAMET) on 11 June 1999 to organise and conduct the public consultation regarding independence.[31] The responsibility for maintaining the peace and security during the public consultation in East Timor was clearly left with the Indonesian military, the very forces that had been responsible for the suppression of the East Timorese population in the past.[32]

The international community finally stepped in when the situation reached the boiling point where the fierce violence following the public consultation mounted the regional pressure upon the Indonesian Government to accept an international force under UN authority. However, even after the violence unfolded, the UN was apparently reluctant to intervene until the deal was struck between Indonesia and the regional actors.[33]

Claiming that the international responsibility to protect was not engaged until the last moment of rebel violence is insurmountable. First, given that the international community continuously denounced Indonesia's occupation of East Timor, it would be wrong to expect the invading country to assume the primary responsibility to protect. It is dubious whether the international community could have been excused for not assuming responsibility to protect the East Timorese relying on Indonesia's responsibility as the occupying power.

Second, the UNAMET could have been a useful and reliable source of early warnings about the potential violence after the public consultation. But the Security Council did not act upon it and rather chose to send another mission to observe the escalation of violence, leaving neighbouring countries with diplomatic negotiations to reach a solution. It is debatable whether the violence could have been curtailed had the Security Council assumed the international responsibility to prevent mass atrocity crimes with more robust and decisive measures. This is because the unrest in East Timor before the popular consultation was sporadic and controllable. Although the violence after the consultation was foreseeable, it was not clear whether it would have involved one of the mass atrocity crimes to which the R2P would have applied.[34]

Third, there is no doubt that the Security Council failed in assuming the international responsibility to react by not taking timely and decisive action, which resulted in the commission of mass atrocity crimes during the violence.[35]

Council Resolution S/RES/389 (1976). The General Assembly, on the other hand, expressed condemnation regularly every year, but stopped adopting a resolution in 1982. See Shearer (2007), p. 434.

31 UN Security Council Resolution S/RES/1246 (1999).

32 See United Nations (1999), Annex 1.

33 Chesterman (2007), p. 195.

34 The Security Council in fact dispatched a mission to Dili and Jakarta to observe the escalation of violence.

35 For details, see, Clinton Fernandez, 'R2P and the East Timor Intervention' in this collection.

This proves the weak linkage between the responsibility to prevent and the responsibility to react, and the unco-ordinated transition from the former to the latter. The incremental approach could well be justified on the grounds of precautionary criteria requiring the use of military coercion only as the last resort and only when it stands a reasonable chance of success.[36] However, it is arguable that the international community failed to protect the East Timorese by strictly following the precautionary criteria under the R2P concept.

International Community and the Responsibility to Prevent

The theoretical foundation of the R2P concept leaving the primary responsibility to protect in the hands of the sovereign state may hinder the international community from taking collective action at an early stage of conflict to err on the side of respecting sovereignty especially when the threshold for intervention is set so high.[37] One may point to the situations in the Democratic Republic of the Congo and Darfur as examples where the international community should have become more actively engaged in deteriorating situations where the State was found to be manifestly failing to protect its population.[38] The division of responsibilities by different stages and pillars means that there is nothing to prevent states from using the first stage of responsibility as an aegis against foreign intervention even in serious humanitarian emergencies, as evident in the R2P language used by several Security Council members to oppose intervention against Sudan.[39]

A brief examination of two cases – Kosovo and East Timor – that occurred when the R2P concept was about to emerge indicates that had the R2P been applicable in Kosovo and East Timor, the concept would not have provided any guidance as to what measure or approach the international community should have taken to prevent mass atrocities. The real value of the R2P concept suffers a conceptual gap by leaving the responsibility to prevent entirely in the hands of each state, whilst limiting the international commitment to intervention within the realm of the responsibility to react as the last resort.

Greater clarity is therefore called for regarding the interface between the responsibility to prevent and the responsibility to react. The Special Advisor to UN Secretary-General on the Responsibility to Protect, Edward C. Luck, appreciates that policymakers have increasingly been recognising the significance of closer collaboration among states, international bodies and civil society as the best way to sustain and deepen sovereignty.[40] However, it remains unclear

36 International Commission on Intervention and State Sovereignty (2001), p. 37, paras 4.41–4.43.

37 Stahn (2007), p. 117.

38 Stanley Foundation (2008), p. 35.

39 Bellamy (2005), p. 31.

40 Statement by Luck (1 December 2008).

how such collaboration is to be played out, or how the ultimate responsibility is to be allocated or shared in the grey area. There are three important questions to be addressed for the purpose of clarifying the international responsibility to prevent as part of the R2P concept: (1) how international political will can be generated at an early stage; (2) how the issue of self-determination and secession can be addressed; and (3) what is the nature of the international responsibility to provide assistance or to take collective action, as opposed to a sovereign state's responsibility towards its own people.

Political Will

Conflict prevention has been one of the core UN activities since the former UN Secretary-General Dag Hammarskjold launched preventive diplomacy in the late 1950s. Despite the development of preventive diplomacy and various measures for the purpose of conflict prevention ranging from early warning to preventive deployment, the UN's policies on conflict prevention have been inevitably haunted by the difficulty of seeking to pacify 'the dog that didn't bark'.[41] As long as state sovereignty is placed at the centre of the debate, this difficulty for conflict prevention will also apply to the R2P concept permeating through the realm of prevention, creating a gulf between rhetorical support and tangible commitment.

The general inclination among states against taking action for prevention may well involve pragmatism that poses an impediment to preventive action – the view, widespread among government officials and experts, which is that peace enforcement actions to prevent the real crisis are ten times more costly in terms of manpower and money than post-conflict prevention.[42]There is also a fear that collective engagement at an early stage will internationalise the problem starting down a slippery slope to intervention and help legitimate rebel violence or secessionist movement against the governments in power.[43]

No matter what the reason might be, the lack of political will certainly constitute a major obstacle to making a collective decision to provide international assistance in a situation that potentially results in mass atrocities. While a number of preventive policy tools such as early warning and confidence-building have been proposed and developed, little attention has been given to how the information gained and confidence built through those mechanisms can be carried through to generate required political will to deal swiftly and decisively with the situation at hand. In an age of high-speed communications and sophisticated fact-finding activities, however, a lack of credible information has become implausible, and even preposterous, as an excuse for inaction to avert or stop atrocities.[44] In

41 Sucharipa-Behrmann and Franck (1998), pp. 493, 497.

42 Stanley Foundation (2008). Cf. Tanguy (2003), p. 144.

43 International Commission on Intervention and State Sovereignty (2001), p. 25, paras 3.34–3.35.

44 Arbour (2008), p. 455.

fact, 'the dog is already barking' in many of the alarming situations.[45] As was the case in Rwanda as early as 1993 and in Zimbabwe more recently, there were abundant serious warnings about the deterioration of the situation, and yet absent was the reaction of intergovernmental organs to this information and the credible commitments by states.[46] Early warning and other preventive policy tools could only be meaningful if the international community reacted to early warnings in a timely and decisive manner.

The key to this issue is therefore how to generate sufficient political will at an early stage to prevent violence from escalating into mass atrocities. The 2009 Report of the Secretary-General notes a host of proposals for creating a standing or standby rapid-response civilian and police capacity for emergencies.[47] The same report also indicates that the use of military force is not reserved to the responsibility to react under Pillar 3, stating in relation to Pillar 2 that:

> ... the early, targeted and restrained use of international military assets and armed forces may be able to save lives and bring a measure of stability so that diplomacy, domestic political processes, healing and reconciliation can have time and space to operate.[48]

Deploying peacekeeping observers and forces would assist the international community in meeting the need for an early and flexible response under Pillar 2 in the way that is tailored to the circumstances of the situation. Those on-site missions can provide opportunities for delivering messages directly to key decision-makers acting on behalf of the larger international community.[49] Adequately equipped and well-resourced peacekeeping forces can also handle the changing situation flexibly even if sufficient political will cannot be generated to adopt a fully fledged enforcement action.

The presence of peacekeeping forces does not, in itself, mobilise sufficient political will to provide reinforcement enough to prevent mass atrocities, as proven in Rwanda and Srebrenica. It is also essential to understand the limited mandate and capacity of peacekeeping forces for a broader purpose of maintaining peace and security and, in contrast, the specific need for protecting populations from the risk of mass atrocities during the conflict. There may not be enough political will to send a large military contingent capable of handling numerous tasks, yet there might be political will just enough to send a tailored mission for the specific purpose of protecting civilians from the risk of mass atrocities in co-ordination with other agencies and missions already deployed. A better understanding about

45 A remark made by William Maley during the International Workshop on 'Sovereignty and R2P 10 Years After East Timor and Kosovo', 16–17 July 2009, Griffith University, Brisbane, Australia.

46 Stanley Foundation (2008), p. 34.

47 Secretary-General Ban Ki-moon (12 January 2009), para. 39.

48 Secretary-General Ban Ki-moon (12 January 2009), para. 40.

49 Secretary-General Ban Ki-moon (12 January 2009), para. 53.

the scope of each mission, a greater co-ordination among different missions and agencies involved in international assistance and new ideas about effective ways to protect civilians such as the use of military police,[50] all may help us in finding a stronger operational link between the responsibility to prevent and the responsibility to react by the international community.

Self-determination and Secession

As Gareth Evans notes, the primary focus of the responsibility to prevent is given to what states at risk can do for themselves with minimum external intrusion.[51] The 2009 Report of the Secretary-General suggests further that the international assistance under Pillar 2 'could also encompass military assistance to help beleaguered States deal with armed non-sate actors threatening both the State and its population'.[52] Deferring to sovereign states, however, may send a wrong message both to the government at issue and the population under threat of violence, which could in turn inflame the conflict. In fact, the UN's commitment to the sovereignty and territorial integrity of the FRY at an earlier stage of conflict[53] arguably tolerated the FRY Government in suppressing Kosovars' secessionist movement, whereas the Kosovo Liberation Army (KLA) strengthened its case for armed struggle to draw more international attention to achieve self-determination.[54] Therefore, the fundamental presumption of sovereign protection underpinning the R2P concept as currently formulated requires a more careful and critical examination.

The East Timorese population expressed their desire for establishing an independent state by an overwhelming majority in the 1999 popular consultation. East Timor represented one of the remaining cases of non-self-governing territories,[55] wherein people retained the right to self-determination as a positive entitlement to secession.[56] It is clearly questionable in cases of colonial or alien domination whether the basic foundation of the R2P concept conferring the primary responsibility to protect upon the administering sovereign state should prevent the international community from engaging proactively to protect the local population simply because the situation does not reach the stage where the international community is required to react by an application of the R2P concept.

It is not always clear, however, whether the people oppressed or otherwise prejudicially treated by the state authorities are entitled to seek another 'right' authority by secession. This question is deep-rooted in the indeterminate definition

50 See, for example, Eaton (2008).

51 Evans (2008), p. 86.

52 Ki-moon (12 January 2009), para. 29.

53 UN Security Council Resolution S/RES/1160 (1998), para. 5.

54 See Economides (2007), p. 222.

55 UN General Assembly (1960). East Timor was removed from the list of non-self-governing territories upon independence on 20 May 2002.

56 See *East Timor (Portugal v Australia) (Judgment)* [1995] ICJ Rep 90, at 103.

of 'self' in the application of the right to self-determination.[57] In the case of Kosovo, the political fate of Kosovars was deliberately left unresolved,[58] although arguably they were entitled to secession in an exercise of their right to self-determination.[59] Establishing an office of self-determination issues on a regional or international scale, modelled on the post of High Commissioner on National Minorities for the Balkans under the auspices of the Organization for Security and Cooperation in Europe (OSCE) to identify and seek early resolution of ethnic tensions before they escalate,[60] may well be a plausible way forward to assess self-determination claims.

Even if an institutional mechanism is established to assess self-determination claims, an unresolved issue will remain as to the circumstances under which the international community should be required to assume responsibility to protect a population and what actions it may take to assist in vindicating their right to self-determination.[61] Some warn that '[e]ncouraging secessionist minorities by giving them the often false impression that the sole Superpower will come to their rescue in case they are repressed, leads to more violence, hatred and death, not less'.[62] Thus the R2P concept poses an unresolved, if not irreconcilable, dilemma – it should not be seen as too deferring to state sovereignty to oppose any realisation of self-determination against the existing state authorities, nor should it be used as propaganda for independence by anyone who claims that they are not protected from the risk of mass atrocities.

This issue poses a fundamental question about finding a right balance between the deference to and respect for state sovereignty ('a factor of stability') and the need for protecting people including any minorities from the risk of mass atrocities, which may well require changes to the existing polity of the state ('a motor of change').[63] The conventional understanding is that the right to secede does not exist as part of the right to self-determination in international law outside the context of decolonisation.[64] It is also arguable, however, that international law does not necessarily prohibit secession as an exercise of the right to self-determination.[65] There is no doubt that the current international legal system is structured in such a way as to help the central government of states ensure the defeat of internal

57 See, generally, Cass (1992), p. 37; Knop (2002), p. 51; Koskenniemi (1994), p. 260.

58 UN Security Council Resolution S/RES/1244 (1999) provides that Kosovo would enjoy 'substantial and meaningful self-administration'.

59 See Seidel (2002); Tomuschat (2006). But see Bing Bing Jia (2009).

60 For details of its activities, see its website available at http://www.osce.org/hcnm/ (last accessed 12 January 2010).

61 Grant (1999), p. 22.

62 Bricmont (23 July 2009), p. 3. See also, Bilder (2008), p. 174.

63 The expression in the brackets is used by Hilpold (2009), p. 55.

64 See, for example, Musgrave (1997).

65 For discussion, see, Hilpold (2009); Orakhelashvili (2009). The ICJ in its advisory opinion on Kosovo avoided adjudication on this legal issue by narrowly construing the question as whether or not the declaration of independence was in accordance with international law, without dealing with the legal consequences of the declaration. International Court of Justice (2010), para. 51. Cf. Separate Opinion of Judge Yusuf, paras 4–17.

secessionist movements, unless the self-determination claim is settled in one way or another.[66] The real challenge to the R2P concept is how the international community should act to reconcile those competing rights and interests, whilst achieving the protection agenda before the recourse is made to violence and armed force.

The starting point is to explore the operational and flexible link between the responsibility to prevent and the responsibility to react by the international community through a gradual shift of responsibility or simultaneously with the sovereign state. The R2P concept will then need to explore the limits of its operation by placing the right of people to self-determination at the centre of the concept,[67] rather than relying on the rigid, formalistic notion of state sovereignty, in order to maintain the normative and practical coherence.

Nature of International Responsibility

The basic premise of the R2P concept lies with the proposition that while sovereign states have the primary responsibility to protect their own citizens from mass atrocities, the responsibility will shift to the international community when the national authorities are manifestly failing to protect their population from genocide, war crimes, ethnic cleansing or crimes against humanity.[68] It is also stated that the international community has the responsibility to use appropriate diplomatic, humanitarian and other peaceful means to help protect populations from mass atrocities, even before the national authorities are found unable or unwilling to discharge their own responsibility.[69] The distinction appears to be made by referring to the nature of international engagement – whether it is consensual or coercive. Yet, this distinction leaves unclear what the international community's responsibility actually entails especially with an early engagement for the purpose of prevention.

It is thus arguable that the expanded conception of responsibility of the international community is sending a mixed (or even contradicting) message – to respect state sovereignty and the principle of non-intervention unless there are exceptional circumstances that genuinely 'shock the conscience of mankind', whilst at the same time urging the international community to commit to early peaceful engagement to prevent mass atrocities.[70]

This confused message may be reflected in the mixed reaction of the international community to the situations in East Timor and Kosovo. In East Timor, the responsibility for maintaining the peace and security during the public

66 For a thorough examination of self-determination settlements, see Weller (2009); Weller and Metzger (2007).

67 In the context of peace-building, see Daglish and Nasu (2007).

68 UN General Assembly (24 October 2005), para. 139.

69 See International Commission on Intervention and State Sovereignty (2001); UN General Assembly (24 October 2005), pp. 23–5, para. 139. Cf. High-Level Panel on Threats (December 2004), para. 201.

70 See Chandler (2004), p. 66.

consultation was clearly left with the Indonesian military – the occupying force – whilst the UN was apparently reluctant to intervene until the deal was struck between Indonesia and the regional actors. In Kosovo, the Security Council adopted a series of measures to prevent the escalation of the conflict, whilst confirming the territorial integrity and political independence of Serbia over Kosovo, which was not enough to stop the NATO states from unilaterally intervening by aerial bombing to achieve what they considered a humanitarian aim. Should the international community have been blamed for its reluctance in relation to East Timor, leaving the maintenance of security in the hands of Indonesian military, even though an early intervention might have inflamed mass atrocity crimes? In contrast, should the international community have been praised for its peaceful engagement in Kosovo, even though it might not have been as effective as coercive measures?

Due to ambiguity of the international community and its responsibility, it is not necessarily clear who is expected to exercise this responsibility and what is expected of the international community in discharging its responsibility to protect.[71] There are general guidelines as to what can be done, as can be found in the 2001 ICISS Report and 2009 Report of the Secretary-General. Although those reports regard the Security Council as the primary actor to represent the international community, it may well not be an appropriate organ to be entrusted with the responsibility to protect, given the inaction and ineffectiveness of the organ in dealing with the people at risk of mass atrocities in the past and because of the systemic political constraints on its decision-making process.[72]

The Security Council is a creation of the post-World War II politics, reflecting states' pre-occupation with the maintenance of international peace and security, as opposed to the protection of people from mass atrocities. The increased activities of the Security Council in response to massive human rights violations have been seen as positive development. Yet, the inaction and ineffectiveness of this organ in dealing with populations at risk of mass atrocities in the past raises doubt about the extent to which the Security Council, as the authorising body of choice, can implement the responsibility to protect. The international community's responsibility to prevent may well be better engaged through a greater dialogue between the Security Council and the Economic and Social Council (ECOSOC) to facilitate an early response to human rights violations.[73] The creation of a new UN subsidiary body, such as a Human Security Council to provide leadership in addressing military and non-military security issues,[74] and a Human Protection Council in a more specific context of protecting civilians during armed conflict,[75] can also be pursued without requiring more politically sensitive Security Council reform.

71 See generally Glanville (2010); Menon (2009).

72 See, for example, Brown (2001), p. 92; Levitt (2003).

73 Breen (2007).

74 Mahbub ul-Haq (1999), p. 88.

75 Nasu (2009), p. 238.

The difficulty in understanding what exactly the international community's responsibility entails is even more obvious when it is compared with the primary responsibility of each sovereign state. While the concept of responsibility can be understood variably in a moral, political or legal sense, the international community's responsibility to provide assistance or to take collective action appears to be different in nature from sovereign responsibility towards its own population, and more challenging for turning into legal norms.[76] It would be wrong to assume that the same or a similar legal liability regime would apply to the international community's responsibility as state responsibility.[77] There is no guideline that serves as criteria by reference to which the action or inaction of the international community can be assessed with regard to the extent to which its responsibility to protect is discharged.[78] The legal consequences arising from the failure of the international community to provide assistance or to take collective action to protect a population from mass atrocities cannot be understood within the framework of a traditional legal liability regime.

If the R2P is nothing more than a political concept based on the existing rules of international law,[79] it appears to suggest that the failure by the international community to provide assistance or to intervene to protect a population from mass atrocities does not entail any legal consequences. However, any action or inaction, success or failure, by the international community will have an impact on the normative force and interpretation of basic principles of international law,[80] such as non-use of armed force and the right of self-determination, which could otherwise pull in potentially conflicting directions. A lack of attention to and understanding of this normative link would be fatal to the discussion of the R2P concept, as illustrated by the debate on humanitarian intervention, which underlines the indeterminacy of competing basic principles and the extent to which the international rule of law 'constitutes a highly manipulable regime that lends itself to politicization'.[81]

Conclusion

The decision made by the world leaders in 2005 to restrict the scope of the R2P concept only in relation to four types of mass atrocity crimes arguably exacerbated

76 For discussion, see Nasu (2009b); Nasu (2011).

77 Cf. Alvarez (2008), p. 281.

78 An attempt to set out guidelines for military intervention by the Security Council failed during the 2005 World Summit due to the strong refusal of China, Russia and the United States. See Bellamy (2009), p. 83; Wheeler (2005), p. 99.

79 Luck (2009), p. 3.

80 The idea of connecting the legal nature of responsibility to the normative force and interpretation of international principles is more fully elaborated in Nasu (2007); Nasu (2009b).

81 Teitel (2002), p. 387.

the conceptual predicament in relation to the responsibility to prevent and diluted the significance of the international community's commitment in an early phase of conflict. A critical reflection of the international community's engagement with the situations in Kosovo and East Timor in 1999 demonstrates that the R2P concept, as understood by the world leaders in 2005, would not have provided any guidance as to what measure or approach the international community should have taken to prevent mass atrocities.

The conceptual gulf can only be bridged by examining how collaboration between the sovereign state and the international community is to be played out, and how the ultimate responsibility is to be allocated or shared in the grey area. In considering this question, this chapter identified three problems that confronted the international community in dealing with Kosovo and East Timor: (1) how international political will can be generated at an early stage; (2) how the issue of self-determination and secession can be addressed; and (3) what is the nature of the international responsibility to provide assistance or to take collective action.

Difficult as those problems might be, the international community should not refrain from collective engagement at an early stage of conflict. There is a need for finding a closer operational and flexible link between the responsibility to prevent and the responsibility to react so that the international community can take a more proactive approach without always deferring to sovereign states even in a preventive phase. In exploring this close operational link, the R2P concept will have to ascertain the limits of its operation by placing the right of people to self-determination at the centre of the doctrine and by facilitating the better understanding of the normative link between the R2P and principles of international law.

Care has to be taken, however, of the way in which the closer operational link is explored. Any rule-setting has to have due regard to Third World anxieties driven by the history of Western colonisation over the centuries and the strong sense of scepticism against any Western sponsored enterprises promoting Western values. Recently, in July 2009, the UN General Assembly interactive thematic dialogue on the R2P chorused such anxieties.[82] The R2P concept in the Third World could well be suspected of having a 'donor driven agenda', concerned about achieving the donor's political and economic aims rather than what developing countries truly value or require.[83] The first step towards operationalising the R2P concept should thus be taken by clarifying what is acceptable to and needed by Third World counties in facilitating the international community's engagement to achieve its responsibility to protect in a preventive phase.

82 UN General Assembly (23–28 July 2009). See also Thakur (2011), p. 156.

83 See Upadhyaya (2004), p. 86.

References

J.E. Alvarez (2008) 'The Schizophrenias of R2P', in Philip Alston and Euan MacDonald (eds) *Human Rights, Intervention, and the Use of Force*, OUP 275.

L. Arbour (2008) 'The Responsibility to Protect As a Duty of Care in International Law and Practice', 34, *Review of International Studies* 445.

A.J. Bellamy (2005) 'Responsibility to Protect or Trojan Horse? The Crisis in Darfur and Humanitarian Intervention after Iraq', 19, *Ethics & International Affairs* 31.

A.J. Bellamy (2006) 'Whither the Responsibility to Protect? Humanitarian Intervention and the 2005 World Summit', 20, *Ethics and International Affairs* 143.

A.J. Bellamy (2009) *Responsibility to Protect: The Global Effort to End Mass Atrocities*, Polity.

R.B. Bilder (2008) 'The Implications of Kosovo for International Human Rights Law', in Philip Alston and Euan MacDonald (eds) *Human Rights, Intervention, and the Use of Force*, OUP 139.

B.B. Jia (2009) 'The Independence of Kosovo: A Unique Case of Secession?', 27, *Chinese Journal of International Law* 31.

C. Breen (2007) 'The Necessity of a Role for the ECOSOC in the Maintenance of International Peace and Security', 12, *Journal of Conflict & Security Law* 261.

J. Bricmont (23 July 2009) *A More Just World and the Responsibility to Protect*, Statement at the UN General Assembly Interactive Thematic Dialogue on the Responsibility to Protect, available at http://www0.un.org/ga/president/63/interactive/protect/jean.pdf (accessed 4 January 2010).

C. Brown (2001) 'Moral Agency and International Society', 15, *Ethics and International Affairs* 87.

D.Z. Cass (1992) 'Rethinking Self-Determination: A Critical Analysis of Current International Law Theories', 18, *Syracuse Journal of International Law and Commerce* 21.

D. Chandler (2004) 'The Responsibility to Protect? Imposing the "Liberal Peace"', 11, *International Peacekeeping* 59.

J.I. Charney (1999) 'Anticipatory Humanitarian Intervention in Kosovo', 93, *American Journal of International Law* 834.

S. Chesterman (2007) 'East Timor', in Mats Berdal and Spyros Economides (eds) *United Nations Interventionism, 1991–2004*, London School of Economics and Political Science.

N. Chomsky (23 July 2009) *Statement to the United Nations General Assembly Thematic Dialogue on the Responsibility to Protect*, available at http://www.un.org/ga/president/63/interactive/protect/noam.pdf (accessed 4 January 2010).

K. Daglish and H. Nasu (2007) 'Towards a True Incarnation of the Rule of Law in War-Torn Territories: Centring Peacebuilding in the Will of the People', 54, *Netherlands International Law Review* 81.

D. Eaton (2008) 'Pointsman', *The Role of the Military Police in Enhancing ADF-AFP Interoperability on Peace and Stability Operations* 29.

S. Economides (2007) 'Kosovo', in Mats Berda and Spyros Economides (eds) *United Nations Interventionism 1991–2004*, 217.

G. Evans (2008) *The Responsibility to Protect: Ending Mass Atrocity Crimes Once and for All*, Brookings Institution Press.

G. Evans (23 July 2009) *Statement to United Nations General Assembly Informal Interactive Dialogue on the Responsibility to Protect*, available at http://www0.un.org/ga/president/63/interactive/protect/evans.pdf (accessed 4 January 2010).

R.A. Falk (1999) 'Kosovo, World Order, and the Future of International Law', 93, *American Journal of International Law* 847.

L. Glanville (2010) 'The International Community's Responsibility to Protect', 2, *Global Responsibility to Protect* 287.

T.D. Grant (1999) 'Extending Decolonization: How the United Nations Might Have Addressed Kosovo', 28, *Georgia Journal of International and Comparative Law* 10.

F.O. Hampson and David M. Malone (2002) *From Reaction to Conflict Prevention: Opportunities for the UN System*, Lynne Rienner.

Challenges and Change (HLP) High-Level Panel on Threats (December 2004) *A more secure world: our shared responsibility*, United Nations A/59/565.

P. Hilpold (2009) 'The Kosovo Case and International Law: Looking for Applicable Theories', 8, *Chinese Journal of International Law* 47.

P. Hilpold (2009) 'What Role for Academic Writers in Interpreting International Law? – A Rejoinder to Orakhelashvili', 8, *Chinese Journal of International Law* 291.

International Commission on Intervention and State Sovereignty (2001) *The Responsibility to Protect: Report of the International Commission on Intervention and State Sovereignty*, International Development Research Centre.

International Court of Justice (2010) *Accordance with International Law of the Unilateral Declaration of Independence in respect of Kosovo (Advisory Opinion) ICJ Rep*, General List No. 141, available at http://www.icj-cij.org/docket/files/141/15987.pdf (accessed 16 December 2011).

B.W. Jentleson (ed.) (2000) *Opportunities Missed, Opportunities Seized: Preventive Diplomacy in the Post-Cold War World*, Rowan and Littlefield.

B. Ki-moon (12 January 2009) *Implementing the responsibility to protect: Report of the Secretary-General UN: A/63/677*, available at http://www.un.org/sg (accessed 4 January 2010).

K. Knop (2002) *Diversity and Self-Determination in International Law*, OUP.

M. Koskenniemi (1994) 'National Self-Determination Today: Problems of Legal Theory and Practice', 43, *International and Comparative Law Quarterly* 241.

J.I. Levitt (2003) 'Book Review: The Responsibility to Protect: A Beaver without a Dam?', 153, *Michigan Journal of International Law* 169.

E.C. Luck (2008, August) 'The United Nations and the Responsibility to Protect', in *Policy Analysis Brief*, The Stanley Foundation.

E.C. Luck (1 December 2008) *Statement to Arria Formula Meeting on the Responsibility to Protect (Working Group on Conflict Prevention and Resolution in Africa, UN Security Council)*, available at http://www.ipacademy.org/asset/file/409/LArria.pdf (accessed 4 January 2010).

E.C. Luck (2009) *Remarks to the General Assembly on the Responsibility to Protect*, available at http://www.un.org/ga/president/63/interactive/protect/luck.pdf (accessed 4 January 2010).

M.S. Lund (1996) *Preventing Violent Conflicts: A Strategy for Preventive Diplomacy*, United States Institute of Peace Press.

M. ul-Haq (1999) 'Global Governance for Human Security', in Majid Tehranian (ed.) *Worlds Apart: Human Security and Global Governance*, Tauris 79.

R. Menon (2009) 'Pious Words, Puny Deeds: The 'International Community' and Mass Atrocities', *Ethics & International Affairs* 235.

H. Miall et al. (1999) *Contemporary Conflict Resolution: The Prevention, Management and Transformation of Deadly Conflicts*, Polity.

G. Molier (2006) 'Humanitarian Intervention and the Responsibility to Protect After 9/11', 53, *Netherlands International Law Review* 48.

T. Musgrave (1997) *Self-Determination and National Minorities*, OUP.

H. Nasu (2007) 'Responsibility to React? Lessons from the Security Council's Response to the Southern Lebanon Crisis of 2006', 14, *International Peacekeeping* 339.

H. Nasu (2009) 'Operationalizing the "Responsibility to Protect" and Conflict Prevention: Dilemmas of Civilian Protection in Armed Conflict', 14, *Journal of Conflict & Security Law* 209.

H. Nasu (2009b) *International Law on Peacekeeping: A Study of Article 40 of the UN Charter*, Nijhoff.

H. Nasu (2011) 'The UN Security Council's Responsibility and the "Responsibility to Protect"', 15, *Max Planck Yearbook of United Nations Law* 377.

N. wa Thiong'o (23 July 2009) *Uneven Development Is the Root of Many Crimes*, Address to the United Nations General Assembly Thematic Dialogue on the Responsibility to Protect, United Nations, New York, available at http://www.un.org/ga/president/63/interactive/protect/ngugi.pdf (accessed 4 January 2010).

A. Orakhelashvili (2009) 'The Kosovo UDI between Agreed Law and Subjective Perception: A Response to Hilpold', 8, *Chinese Journal of International Law* 285.

A. Roberts (1999) 'NATO's 'Humanitarian War' over Kosovo', 41, *Survival* 120.

S.P. Rosenberg (2009) 'Responsibility to Protect: A Framework for Prevention', 1 *Global Responsibility to Protect* 422, available at http://responsibilitytoprotect.org/.

Secretary-General (17 June 1992) *An Agenda for Peace*, Report of the Secretary-General pursuant to the statement adopted by the Summit Meeting of the Security Council on 31 January 1992A/47/277 – S/24111, available at http://www.un.org/Docs/SG/agpeace.html (accessed 4 January 2010).

Secretary-General (Ban Ki-moon) (12 January 2009) *Implementing the Responsibility to Protect: Report of the Secretary-General A/63/677*, available at http://www.un.org/sg/ (accessed 4 January 2010).

Secretary-General's High-level Panel (2004) *Challenges and Change, A more secure world: Our shared responsibility*, United Nations.

G. Seidel (2002) 'A New Dimension of the Right of Self-Determination in Kosovo?', in Christian Tomuschat (ed.) *Kosovo and the International Community: A Legal Assessment*, CUP 203.

I. Shearer (2007) 'A Pope, Two Presidents and A Prime Minister', 7, *ILSA Journal of International and Comparative Law* 429.

C. Stahn (2007) 'Responsibility to Protect: Political Rhetoric or Emerging Legal Norm?', 101, *American Journal of International Law* 99.

E. Stamnes (2008) *Operationalising the Preventive Aspects of the Responsibility to Protect*, Norwegian Institute of International Affairs Report.

Stanley Foundation (2008) *Actualizing the Responsibility to Protect*, Report of the 43rd Conference on the United Nations of the Next Decade, 20–25 June Stanley Foundation, available at http://www.stanleyfoundation.org/publications/report/UNND808.pdf (accessed 4 January 2010).

L.R. Sucharipa-Behrmann and Thomas M. Franck (1998) 'Preventive Measures', 30, *New York University Journal of International Law and Politics* 485.

J. Tanguy (2003) 'Redefining Sovereignty and Intervention', 17, *Ethics & International Affairs* 141.

R.G. Teitel (2002) 'Humanity's Law: Rule of Law for the New Global Politics', 35, *Cornell International Law Journal* 355.

R. Thakur (2011) *The Responsibility to Protect: Norms, Laws and the Use of Force in International Politics*, UNU Press.

C. Tomuschat (2006) 'Secession and Self-Determination', in Marcelo Kohen (ed) *Secession: International Law Perspectives*, CUP 23.

UN General Assembly (1960) *GA Res 1542(XV)*, available at http://daccess-dds-ny.un.org/doc/.

UN General Assembly (24 October 2005) *World Summit Outcome GA Res. 60/1*, http://available at www.un.org/depts/dhl/resguide/r60.htm (accessed 4 January 2010).

UN General Assembly (23–28 July 2009) *UN GAOR, 63rd sess, 97th-101st mtgs, UN Doc A//63/PV.97-101*, available at http://responsibilitytoprotect.org/.

UN General Assembly (24 July 2009) *General Assembly Sixty-third session 98th plenary meeting A/63/PV.98*, available at http://responsibilitytoprotect.org/98thPlenary%281%29.pdf.

UN Security Council Resolution S/RES/384 (1975), available at http://www.un.org/Docs/sc/unsc_resolutions (accessed 4 January 2010).

UN Security Council Resolution S/RES/389 (1976) 22 April, available at http://www.un.org/Docs/sc/unsc_resolutions (accessed 4 January 2010).

UN Security Council Resolution S/RES/1160 (1998) 31 March, available at http://www.un.org/Docs/sc/unsc_resolutions (accessed 4 January 2010).

UN Security Council Resolution S/RES/1199 (1998) 23 September, available at http://www.un.org/Docs/sc/unsc_resolutions (accessed 4 January 2010).

UN Security Council Resolution S/RES/1244 (1999) 10 June, available at http://www.un.org/Docs/sc/unsc_resolutions (accessed 4 January 2010).

UN Security Council Resolution S/RES/1246 (1999), available at http://www.un.org/Docs/sc/unsc_resolutions (accessed 4 January 2010).

United Nations (1999) *Agreement between the Republic of Indonesia and the Portuguese Republic on the Question of East Timor, UN Doc. A/53/951-S/1999/513/Annex I*, 5 May, available at http://reliefweb.int/node/52700 (accessed 4 January 2010).

P. Upadhyaya (2004) 'Human Security, Humanitarian Intervention, and Third World Concerns', 33, *Denver Journal of International Law and Policy* 71.

M. Weller (2009) 'Settling Self-Determination Conflicts: Recent Developments', 20, *European Journal of International Law* 111.

M. Weller and B. Metzger (2007) 'Settling Self-Determination Conflicts', 20, *European Journal of International Law* 111.

N.J. Wheeler (2005) 'A Victory for Common Humanity? The Responsibility to Protect after the 2005 World Summit', 2, *Journal of International Law and International Relations* 95.

S. Wills (2009) *Protecting Civilians: The Obligations of Peacekeepers*, OUP.

Chapter 7

Sovereignty and R2P Ten Years after East Timor and Kosovo: A Failure to Protect: The UN Human Rights Council and Darfur

Kevin Boreham

When there is genocide in Darfur ... – there must be consequences.

President Obama's speech at the acceptance of the Nobel Peace Prize, Oslo, 10 December 2009

This was the least convincing passage of the speech: so far, there have been no consequences in places like Darfur.

George Packer, 'Peace and War', *The New Yorker*, 21 December 2009

Introduction

This chapter analyses the United Nations Human Rights Council's response to mass atrocity crimes in the Darfur region of Sudan from 2006 to 2010. The objectives of the chapter are to show:

- That the practice of the Human Rights Council in dealing with Darfur proves that the Responsibility to Protect (R2P) is not yet an emerging 'soft law' norm; and
- That the experience of Darfur suggests that as yet R2P has little potency as a framework for international decision making in response to mass atrocity crimes.

The violence associated with the attacks by the Government of Sudan and its allies, the janjaweed militia, on armed opposition groups, which peaked in 2004,[1] was generally acknowledged to be 'on any analysis, "an R2P situation"'.[2] It was widely agreed that 'the responsibility to react had shifted to the international community' because of Khartoum's 'manifest abdication of its own sovereign responsibility'.[3]

1 United Nations Human Rights Council (2010d), para. 46.
2 Evans (2008b), p. 61.
3 Evans (2008a), p. 292.

It was widely seen as a test of whether the international community would shoulder its responsibilities under the R2P doctrine.[4]

United Nations bodies themselves used R2P as a framework for addressing Darfur. The Security Council's Resolution 1769 of 31 July 2007 authorising the deployment of the 26,000-person United Nations-African Union Mission in Darfur (UNAMID) invoked the Council's Resolution 1674 which reaffirmed the endorsement of R2P by the 2005 World Summit.[5]

The Human Rights Council appointed a High Level Mission on the situation in Darfur at its Special Session on Darfur in 2006. The Report of the High Level Mission used R2P as the framework of its analysis. The Report concluded:

> [T]hat the Government of the Sudan has manifestly failed to protect the population of Darfur from large scale international crimes, and has itself orchestrated and participated in these crimes. As such, the solemn obligation of the international community to exercise its *responsibility to protect* has become evident and urgent.[6]

The main conflict in Darfur between the government, the janjaweed and rebel groups has subsided but criminal violence continues.[7] The Independent Expert on Sudan appointed by the Human Rights Council in his first report to the Council in May 2009 said that:

> Today, the fighting between the Government of the Sudan and its allied militia groups against armed opposition movements is not the only source of insecurity in Darfur. The conflict is characterized by several distinct patterns of violence, including armed hostilities, acts of banditry and criminality, direct and indiscriminate attacks against civilians by all parties and intertribal fighting.[8]

In his second report to the Council in September 2010, the Independent Expert in Darfur reported that clashes in Darfur between government forces and the armed movements as well as inter-communal violence continued to cause further death and displacement among the civilian population.[9]

The violence in Darfur today has its direct roots in the conflict between the government and rebel groups. In his first report, the Independent Expert reported that:

> After more than seven years of conflict, armed men on all sides were benefiting from the near total collapse of law and order in certain areas of Darfur, and a

4 Flint and Alex de Waal (2008), p. 191.
5 United Nations Security Council (2006), para. 4.
6 United Nations Human Rights Council (2007c), para. 76.
7 Gettleman (2010).
8 United Nations Human Rights Council (2010a), para. 46.
9 United Nations Human Rights Council (2010b), para. 37.

> lack of response by local governance structures, to directly and indiscriminately attack civilians, loot the livestock of vulnerable people and prey on humanitarian personnel and their assets.[10]

The security problems and threats to civilian populations are now too diffuse for any effective international intervention. It is timely to assess, first, whether the R2P doctrine played any useful role in stopping or moderating mass atrocity crimes in Darfur at the time when the reasonably clear distinctions among the government, its janjaweed militia and the organised rebel groups provided the potential for an effective intervention and, second, what that experience can tell us about the status of R2P in international law and about its utility in dealing with mass atrocity crimes.

The Status of R2P as a Norm of International Law

R2P has been claimed as a 'conceptual breakthrough' which 'enable entrenched opponents to find new ground on which to more constructively engage'.[11] About six years on from the endorsement of the concept by the World Summit, it is timely to assess whether the concept has evolved to the point where states are accepting it *as* a responsibility.

The proponents of R2P do not claim that it has gained the status of a norm of customary international law. The International Commission on Intervention and State Sovereignty which first introduced the concept into the international discourse on humanitarian intervention said that:

> While there is not yet a sufficiently strong basis to claim the emergence of a new principle of customary international law, growing state and regional organization practice as well as Security Council precedent suggest an emerging guiding principle – which in the Commission's view could properly be termed 'the responsibility to protect'.[12]

Gareth Evans, the co-chair of ICISS, assesses that, following the endorsement of R2P by the 2005 United Nations World Summit, 'R2P had the pedigree to be described, at the very least, as a broadly accepted international norm, and maybe even one with the potential to evolve further into a full-fledged rule of customary international law'.[13]

It is difficult objectively to evaluate whether R2P is a 'guiding principle' or a 'broadly accepted international norm', which are not terms of art in international law. However, the 2004 Report to the then Secretary General of his High Level Panel on Threats, Challenges and Change stated that there was an '*emerging norm*

10 United Nations Human Rights Council (2010a), para. 46.

11 Evans (2008b) pp. 38–42.

12 International Commission on Intervention and State Sovereignty (2001), para. 15.

13 Evans (2008b) p. 52.

that there is a collective international responsibility to protect' (emphasis added).[14] Citing this reference, the Secretary General in his subsequent report *In Larger Freedom*, said 'I strongly agree with this approach'.[15]

The task of international law analysis is therefore to assess whether R2P is emerging as a rule of customary international law, that is 'an evolving norm [which] does not yet satisfy the requirements for the creation of custom but is regarded as likely to do so over time'.[16]

Carsten Stahn's analysis of the formulation of R2P as an 'emerging norm' in the High Level Panel report was that it was 'misleading'.[17] Stahn assessed that the World Summit Outcome left 'considerable doubt concerning whether and to what extent states intended to create a legal norm'.[18]

What is the relevant test to determine whether R2P is an emerging norm of customary international law? R2P is the product of a process of 'soft law' making as described by Jonathan Charney:

> [T]he traditional way [of identifying customary norms by state practice and *opinio juris*] has increasingly given way to a more structured method, especially in the case of important normative developments. [M]ultilateral forums often play a central role in the creation and shaping of international law. Sometimes these efforts result in a consensus on solving the problem and express it in normative terms of general application. At other times, the potential new law is developed through the medium of international relations ... and at later stages is addressed in international forums. That process draws attention to the rule and helps to shape and crystallize it.[19]

The process of soft law making described by Charney put R2P on the international agenda. The relevant test is whether multilateral forums, most relevantly the Human Rights Council, are in fact in the process of shaping and crystallizing R2P as a soft law norm.

Such an assessment would also provide an indicative test of whether the evolution or emergence of a 'soft law' norm can be objectively tested.

The Council's Record on Darfur

What is the role of the Council, indeed the role of the United Nations human rights mechanisms, in implementing R2P?

14 Secretary-General's High-level Panel (2004), para. 203.
15 Secretary-General (2005, 21 March), agenda items 45 and 55, para. 135.
16 Triggs (2011), pp. 48–9.
17 Stahn (2007), p. 110.
18 Stahn (2007), p. 101.
19 Charney (1993), pp. 529, 543–4.

The role of human rights mechanisms in R2P has been best summed up by Héléne Ruiz Fabri: the procedures developed by the former Commission on Human Rights, particularly the Special Procedures mechanism under which Special Rapporteurs were appointed, were 'an accumulation of non binding elements [which] can give rise to constraints that, if not themselves "legal", are none the less genuine'.[20]

The 2001 Independent Commission on Intervention and State Sovereignty acknowledged that in the post war period '[w]hat has been gradually emerging is a ... transition from a culture of sovereign impunity to a culture of national and international accountability'.[21] Gareth Evans acknowledges the momentum of human rights protections as an aspect of the international community's 'responsibility to prevent' mass atrocity crimes: 'states do feel themselves under constant international pressure to avoid more egregious violations'.[22]

The Council inherited a poor record on Darfur from its predecessor, the Commission on Human Rights. Although in the period 2003–04 the great majority of deaths in Darfur were caused by attacks on Darfur's African tribes by Sudanese army and government-backed Arab janjaweed militia,[23] the Commission did not adopt a Resolution on Darfur at its final session in 2005, a 'shameful failure' in the words of the American Bar Association.[24]

The Council first took up the issue of Darfur at its second session in November 2006, passing a resolution that noted the situation in Darfur 'with concern'.[25] Amendments put forward by the European Union (EU) proposing an operational mechanism to follow up on the situation were defeated. In a pattern which has been followed in later Council votes on Darfur, Sub Saharan African delegations did not vote with the Organization of the Islamic Conference (OIC) member states, Ghana and Zambia abstaining on the final vote after the EU amendments were defeated.

The Council held its Fourth Special Session, devoted to Darfur, in December 2006, prompted not only by the gravity of the situation in Sudan but also by a statement from the then United Nations Secretary General, Kofi Annan, to the third regular session of the Council, that after the Council had devoted its first three Special Sessions to the situation in the Occupied Palestinian territories, there were surely 'other situations, besides the one in the Middle East' which warranted a special session and suggested that Darfur merited convening a special session.[26]

The Fourth Special Session achieved a consensus Resolution which expressed the Council's 'concern about the seriousness of the human rights and humanitarian situation in Darfur' and decided 'to dispatch a High-Level Mission to assess the

20 Fabri (2008), pp. 33.
21 International Commission on Intervention and State Sovereignty (2001), p. 14.
22 Evans (2008b) p. 96.
23 Flint and Alex de Waal (2008), p. 187.
24 Nanda (2007), p. 358.
25 United Nations Human Rights Council (2006a), para. 2.
26 International Service for Human Rights (ISHR) (12–13 December 2006).

human rights situation in Darfur and the needs of the Sudan in this regard'.[27] As noted above, the Mission assessed that Sudan had failed its responsibility to protect its own population and recommended that:

> The Human Rights Council should … regret the Government's manifest failure in its responsibility to protect civilians, condemn the continuing violations, and call for effective protection for civilians, accountability for perpetrators (including through action by the ICC [the International Criminal Court]) and compensation and redress for victims.[28]

Alex Bellamy comments that '[t]he HRC was thus presented with an opportunity to operationalise the R2P into its human rights diplomacy'.[29]

The ensuing contentious discussion in the Council focused on debating the legitimacy of the Mission's report, which was attacked by member states of the Organisation of the Islamic Conference, particularly because it had not visited Darfur (the Government of Sudan had not granted the members of the Mission visas).

Algeria, speaking for the League of Arab States, and Pakistan, speaking for the OIC, specifically objected to the Mission's adoption of R2P as its frame of reference. Pakistan's delegate said:

> The mandate adopted for the mission by consensus at the fourth special session clearly stated that the mission was to assess the human rights situation in Darfur and the needs of the Sudan in this regard. At no place was the concept of the 'responsibility to protect' reflected in the Council's decision. This concept, as the Member States of the Council knew, had multiple political and security dimensions, that went beyond the mandate given to the mission.[30]

The head of the High Level Mission, Jody Williams, joint winner of the 1997 Nobel Peace Prize as coordinator of the International Campaign to Ban Landmines, spoke with particular passion at the end of this contentious discussion, saying that she 'felt that if the Council were to send the same people with the same mandate, but they were asked to assess the situation with regard to the situation in Palestine, the discussions in the Council would be amazingly different'. (This statement was an amazingly candid but entirely valid criticism of the Council's preoccupation with and bias on this subject.)

Professor Williams concluded that:

> [I]t did not matter what country it was. What mattered was the people who were being violated. Regarding credibility of the mission, she said that that word

27 United Nations Human Rights Council (2007b).
28 United Nations Human Rights Council (2007c), para. 77.
29 Bellamy (2009), p. 126.
30 United Nations (16 March 2007a), p. 6.

> seemed to have a rarefied meaning in this Council that was not shared by the public at large … If the Council chose not to consider the report, that decision would have an impact on the Council – not on the members of the mission.[31]

The Council did *not* consider the report, as emphasised by China in its explanation of vote on the consensus Resolution adopted by the Council.[32] The Council adopted a Resolution which 'took note' of the report, expressed its 'deep concern' about the violations in Darfur and decided to convene a Group of Experts to be presided over by the Special Rapporteur on the situation of human rights in the Sudan, with a mandate:

> [T]o ensure the effective follow-up and to foster the implementation of resolutions and recommendations on Darfur, as adopted by the Human Rights Council, the Commission on Human Rights and other United Nations human rights institutions as well as to promote the implementation of relevant recommendations of other United Nations human rights mechanisms, taking into account the needs of the Sudan in this regard, to safeguard the consistency of these recommendations and to contribute to monitoring the human rights situation on the ground.[33]

Following the adoption of this Resolution, an editorial in the *New York Times* vividly castigated the Human Rights Council and the United Nations as whole for its 'half-hearted and inadequate response to the gravest human rights challenge it has faced since it failed the same test in Rwanda'. The *Times* said:

> Yesterday, the United Nations Human Rights Council at last expressed its deep concern over human rights violations in Darfur. That modest advance was made possible by the welcome willingness of several African countries to set aside their usual reluctance to talk about their continent's human rights problems. But in practical terms, it was only a baby step …
>
> The Human Rights Council, which should focus moral pressure on the Sudanese government, holds back from doing so. China and a shrinking bloc of nonaligned nations have repeatedly put the sovereign right of Sudan's rulers to annihilate minorities ahead of the international community's *legal responsibility to prevent genocide and protect human rights* (emphasis added).[34]

The Group of Experts reported to the Council at its fifth session in June 2007.[35] It reiterated 'the seriousness of ongoing violations of human rights and international humanitarian law in Darfur as well as the lack of accountability of perpetrators of

31 United Nations (16 March 2007b), p. 11.
32 United Nations (30 March 2007), p. 8.
33 United Nations Human Rights Council (2006b), para. 7.
34 Talking Darfur to Death (2007).
35 United Nations Human Rights Council (2007d).

such crimes' and welcomed 'the expressed commitment of the Government of the Sudan to work with the Council and the United Nations in order to implement pre-existing human rights recommendations'.[36] The Council deferred action on the report.

At its sixth session in December 2007, the Council terminated the mandate of the Experts Group.[37] The Council took this decision although the Experts Group's final report said that it had concluded:

> that the information available does not confirm the [Sudanese] Government's positive assessment of the impact on the ground of its activities aimed at implementing [the Expert Groups's] recommendations.[38]

In a 'tense atmosphere', the Council compromised by folding the mandate of the Experts Group into the mandate of its Special Rapporteur on Sudan[39] who was requested 'to ensure effective follow up to the first report of the Group of Experts … taking account of [their] final report'.[40]

The International Service for Human Rights commented that a year after the Fourth Special Session on Darfur, much of the progress in the Council's focus on Darfur had been lost.[41]

At its seventh session in March 2008, the Council passed a 'disturbingly weak'[42] Resolution which 'took note with interest' of the Sudanese Government's engagement with the international community on human rights issues' although it also expressed 'its deep concern at the seriousness of the ongoing violations of human rights and international humanitarian law in some parts of Darfur'.[43]

At its ninth regular session in September 2008, the Council decided to extend the mandate of the Special Rapporteur on the situation of human rights in Sudan until June 2009, 'a serious departure from the one year duration stipulated by the [Council's] institution building text'.[44]

At the Council's eleventh session in June 2009 the Special Rapporteur reported to the Council that in Darfur 'violations of human rights and IHL continue unabated. One key concern remains the direct and indirect attacks on civilians by government security forces, government supported militia groups, and armed movements'.[45]

Despite the Special Rapporteur's grim report on the situation in Darfur, the Council ended the Special Rapporteur's mandate, and only very narrowly decided (by a vote

36 United Nations Human Rights Council (2007d), paras 37, 39.
37 United Nations Human Rights Council (2007e).
38 United Nations Human Rights Council (2007f), para. 56.
39 International Service for Human Rights (ISHR) (2007).
40 United Nations Human Rights Council (2007g), para. 5.
41 International Service for Human Rights (ISHR) (2007).
42 Human Rights Watch (28 March 2008).
43 United Nations Human Rights Council (2008a).
44 International Service for Human Rights (ISHR) (2008).
45 United Nations Human Rights Council (2009b), para. 11.

of 20–18–9) to maintain a vestige of independent monitoring of the situation in Darfur by establishing the position of 'independent expert' on Sudan for a one-year period, against the strenuous opposition of the OIC member states.[46] During the debate on the establishment of this position, the representative of Sudan said 'Sudan did not want to be a horse that was pushed to drink water that it did not want to drink'.[47] Notably, among members of the African Group, two Sub Saharan Council members (Zambia and Mauritius) voted for the Resolution and two (Madagascar and Angola) abstained.

The Independent Expert, Mohammed Chande Othman, inherited the mandate of the Special Rapporteur to ensure follow up to the Group of Experts' recommendations.[48]

At the twelfth session of the Council in September 2009, several states expressed 'particular alarm' about the situation in Darfur 'with continuing attacks against civilians by the government and armed forces continuing. Austria noted with concern that there were still two million internally displaced people and that sexual assault and attacks on women still take place with impunity. Sweden (on behalf of the EU) urged the Sudan to launch investigations into human rights violations and prosecute perpetrators. Sudan rejected all these concerns 'and ended by expressing concern over the Council's use of "politicisation and double standards" regarding human rights situations'.[49]

Mohammed Chande Othman presented to the fifteenth session of the Council in September 2010 his report on the status of implementation of the recommendations made by the Group of Experts in 2007. He reported that 'a significant number of the [Expert Group's] recommendations still remain without implementation in spite of the fact that the time frame for implementation elapsed more than two years ago'.[50]

The Independent Expert reported 'no implementation at all' of some recommendations which had 'direct bearing on concretely improving the human rights situation on the ground'.[51] This included 'no implementation at all' of the Expert Group's recommendation that the government should:

> Issue and enforce clear instructions to the law enforcement agencies, the armed forces and any militias under the Government's control that summary executions, arbitrary detention, enforced or involuntary disappearances and torture are illegal and will not be tolerated; that they can amount to war crimes and crimes against humanity, that suspects will be investigated and brought to justice and any immunities would be waived.[52]

Mr Mohammed Chande Othman reported in his own report to the Council 'a significant deterioration in the security situation in Darfur' in which 'a significant

46 International Service for Human Rights (ISHR) (2009a).
47 United Nations (18 June 2009), p. 6.
48 United Nations Human Rights Council (2009a), para. 19.
49 United Nations Human Rights Council (2010c).
50 United Nations Human Rights Council (2010c), para. 39.
51 United Nations Human Rights Council (2010c), para. 39.
52 United Nations Human Rights Council (2010c), para. 26.

number of civilians were killed, displaced or lost their livelihoods as a result of the fighting'.[53]

Despite this continued stream of reporting of 'death and displacement among the civilian population of Darfur',[54] the draft resolution introduced by the African Group at the Council's fifteenth session failed to recommend an extension of the mandate of the Independent Expert. The Council 'was deeply divided on the need for the mandate'.[55] An amendment moved by the United States and supported by the EU member states, Japan and most of the sub-Saharan Africans extended the mandate of the Independent Expert for one year,[56] but on a sharply divided vote of 25–18–3, with most of the OIC states voting against the amendment (Gabon and the Maldives voted in favour while Kyrgystan abstained).

The debate over the US amendment vividly reflected the continuing resistance of many States to the underlying principles of R2P. Brutally inverting the concept, the representative of Sudan said that:

> The root cause of the eruption of violation of human rights in Darfur was the rebels from the Justice and Equality Movement; the Government had a responsibility to protect its citizens and had therefore deployed its security forces.[57]

The representative of Pakistan said that 'Pakistan believed that all mandates required the consent and willing participation of the concerned country and the proposed amendment contradicted this fact'. Most significantly, China 'expressed great regret ... that the amendment ran against the will of Sudan as a sovereign State' and would vote against the amendment.[58]

Darfur is widely regarded as having been a test of R2P which international institutions have failed.[59] As far as the role of the Human Rights Council is concerned, despite the struggle of Western delegations and, very honourably, sub-Saharan Africans, to maintain a focus on the mass atrocity crimes in Darfur, Gareth Evans' comment still applies: 'The international community has so far failed dismally in its responsibility to protect the people of Darfur from mass atrocity crimes'.[60]

Why Did the Human Rights Council Fail Darfur?

The determination of the OIC bloc on the Council to prevent any firm action on Sudan has undoubtedly been the main factor in frustrating efforts by other Council members

53 United Nations Human Rights Council (2010b), para. 14.
54 United Nations Human Rights Council (2010b), para. 37.
55 International Service for Human Rights (ISHR) (7 October 2010).
56 United Nations Human Rights Council (2010e), para. 10.
57 United Nations Human Rights Council (1 October 2010).
58 United Nations Human Rights Council (1 October 2010).
59 Human Rights Watch (19 September 2007).
60 Evans (2008b), p. 61.

to put pressure on the Government of Sudan over the continued mass atrocity crimes in Darfur.[61] In March 2007, when the Council dealt with the report of the High Level Mission, the 'influential' OIC had 17 members of the Council's total of 47.[62]

China and many Third World states are wary about giving R2P *any* status. China, in a December 2006 Security Council debate on the protection of civilians in armed conflict said that:

> The World Summit Outcome last year gave an extensive and very cautious representation of the responsibility to protect populations from genocide, war crimes, ethnic cleansing and crimes against humanity, and went on to request the General Assembly to continue to explore this concept. As many Member States have expressed their concern and misgivings in that regard, we believe that it is not appropriate to expand, wilfully interpret or even abuse this concept. Resolution 1674 (2006) only reaffirmed in principle the relevant statement as contained in the Summit Outcome, without any further elaboration.[63]

In the United Nations General Assembly debate on R2P in July 2009, the Egyptian delegate, speaking on behalf of the Non Aligned Movement, said that:

> [M]ixed feelings and thoughts on implementing R2P persist. There are concerns about the possible abuse of R2P by expanding its application to situations that fall beyond the four areas defined in the 2005 World Summit Outcome, and by misusing it to legitimize unilateral coercive measures or intervention in the internal affairs of States.[64]

Sixteen speakers in the UNGA debate, including Russia and China, expressed concerns about R2P's implications for state sovereignty.

An honest evaluation, however, of the Council's failure over Darfur should take account of the international context in which efforts to implement R2P have taken place. The US-UK-Australian intervention in Iraq in 2003 has overshadowed the R2P project. Gareth Evans says that:

> [f]ew misunderstandings have been more persistent, or have done more to undermine global acceptance of R2P, than the perception that the coalition invasion of Iraq in 2003 was a good example of the responsibility to protect principle at work.[65]

There are numerous indications that the Iraq experiment has played into the hands of the Government of Sudan. The former United Nations Secretary General Kofi

61 Hoge (2007).

62 MacInnis (2007), p. 10.

63 United Nations Security Council (2006), para. 8.

64 United Nations General Assembly (23–28 July 2009), paras 5–6.

65 Evans (2008b), p. 69.

Annan, spoke to a press conference in 2006 that in Darfur 'we are heading for a disaster, and I don't think we can allow that to happen, particularly since we have only recently passed the Responsibility to Protect resolution'.[66] Speaking about the problem of having to obtain the consent of the Sudanese Government (which has proven highly adept at bureaucratic obstruction) to the deployment of UNAMID Annan said:

> [T]here has also been Iraq. The Sudanese have been very clear in exploiting some of these issues, saying 'If you want to have another Iraq, come there'. This has scared away some Governments. So not only would I not have troops, if I do not have the consent of the Sudanese Government, I'm not sure if a coalition of the willing were to be formed that there will be members.[67]

An aid worker in Darfur reported that strong statements by US and UK leaders about Darfur 'only played into the paranoia that the West was only interested in Darfur to justify taking Sudan's oil and stealing Muslim territory as they did in Iraq'.[68]

The Human Rights Council, Darfur and R2P as an 'Emerging Norm'

We should now address the questions suggested above to test whether R2P should be regarded as an emerging norm of customary international law.

First, the institutional state practice of the Human Rights Council has been to directly repudiate the application of R2P to the mass atrocity crimes in Darfur. Second, the Council has generally responded with stubborn ineffectiveness to the situation in Darfur.

If we apply the 'structured method' for creating a soft law norm through international institutions to the Human Rights Council's response to the situation in Darfur, we can see that R2P does not satisfy the test of an 'emerging norm'. We cannot regard it, on this evidence, as likely to satisfy the requirements for the creation of a customary norm in the future.

Conclusion: Testing Soft Law Norms

This examination of whether R2P is an emerging soft law norm should not be taken as a critique of the soft law theory that 'the products of multilateral forums substantially advance and formalize the international lawmaking process'.[69] Indeed, the reverse is true: soft law theory, like any theory of law-making, must be

66 United Nations Secretary General (13 September 2006), para. 1.

67 United Nations Secretary General (13 September 2006), para. 4.

68 Flint and Alex de Waal (2008), p. 188.

69 Charney (1993), p. 547.

capable of empirical testing: if the creation of a soft law norm is matter merely of assertion, incapable of proof, then a soft law norm is not a legal norm.

The above assessment of whether R2P is an emerging soft law norm shows that the emergence of a soft law norm is, as Charney suggests, capable of testing by reference to the 'structural method' by which a soft law norm is developed and applied in multilateral forums. This suggestion may be a partial answer to the assessment that 'the redefinition of custom to encompass international consensus manifested in non binding form' is a 'radical departure from traditional jurisprudence'.[70] If whether a soft law norm is emerging can be tested by objective criteria, by reference to the institutional practice of United Nations forums, then it is assessable by recognisable objective judicial method.

References

A.J. Bellamy (2009) *Responsibility to Protect: The Global Effort to End Mass Atrocities*, Polity.

H. Charlesworth (1991) 'Customary International Law and the Nicaragua Case', in D.W. Greig (ed) *Australian Yearbook of International law 1984–1987*, AustLii.

J.I. Charney (1993) 'Universal International Law', 87, *American Journal of International Law* 529.

G. Evans (2008a) 'The Responsibility to Protect: An Idea Whose Time Has Come and Gone?', 22, *International Relations* 293, available at http://ire.sagepub.com/content/22/3/283.full.pdf+html (accessed 15 December 2011).

G. Evans (2008b) *The Responsibility to Protect: Ending Mass Atrocity Crimes Once and for All*, Brookings Institution Press.

H.R. Fabri (2008) 'Human Rights and State Sovereignty: Have the Boundaries been Significantly Redrawn?', in Philip Alston and Euan MacDonald (eds) *Human Rights, Intervention and the Use of Force*, OUP.

J. Flint and A. de Waal (2008) *Darfur*, Palgrave MacMillan.

J. Gettleman (2010) 'Fragile Calm Holds in Darfur After Years of Death', *New York Times* 2 January.

W. Hoge (2007) 'Dismay Over New UN Human Rights Council', 11 March edn, *New York Times*, available at http://www.nytimes.com/2007/03/11/world/11rights.html?scp=6&sq=%22human+rights+council%22+and+%22darfur%22&st=nyt (accessed 15 December 2011).

Human Rights Watch (19 September 2007) 'Darfur 2007: Chaos by Design', available at http://www.hrw.org/en/reports/2007/09/19/darfur-2007-chaos-design (accessed 15 December 2011).

Human Rights Watch (28 March 2008) *UN Rights Council Chooses Consensus Over Victims*, Press Release, available at http://www.hrw.org/en/news/2008/03/27/un-rights-council-chooses-consensus-over-victims (accessed 15 December 2011)

70 Charlesworth (1991), pp. 1, 15.

International Commission on Intervention and State Sovereignty (2001) *The Responsibility to Protect: Report of the International Commission on Intervention and State Sovereignty*, International Development Research Centre.

International Service for Human Rights (ISHR) (12–13 December 2006) 'Human Rights Council Fourth Special Session', available at http://olddoc.ishr.ch/hrm/council/other/cmreports/specialsessions/Fourth_Special_Session.pdf (accessed 15 December 2011).

International Service for Human Rights (ISHR) (2007) *Human Rights Council*, sixth session overview, available at http://www.ishr.ch/council-monitor/session-overviews?task=view. (accessed 15 December 2011).

International Service for Human Rights (ISHR) (2008) 'Analytical Overview, Human Rights Council, 9th session', available at http://www.ishr.ch/index.php?option=com_content&task=view&id=15&Itemid=262.

International Service for Human Rights (ISHR) (2009a) *Council creates Independent Expert on the Sudan*, available at http://www.ishr.ch/index.php?option=com_content&task=view&id=471&Itemid=513 (accessed 15 December 2011).

International Service for Human Rights (ISHR) (7 October 2010) 'Council creates new mandate on discrimination against women and renews mandate on the Sudan', available at http://www.ishr.ch/archive-council/926-council-creates-new-mandate-on-discrimination-against-women-and-renews-mandate-on-the-sudan (accessed 15 December 2011).

L. MacInnis (2007) *Islamic States seek new UN rights probe of Darfur*, 14 March edn, *Washington Post*, available at http://www.reuters.com/article/idUSL14491837._CH_.2400 (accessed 15 December 2011).

V.P. Nanda (2007) 'The Protection of Human Rights under International Law: Will the Human Rights Council and the Emerging New Norm "Responsibility to protect" Make a Difference?', 35, *Denver Journals of Int'l Law and Policy* 353.

Secretary-General (2005, 21 March) *In larger freedom: towards development, security and human rights for all*, UN GAOR, 59th sess, UN Doc A/59/2005.

Secretary-General's High-level Panel (2004) *Challenges and Change, A more secure world: Our shared responsibility*, United Nations.

C. Stahn (2007) 'Responsibility to Protect: Political Rhetoric or Emerging Legal Norm?', 101, *American Journal of International Law* 99.

'Talking Darfur to Death' (2007) *New York Times* 31 March.

G.D. Triggs (2011) *International Law: Contemporary Principles and Practices*, 2 edn, LexisNexis: Butterworths.

United Nations General Assembly (23–28 July 2009) 63rd sess, 97th–101st mtgs, UN Doc A//63/PV.97–101 (accessed 15 December 2011).

United Nations Secretary General (13 September 2006) Press Conference, available at http://www.un.org/apps/sg/printoffthecuff.asp?nid.

United Nations Security Council (2006) *Protection of Civilians in Armed Conflict*, 5577th mtg, UN Doc S/PV.5577.

United Nations (30 March 2007) *Human Rights Council Adopts ... Text on Darfur*, Press Release.

United Nations (16 March 2007a) *Human Rights Council Discusses Report of High Level Mission on Situation of Human Rights in Darfur*, Press Release.

United Nations (16 March 2007b) *Human Rights Council Concludes Debate on Report of High Level Mission Situation of Human Rights in Darfur*, Press Release.

United Nations (18 June 2009) *Human Rights Council Establishes Mandate of Independent Expert on Sudan for One Year*, Press Release.

United Nations Human Rights Council (2006a) Darfur, Decision 2/115, 2nd sess, 34th meeting, UN Doc A/HRC/DEC/2/115, available at http://www2.ohchr.org/english/bodies/hrcouncil/ (accessed 15 December 2011).

United Nations Human Rights Council (2006b) *Follow-up to decision S-4/101 of 13 December 2006 adopted by the Human Rights Council at its fourth special session entitled "Situation of human rights in Darfur"*, 31st mtg HRC Res 4/8.

United Nations Human Rights Council (2007b) *Situation of human rights in Darfur*, Decision S-4/101, 4th special sess, 4th mtg, UN Doc A/HRC/S-4/5, available at http://www2.ohchr.org/english/bodies/hrcouncil/specialsession/4/docs/A_HRC_S_4_5_en.pdf (accessed 15 December 2011).

United Nations Human Rights Council (2007c) *Report of the High Level Mission on the situation of human rights in Darfur pursuant to Human Rights Council Decision S-4/101*,4th session, UN Doc A/HRC/4/80.

United Nations Human Rights Council (2007d) *Report on the situation of human rights in Darfur prepared by the group of experts mandated by Human Rights Council resolution 4/8*, 5th sess, UN Doc A/HRC/5/6.

United Nations Human Rights Council (2007e) *Human Rights Council Group of Experts on the situation of human rights in Darfur*, HRC Res 6/35, 34th mtg, UN Doc A/HRC/6/72.

United Nations Human Rights Council (2007f) *Final report on the situation of human rights in Darfur prepared by the groupof experts mandated by the Human Rights Council in its resolution 4/8*, 6th sess, UN Doc A/HRC/6/19.

United Nations Human Rights Council (2007g) *Mandate of the Special Rapporteur on the situation of human rights in Sudan*, HRC Res 6/34, 34th mtg, UN Doc A/HRC/6/22.

United Nations Human Rights Council (2008a) *Situation of human rights in the Sudan HRC Res 7/16*, 7th sess, 40th mtg, UN Doc A/HRC/RES/7/16, available at http://www2.ohchr.org/english/bodies/hrcouncil/7session/reports.htm (accessed 15 December 2011).

United Nations Human Rights Council (2009a) *Situation of human rights in the Sudan, HRC Res 1/10*, 29th mtg, UN Doc A/HRC/Res 11/10.

United Nations Human Rights Council (2009b) *Report of the Special Rapporteur on the Situation of Human Rights in the Sudan*, Samir Samar, UN Doc A/HRC/11/14.

United Nations Human Rights Council (1 October 2001) *Human Rights Council establishes Working Group on activities of Private Security Companies*, renews mandates on Sudan and Somalia Press Release, available at http://www.ohchr.org/EN/NewsEvents/Pages/DisplayNews.aspx?NewsID=10407&LangID=E (accessed 15 December 2011).

United Nations Human Rights Council (2010a) *Report of the independent expert on the situation of human rights in the Sudan*, 14th sess, UN Doc A/HRC/14/41, 46.

United Nations Human Rights Council (2010b) *Report of the independent expert on the situation of human Rights in the Sudan*, 15th sess, UN Doc A/HRC/15/CRP.1.

United Nations Human Rights Council (2010c) *Update on the report of the independent expert on the situation of human rights in the Sudan*, 15th sess, UN Doc A/HRC/15/57.

United Nations Human Rights Council (2010d) *Report of the independent expert on the situation of human Rights in the Sudan*, 15th sess, UN Doc A/HRC/15/CRP.1.

United Nations Human Rights Council (2010e) *Situation of human rights in Sudan*, 15th sess, 34th mtg, UN doc A/HRC/RES/15/27.

Chapter 8
Legality and Legitimacy: A Dozen Years after Goldstone

Charles Sampford

Introduction

It is more than a decade since the release of the Reports of the Independent International Commission on Kosovo (IICK or the Goldstone Commission) and the International Commission on Intervention and State Sovereignty (ICISS), both of which sought to deal with some of the controversies generated by the NATO-Serbian war over Kosovo and 'humanitarian' intervention more generally. Each came up with three-word catch phrases – Goldstone with its conclusion that the Kosovo war was 'illegal but legitimate' (INL), ICISS with the principle 'responsibility to protect' (R2P). Both terms have persisted – though R2P has had a better decade with its beatification at the 2005 World Summit and a reference to it in March 2011 United Nations Security Council (UNSC) Resolution 1973 (though with reference to the Libyan Government's responsibility).[1]

I have written elsewhere about R2P, and will conclude by emphasising its greatest strength. In this chapter, I will concentrate on the Goldstone Report and give notice that I intend to bury it, not to praise it. I have never ceased to admire Justice Goldstone's tremendous contributions as a law reformer and jurist. But I will argue that the Commission was fundamentally flawed in its composition; its analysis of what happened; and its conclusion of 'legitimacy'. Indeed, I will argue that its concept of legitimacy is flawed and the formulation 'illegal but legitimate' was doubly so. This reasoning is not because an illegal action may not be morally justifiable (even morally compelling) but that it is an inaccurate, confusing and a dangerous mode of argument.

In this chapter, I will disagree with the views of my valued colleague, Dr Vesselin Popovski (who co-wrote the UNU brief on Legality and Legitimacy with Nicholas Turner and co-edited a book on the subject).[2]

I will start by mapping out the intellectual and territorial journey by which I first became fascinated by these issues during the course of the war and the Goldstone Committee's deliberations. After dealing with the problems concerning the composition of the Goldstone commission, I will attempt to analyse the concept of legitimacy the Commission appears to use and the factual basis on which that concept is applied: in this case, the Commission's analysis of 'what happened'. I

1 UN Security Council (2011).

2 Falk et al. (2012).

will complete the chapter by identifying the importance the ICISS' R2P concept and its place in the development of legal and political philosophy.

An Intellectual Journey: New York, Canberra and Washington

I first considered these issues when preparing a keynote address for the closing plenary of the World Congress on Legal and Social Philosophy on 'Sovereignty and Intervention' in 1999. The conference was held in the World Trade Centre in New York. The topic had been given great prominence by the British and American decision to bomb Serbian troops and Serbian infrastructure in the Kosovo war. As the bombing intensified, I read as widely as I could and became immersed in the details of the Yugoslavian conflicts. I sympathized with the dilemmas of well-intentioned democrats dealing with ill-intentioned criminal demagogues. I read the legal arguments about the legality of the war and the adamant claims by NATO countries that it was legal. I also noted that they did everything they could to avoid having to argue them before the International Court of Justice (ICJ) when given the opportunity.[3]

Like others at the time (and IIKC and ICISS soon after), I acknowledged that strong theories of sovereignty and non-intervention enshrined and universalised in the UN Charter were potentially limited by the development of human rights (also based on the charter) and the recognition of individual persons by international law (initially as bearers of duties not to commit war crimes then as bearers of human rights).

My original address sought to put this into the larger context of the way that the changes to sovereign states and the international order caused by globalisation and the spread of democracy were leading to a disconnection between the recognition of sovereign legitimacy in international and domestic affairs. (In the latter, but not the former, the criterion has shifted from the 'prior successful use of force' to the prior choice of the governed). The address also made a plea to the United States to practice internationally the values it had done so much to develop domestically.[4]

This larger context reinforced the idea that state sovereignty did not trump the human rights of those who lived within its territory and that international law and institutions should be able to protect the latter from the former. The emerging norm of humanitarian intervention was a tentative recognition of those trends.

The question was: how do progress? I suggested that the process would and should be done by the evolution of international law rather than by 'trashing' it.

---

3 Serbia accepted the compulsory jurisdiction of the ICJ on 24 April, filed suit on 29 April and hearings commenced on 10 May.

4 At the same time, I argued that we needed a global dialogue to rethink enlightenment values (rule of law, democracy, human rights and, of course, liberty equality, fraternity/citizenship). These had been developed in and for strong sovereign states but needed to be developed and applied to a globalising world through a global dialogue involving the rich insights of many longstanding cultures.

Indeed, I argued strongly that those who sought to enforce international law should abide by it – seeking and publishing genuinely independent advice before going to war and accepting the jurisdiction of the ICJ and other tribunals (including the ICC when established). I suggested that, if they did not secure UN approval (that is, through a UNSC General Assembly 'uniting for peace' vote). The Security Council could adopt a 'sue me' approach. For example the Security Council could invite the state in which they were intervening to challenge the intervention in the ICJ, provided that they also agreed to the litigation of the human rights abuses which the intervention was designed to prevent. I expressed confidence that the genuine cases were likely to get UN endorsement and/or be successfully defended. In this way, the norm of humanitarian intervention could be gradually developed through cases litigated or, more likely, not challenged.[5]

I argued that abiding by international law was not only in line with the principles of NATO members but also in their interests (citing the need for genuine co-operation by other countries to enforce other international agreements concerning the protection of copyright and the prevention of terrorism).[6]

The proposition that those who claimed to enforce international law must abide by international law seemed so obvious and its denial so offensive, that I struggled to work out how to make the argument more forceful. As I was finalising my address, I heard an interview in which a journalist asked Clinton whether US personnel might be prosecuted for war crimes before the International Criminal Tribunal for the Former Yugoslavia (ICTY). He looked the reporter in the eye and asserted, 'We did not commit any war crimes'. This bare denial, however, did not satisfy the President's critics in Congress. Instead, they had insisted on a full investigation and public hearing. These same legislators should not be surprised if the rest of the world was also unconvinced by a bare denial of criminality. The United States should be prepared to defend itself in court.[7]

The Canberra Confessional

I returned to Canberra via Washington for our new centre's first major conference: 'From Civil Strife to Civil Society' dealing largely with peacekeeping rather than war making but in which Kosovo and the possible East Timor intervention

5 I also dealt with the way that sovereign states could deal with occasions where they were not confident that they could win that case.

6 I claim no prescience in giving this example in a conference held at the World Trade Centre – I was staying in the WTC hotel that had been bombed by bin Laden six years earlier.

7 When I sat down, the next speaker, a former Nuremberg prosecutor whispered: 'You must be a Republican!' I later reflected that the Republican Right had pulled out all stops in their quest to find some charge they could make stick. But Clinton's apparent breach of the UN Charter (which is part of US law by virtue of its ratification by the Senate) was much more serious than whatever he did to a consenting intern and what he later said about it.

were discussed in open session, private conversation or both. There were several Judge Advocate General (JAG) lawyers from Australia, US and UK. I learnt two interesting things.

Ius ad Bellum

At a session on Kosovo, a young British lawyer who was a Lieutenant Colonel gave the official line that the Kosovo war had been legal: a view not accepted by the majority of those present. He later confided in me that he had been tasked with developing the advice on the legality of the bombing campaign in contemplation. He said that he had done his job as a lawyer to find a legal justification, but he came to the conclusion that it would be unlawful and, as a good lawyer, he told his client that it would not be lawful. He told me that he was thanked for his work and new advice was sought from, what he said with a sad smile, must be much better legal minds than his. I am not sure why he told me this and it seemed like a confessional. For some time, I was concerned that he had committed a very serious breach of legal professional privilege. Fortunately, James Rubin[8] later claimed that Madeleine Albright had been seeking the commitment of Robin Cook, the British Foreign Secretary, who had said that they had problems with their lawyers saying it was illegal. Albright's response was to 'Get More Lawyers'. This admission made it easy to write about the ethical issues for lawyers advising on the legality of wars (Kosovo and Iraq) without mentioning the 'first lawyer'.[9] However, I have thought more on the issue and have realised that the privilege does not generally apply with regard to clients' future criminal acts – sometimes referred to as 'delinquent clients'.[10]

Ius in Bello (Targeting)

I already understood that the JAG lawyers were regularly consulted on targeting decisions. I was fascinated to hear that there was an agreed protocol: if a target was allotted to one air force and its JAG officers advised that the target was illegal, the target would not be given to another air force. However, I was shocked to be told that the US picked up a number of such targets.[11]

The Washington Moment

The following year, as a Senior Fulbright Scholar at Harvard, and I was invited to join a task force on 'Threats to Democracy' by coups and other unconstitutional

8 'A very personal war', in *The Financial Times* on 30 September 2000.

9 Sampford (2003, 2005).

10 The third essay in my trilogy will be called 'Lord Goldsmith's Delinquent Client'.

11 Note that there is no issue of privilege here as the United States was not the client of the JAG lawyers giving the relevant advice.

seizures of power. The task force was co-chaired by Madeleine Albright and Bronislaw Geremek (former foreign minister of Poland). It met several times over the following two years and reported to the Community of Democracies in Seoul. I was surprised and a little embarrassed when Albright twice asked if she was a war criminal. The first time, there were 12 members of the task force present and it was easy for me to remain silent – with someone else coming up with the denial that she was glad to hear. The second time, there were just two of us with Albright – and I was the only lawyer. The Task Force was doing good work and I was pleased that the matter was concerning her. But I did not think that it would serve any purpose saying what I thought and there were a couple of points I wanted to discuss with her.

Had I answered, I would have said the following:

- It is not the job of a law professor to pronounce guilt or innocence. It is for a duly constituted court.
- I thought that she deserved a fair trial – no more and no less.
- As to the legality of the war, I thought that it should be tested in court. But as the views of international law professors are a source of law and because the vast majority said it was illegal, it would be illegal unless trumped by the decision of a court of competent jurisdiction.
- I thought that she was a decent human being with generally admirable motives who, like Sir Anthony Eden, blew up their opponent into a latter day 'Hitler' and seriously overstepped the mark in pushing a strong military response. She was luckier than Eden because Russia was far more quiescent and their allies were not threatening to withdraw finances (as the United States threatened to do in 1956).

In other discussions with former State Department officials, I discovered that the State Department legal advisors had developed similar arguments to the Lieutenant Colonel that I had met.

Composition of Goldstone Commission

The co-chairs, Justice Richard Goldstone and Mr Carl Tham, were from neutral countries. They claimed that selection of other members 'was made on the basis of known expertise and with due regard for the gender and geographical composition of the Commission'.[12] However, they failed to take into account one factor that would usually be considered important: belligerency.

Seven of the 11 chosen were from belligerent nations – Professors Richard Falk and Martha Minow (USA), Mr Michael Ignatieff (Canada), Professor Mary Kaldor (UK), Professor Jacques Rupnik (France), Theo Sommer (Germany), Mr

12 Independent International Commission on Kosovo (2000), p. 8.

Jan Urban (Czech Republic).[13] And all were from the one side of the war. While some were prepared to criticise their own countries, that is not a sufficient reason to allay a reasonable apprehension of bias – and domestic political allegiance to the political parties in power at the time may exacerbate the bias. This characteristic would raise a reasonable apprehension of bias. It is surprising that Goldstone, a very distinguished lawyer, was not more sensitive to such issues. Furthermore, as former chief prosecutor at the International Criminal Tribunal for the former Yugoslavia (ICTY), it was totally inappropriate for Goldstone to make judgements on those he had sought to prosecute. While a reasonable apprehension of bias is sufficient for lawyers to advise against such a composition, I would argue that the imbalance was apparent in the findings.[14]

There are numerous examples of apparent bias (or, at the very least, asymmetric credulity and naivety). I will not deal with these in detail but will refer to them as they arise in the cause of other arguments. However, the Commission's comments before the media are a remarkable example. For IICK, the key issue was whether the Western press had done their job critically examining NATO claims. Whether or not 'NATO spokesmen, either intentionally or unintentionally, misled the press and the NATO electorate' is merely a 'related question'.[15]

IICK concedes 'exaggerated claims were made about the accuracy of the bombing campaign' and that 'the Western press and public were led to believe that the bombing was more "surgical" and accurate than it actually was' and that 'far fewer tanks, artillery pieces and other offensive and defensive weapon systems were destroyed from the air than NATO initially claimed'.[16] They refer to a BBC Television documentary on the subject, that 'the war was won by being spun' but come to a far more generous conclusion:

> The Commission is not in a position to know whether these distortions were deliberate or not … War is conducted in a fog, and at the time, it is consistent with what we know about their mode of operation that NATO spokesmen engaged in good faith attempts to establish the accuracy of their public claims. Certainly, NATO spokesmen insisted throughout the campaign that they were not knowingly engaged in propaganda and that they attempted to disclose the full truth in a timely fashion.[17]

The Commission gave credence to this insistence based on their view that 'this was both a moral and a prudential commitment: that is, they believed they ought

13 For details of the 11 members see Independent International Commission on Kosovo (2000), p. 8.

14 The ICISS had four members for belligerent countries and eight from non-belligerents.

15 See Independent International Commission on Kosovo (2000), p. 78.

16 Independent International Commission on Kosovo (2000), p. 78.

17 Independent International Commission on Kosovo (2000), p. 78.

to tell the truth, and they believed that if they did not they would eventually be found out anyway'.[18]

This credulity is belied by what the IICK says and what it does not. They refer to an information war, battle and campaign. The use of such strong terminology does not sit well with the dispassionate image of the NATO spokesmen. They use the 'fog' of war cliché but not the 'first casualty of war is truth' argument.

IICK states that 'maintaining public support for the NATO campaign was vital. NATO leaders realised that their media and public relations campaign was inadequate for the task'.[19] Although the second sentence may be intended to qualify it, the first sentence makes one wonder if they are already siding with NATO. More importantly, the Commission does not state that Alastair Campbell, who was already notorious as the acknowledged master of 'spin' in the Labour government, supplied the extra resources. While they were not to know of Campbell's future role in the 'dodgy dossier' used to justify the Iraq war, they should have paid heed to the journalists (such as those in the BBC documentary) who were criticising Campbell. The comment about the ICTY by Jamie Shea[20] should have alerted the IICK.

One of the most remarkable contrasts is the nature of criticism of NATO and the Federal Republic of Yugoslavia (FRY) actions. With respect to the media, it 'strongly condemned' the FRY's arrest of a journalist but the NATO bombing of the Belgrade TV station that killed journalists is merely queried.[21]

Dealing with Evil People

My disagreements with the actions of NATO and the IICK's attempt to legitimate it should not be seen as an endorsement of Milosevic – any more than my conclusion that the Russians had acted more reasonably than the Americans was an endorsement of Boris Yeltsin whose cronyism, nepotism and sheer incompetence nearly destroyed the Russian economy and who sent tanks to clear the Russian legislature of its members.[22]

My condemnation was as follows:

> In seeking to make Yugoslavia a Serb-controlled state, Slobodan Milosevic re-ignited old ethnic nationalisms, sentiments which had led to enormous suffering of the Serb people in the past and would do so again. It is for this reason, that I have no problem placing primary blame on Milosevic for shamelessly playing

18 Independent International Commission on Kosovo (2000), p. 78.

19 Independent International Commission on Kosovo (2000), p. 78.

20 Shea and Jertz (17 May 1999).

21 See Independent International Commission on Kosovo (2000), p. 80.

22 I regretted that countries I held dear and whose traditions I respected had managed to appear unreasonable in the most unreasonable of company.

> the ethnic card. His attempt at ethnic control led to the demand for an ethnic partition by other ethnic minorities. The problem is that ethnic division is wrong in principle and disastrous in practice. In practice, it is disastrous because it is rarely possible to determine when to stop. If Croatia can secede from Yugoslavia because a majority of its people are Croats who want to leave, then the majority Serbs in Krajina will claim the same right to secede from Croatia (or, in what is a stronger claim, to be exempt from the secession) and pockets of Croats within Krajina do not want to be part of the Krajina secession/retention. This is one of the main reasons why the right to self-determination has never been extended to a right to secession. If self-determination was extended to secession, then there would be no end to the arguments over where lines are to be drawn – and no end to the wars that would be fought to draw them![23]

After the partition of Yugoslavia the Milosevic forces 'took the terrible step of 'ethnic cleansing', leading to the worst massacres in Europe since 1957 and possibly 1945.[24]

How do you deal with such a man and the situation he created? The first point that we should emphasise is that we should act within the law – that criminals engage in criminal behaviour is tautological. It does not justify policemen breaking the law. This is not just a normative plea for those claiming to enforce international law to abide by it. Giving clear guidelines as to what behaviour is acceptable and what will generate the use of force is much more likely to generate compliance. This is the pragmatic and consequentialist argument in favour of the international rule of law that I have been at pains to emphasise ever since.

The Americans started well, recognising inherent difficulties of ethnic partition. Some hoped that membership of the EU could come soon enough to make ethnic divisions less relevant. Unfortunately, Germany, newly confident with its economic miracle and what seemed an even greater political miracle in reunification, stepped in.

My view in 1991 and since is that, on the issue of whether Croatia should separate from Yugoslavia, Germany is under a permanent and bounden duty to be silent.[25] Once the West, with Germany leading and the United States following, made it clear that it supported ethnic partition, areas of Yugoslavia with Serb majorities sought to apply the same principle and sought to either remain within

23 Sampford (2001).

24 Sampford (2001).

25 I emphasised that I have no anti-German sentiments and have many German friends and colleagues whose moral sense is, if anything, over developed and subject to a level of personal guilt for the past deeds of their forebears' leaders that I feel is misplaced. However, their leaders did not share the restraint and sense of history so sensibly displayed by the Americans at that time. Later on, the Americans lost that sense of history completely. The idea that German planes should be asked to bomb targets in Belgrade should never have been contemplated: yet the United States allocated targets and Germany accepted.

the rump of Yugoslavia or at least to become independent of the newly independent republics. These were then blocked on the basis that Slovenia, Croatia, Macedonia and Bosnia were republics with a constitutional right to secession, which had been a symbolic pretence under communist rule but was a real likelihood once that rule was loosened. But having applied the constitutional test with respect to Croatia and the other republics, it was ignored with regard to Kosovo – whose independence was effectively promised to the Kosovo Liberation Army (KLA) at Rambouillet and subsequently delivered in spite of the G8 agreement incorporated in UNSC Resolution 1244.[26] When ethnically based separation of Kosovo was forced on Serbia, the secession of Serb majority areas was forbidden. Russian forces were not permitted control of any area because it was claimed that they might use that power to create a de facto secession of Serb majority areas from Kosovo. This was a rather bizarre claim given the fact that UNSC Resolution 1244 acknowledged FRY sovereignty over Kosovo. It fuelled suspicions that NATO would seek to ensure that the independence condition insisted on at Rambouillet to secure KLA support and which was explicitly excluded in the G8 communiqué that formed the basis of and was appended to UNSC Resolution 1244 was delivered to Kosovo.

Ethnic cleansing was rightly condemned when this was practised by Serbians in Bosnia. But the West did not seem to lift a finger when Croatian forces funded and armed by the USA drove 400,000 ethnic Serbians into Serbia – the most effective ethnic cleansing operation of the Balkan Wars.

In October 1998, the Kosovo Liberation Army (KLA) stepped up their insurgency in flagrant defiance of the agreement brokered by Holbrooke, taking advantage of Serbian force withdrawals in compliance with those agreements.[27] IICK note that criticism of the KLA was muted and no attempt was made to cut off arms or other support to the KLA. Criticism by the West at the time and IICK later was focussed on Serbian responses. The number of casualties actually suggests that the Serb Government was showing uncharacteristic restraint in killing civilians. This may have been due to the presence of the Organisation for Co-operation and Security in Europe (OCSE) or because the Serbs were made very aware of the consequences of atrocities. The Serb general staff certainly sought and gained expert advice of how to conduct a counter-insurgency operation without committing war crimes.[28] The Serbians used a common military practice

26 UNSC (1999).

27 The IICK acknowledges this, *The Kosovo Report* 2000, p. 54, stating it was 'not surprised' but fails to condemn this clear breach. When the FRY sent in troops in response to KLA breaches it is called a 'clear breach'.

28 From none other than Lt Gen John Sanderson, Vietnam veteran and UN Force Commander in Cambodia. He was impressed by the concern to understand effective counter-insurgency measures consistent with international law. This did not mean that the para-military thugs were not capable of misconduct but the level of casualties before the bombing war was relatively limited for this kind of war – generally agreed to be about 2,000. While having no doubt that there were many excesses by the Serbs, I was then, and remain, genuinely

(first devised by General Templar in Malaya) to remove civilians from the area of operations so as to ensure the removal of potential supporters and the drying up of potential recruits, as well as a reduction in civilian casualties (not least by ensuring that there were no civilians to confuse with the guerrilla enemy).[29] I do not doubt that the Serbians relished the fact that adopting these Western tactics could have an effect on the ethnic balance. But it did not approach the levels practised by the Croatians until after the bombing commenced.

Finally, the West's approach to terrorism was hardly consistent with its public stand. While a US ambassador called the KLA terrorists (the shooting of Serb police and officials would justify that term), their demands were supported by the US at Rambouillet. More significantly, Wesley Clark went to Belgrade to threaten Milosevic with bombing if he did not give in to political demands which no sovereign state would accept (and which were not required by the subsequent peace agreement). While the US has not been prepared to define terrorism, threatening illegal[30] bombing, if political demands are not met, falls within most definitions.[31]

NATO and the West floundered inconsistently between ethnic majoritarianism and constitutional nicety. Serbian opponents were permitted to secede, to insist on constitutional texts and to ethnically cleanse. When Serbians did the same, they were sanctioned. When agreements were made, the KLA and NATO countries breached them, dissuading the Serbians from making new agreements. They acted in ways that the Serbians then copied and for which they were sanctioned and eventually bombed. This inconsistency was thought to be justified because Milosevic was a terrible man who would only understand force. But if that is true, it is even more important to be clear about the conditions when force will be used.

---

uncertain that the severity of the response was in any way atypical of responses to guerrilla war. Most reports seem to agree that about 2,000 people were killed over two years – on both sides, and including policemen and public officials who were murdered in a deliberate KLA policy. The worst pre-bombing atrocity complained of during the war involved a number of people killed in an attack on a village that was an admitted KLA headquarters. There would have been hundreds of such actions in the Vietnam War in which the 'body count' was far higher without any intention to hurt innocent civilians. If the Vietnam War produced massacres such as My Lai, I would expect a 'dirty little war' like that between the KLA and the Serbs to produce many more. If the US army had a number of Lt William Calleys, I would expect the Yugoslav army to have many more – especially as the KLA was trying to provoke Serb atrocities to generate Western sympathy and military support.

29 This was a common feature of American military practice in Vietnam where civilian populations were forcibly removed to new areas and the areas vacated treated as a free-fire zone.

30 The IICK acknowledges it was illegal. Independent International Commission on Kosovo (2000), p. 2.

31 It is interesting that the use of the term 'bombing' has gone full circle from terror tactics of nineteenth century anarchists to 'terror bombing' from the air (the term used about German efforts in World Wars I and II), to Palestinian and Tamil separatists.

Legality

I will only briefly discuss whether NATO's war was legal under *ius ad bellum*. At the time, I said the arguments put forward for its legality were 'underwhelming' but that if NATO powers were as confident as they claimed, they should have been happy to fight the case in the International Court of Justice (ICJ). We now know that the weight of internal advice held that it was illegal, in breach of the UN Charter and therefore the treaty constituting NATO. The IICK comes, firmly, to the same view.

However, I think that the IICK treated NATO lightly in relation to *ius in bello* breaches. While it makes many judgments about the actions of FRY, it questions rather than makes judgments on NATO. They '**question** (emphasis added) the selection of targets relating to the civilian infrastructure of the FRY in which the probability of civilians being present and killed was quite high'.[32] It is also 'critical of the use of cluster bombs, the environmental damage caused by the use of depleted-uranium tipped armour-piercing shells and missiles and by toxic leaks caused by the bombing of industrial and petroleum complexes in several cities, and the attack on Serbian television on 17 April 1999'.[33]

Although IICK cite the views of Amnesty International to the contrary, 'the Commission accepts the view of the Final Report of the International Criminal Tribunal for the Former Yugoslavia (ICTY) that there is no basis in the available evidence for charging specific individuals with criminal violations of the Laws of the War during the NATO campaign. Nevertheless some practices do seem vulnerable to the allegation that violations might have occurred and depend, for final assessment, on the availability of further evidence'.[34] This response raises many concerns:

1. What the IICK does not say is that the reason for the limited evidence is the non-co-operation of NATO. One can hardly see the ICTY meekly complying with non-co-operation by FRY. The ICTY would have improved its bona fides as an independent tribunal by publicly insisting on co-operation, and the IICK should surely have made this point.
2. It highlights the concern with appointing someone who had been Chief Prosecutor at the ICTY – that he might be too lenient.
3. At the time the ICTY was dealing with the accusations and President Clinton was breezily insisting that the US had committed no 'war crimes', the ICTY was receiving funding and other support from NATO countries – highlighting the danger of ad hoc tribunals' reliance on funding from one side of a conflict on which it is sitting in judgment.
4. That danger was put in the crudest terms by Jamie Shea when he was asked about the ICTY and NATO pilots. I remember his statement at the time and have recently accessed the text:

32 Independent International Commission on Kosovo (2000), p. 65.
33 Independent International Commission on Kosovo (2000), p. 2.
34 Independent International Commission on Kosovo (2000), p. 66.

> I believe that when Justice Arbour starts her investigation, she will because we will allow her to. It's not Milosevic that has allowed Justice Arbour her visa to go to Kosovo to carry out her investigations. If her court, as we want, is to be allowed access, it will be because of NATO so NATO is the friend of the Tribunal, NATO are the people who have been detaining indicted war criminals for the Tribunal in Bosnia. We have done it, fourteen arrests so far by SFOR,[35] and we will continue to do it. NATO countries are those that have provided the finance to set up the Tribunal, we are amongst the majority financiers, and of course to build a second chamber so that prosecutions can be speeded up so let me assure that we and the Tribunal are all one on this, we want to see war criminals brought to justice and I am certain that when Justice Arbour goes to Kosovo and looks at the facts she will be indicting people of Yugoslav nationality and I don't anticipate any others at this stage.[36]

I was amazed by the crudity of this assertion and the deliberate link drawn between funding and expected results. I wondered about the contempt powers of the ICTY but even if there was no way to formally sanction statements such as this, I would have expected the ICTY to issue a statement condemning Shea's comments and demanding that NATO dissociate itself from the statements and require Shea to apologise and withdraw. The failure of the ICTY to respond only fuels concerns about bias. The fact that IICK do not mention this and profess confidence in the good faith of NATO spokesmen is astonishing. As indicated above, I have been informed that the US accepted targets that JAG officers from other countries had ruled illegal. I am unsure if a relatively well-funded commission could have secured the same information.

Legitimacy

As IICK agree with most commentators that the war was illegal, the major issue is the claim that it was 'legitimate'. Two of the most remarkable points about this conclusion of 'illegal but legitimate' are that they offered no analysis of the meaning of 'legitimacy'[37] and that the legitimacy of the war was not in the terms of reference.

The terms of reference did require the IICK to:

35 The Stabilization Force (*SFOR*) was a NATO-led multinational peacekeeping force deployed to Bosnia and Herzegovina after the Bosnian war.

36 Press conference conducted by NATO spokesperson Jamie Shea and Major Gen. W. Jertz. Brussels, 17 May 1999. Concerns are also raised about comments by Louise Arbour and Madeleine Albright but they were more circumspect.

37 Given the presence of a political theorist (Ignatieff) and a teacher of jurisprudence (Minow) on the Commission, I am even more surprised.

> … identify the norms of international law and diplomacy brought to the fore by the Kosovo war and the adequacy of present norms and institutions in preventing and responding to comparable crisis in the future.[38]

This term of reference asked the IICK to consider current norms and asked if changes were recommended. The IICK does recommend changes (discussed below), which would cover such situations. This raised the issue of what the commission might say about an intervention that, in their view, stimulated the need for change – one that was illegal under current laws; or, legal under proposed reforms but which the IICK felt should have been pursued even before the legal reform that would make such interventions legal and provide the key driver for legal change. There are a number of ways in which this argument could be put but 'legitimacy' is a strange term to use and, in my view, clearly inappropriate.

The concept of 'legitimacy' has a long history in the law and politics within sovereign states and the relations between them. It started when sovereign states were seen in terms of individual sovereigns – individuals that were not so much the head of state but the state itself.[39] Legitimacy was the key to dynastic succession in the same way as it was in the inheritance of titles and property – based on those born in wedlock (with complex rules for each when the sovereign or property holder did not have a direct male heir).[40] This does not mean that sovereign power was always transferred according to the faithful application of those rules. The availability and application of force was always relevant. However, even when a palace coup was staged, the usurpers had to claim lineage and if they could not do so, they exercised power as a regent, strongman or 'kingmaker'. As it was domestically, so it was internationally. Invasions were generally based on purportedly superior claims to being the legitimate heir (from the Hundred Years War between England and France to Spanish and Austrian wars of succession in the late seventeenth and eighteenth centuries).

In Christian Europe, this concept of legitimacy was linked to divine authority – first that he blessed the royal household with a son and secondly that the successor was deemed to be anointed by God, something that his earthly Bishop confirmed in coronation ceremonies. Links to divine authority were found in other polities – from the claims that the pharaoh, king/emperor were gods (for example, Egypt), to claims that they were descended from Gods (for example, Japanese), became Gods on death (for example, Rome) or held the highest religious office (for example, the Caliph). The Chinese deduced a mandate of heaven based on the very fact that power had been successfully seized or retained.

---

38 Independent International Commission on Kosovo (2000), p. 9.

39 Louis XIV's famous statement '*l'état c'est moi*' is not significant as a new claim but of an old claim that was already becoming out of date.

40 This is related to two *Oxford English Dictionary* definitions. It defines legitimacy of a child as 'born of parents lawfully married to each other'; and legitimacy of a sovereign as 'having a title based on strict hereditary right'.

As modern states developed into complex entities in which power was divided among a number of officials – few, if any, officials attained office through birth alone. Sovereign legitimacy in domestic and international law was based upon the effective control of territory by what Austin called an 'independent political community'.[41] The test was not the genetic material of the king but whether or not the regime in which those officials worked was in effective control of a territory – what Kelsen called 'by and large efficacious'[42] and which I referred to as the 'prior successful use of force'.[43]

The democratic revolutions from the eighteenth century onwards generated a different concept of sovereignty – initially based on acquiescence,[44] then consent, then the active choice of the governed. That active choice of the governed (according to constitutional rules about how that choice is exercised) is now the basis for legitimacy in the domestic polities of the majority of states (including a majority in numbers, residents and gross domestic product (GDP)). Active choice has also come to be the basis of legitimacy of international agencies – which are established by treaty and which, with very few exceptions, only apply to those who have signed those treaties. However, it is not the basis for the recognition and legitimacy of states within the international system – where the 'prior successful use of force' remains the criterion.[45]

This history lies behind the various definitions of legitimacy found in the literature.

For example, Sternberger describes legitimacy as 'the foundation of such governmental power as is exercised both with a consciousness on the government's part that it has a right to govern and with some recognition by the governed of that right'.[46] For Lipset, it 'involves the capacity of a political system to engender and maintain the belief that existing political institutions are the most appropriate and proper ones for the society'.[47] Weber saw three forms of legitimacy: charismatic, traditional (through long acceptance) and rational/legal authority – determined by rules.[48] In the Stanford Dictionary of Philosophy, Fabienne[49] describes 'political

41 Austin and Austin (1861).

42 Kelsen (1989); Kelsen (1945).

43 The 'prior successful use of force' by Sampford and Palmer (2005).

44 Demonstrated through the non-exercise of the right to depose sovereigns who had breached a Lockean social contract.

45 See Sampford (2001). Here I discuss the causes of this disconnect, the potential resolutions of it and the consequences of its elimination including: liability for sovereign debt; the inefficacy of rigged elections; the convergence of 'Public Law' and 'Public International Law' and the influence of the former on the latter; international legal personality; the unification of sovereignty and human rights; and, most particularly in this case, the legitimating of what is now seen as 'intervention' to protect civilian populations from governmental authorities which are not accountable to them.

46 Sternberger (1968), p. 244.

47 Lipset (1960).

48 M. Weber (Trans H. Gerth) (1958), p. 1.

49 Fabienne (2010).

legitimacy' as 'a virtue of political institutions and the decisions – about laws, policies and candidates for political office – made within them'. There is, of course, much room for difference. Descriptive theories of legitimacy (such as Weber's and Austin's) concentrate on whether those subject to political authority believe that authority to be justified. Normative theorists examine whether that authority is justified. The primary focus of each is on the relevant institutions and the way they make decisions. Wikipedia sums it up very well: 'legitimacy in political science is the popular acceptance of a governing regime or law as an authority. Whereas authority refers to a specific position in an established government, the term legitimacy is used when describing a system of government itself'. For me, legitimacy concerns the source of the power, not its exercise. It is the way laws are made, not the content of laws – unless there are content provisions (typically found in a constitutionally enforced bill of rights) within the rules that cover the making of laws.

What is common to all these concepts of legitimacy is that it is a quality of an individual or institution that makes decisions, legislative, executive, judicial or mixed. It is not a quality of an action or norm which is made – and in applying the word 'legitimate' to actions or norms is to make what Gilbert Ryle called a 'category mistake'.[50] Although one might extend the word legitimate to the decisions of a legitimate authority, it seems strange to use that term where the authority is not legitimate. If the intervention is legitimate, it is not because the action is justified but because the body that decided to intervene is a legitimate one to make that decision. Legitimate institutions may produce illegitimate decisions (for example, by failing to follow constitutional requirements); but decisions are not legitimate in the absence of legitimate institutions.

This is not to say that the content of decisions and the fairness with which they are made are irrelevant over the longer term. A series of decisions that are seen as procedurally just, transparent and generally sound may bolster the legitimacy of any institution – and may mean that a group of usurpers come to be seen as legitimate by those on whom the decisions are imposed (especially if they make themselves accountable). Similarly, a body with unquestioned legitimacy may lose all that legitimacy by a series of unfair, unaccountable and generally bad decisions. However, this only underlines the point that legitimacy lies with the decision-maker, not the decision.[51] And Thakur points out that the NATO decision

50 Ryle (1949), p. 16.

51 Note that Anne-Marie Slaughter's attempt to construct a concept of 'retrospective legitimacy' may be partly due to this phenomenon by which decision-making bodies may grow in legitimacy by making good decisions – but it is the body that develops legitimacy not the decision. The decision itself may come to be seen as more or less wise and more or less morally justified which is why she claims the Kosovo bombing to be retrospectively 'legitimate'. However, even if this were the case (and I argue against that claim below), it might not make the decision-maker any more legitimate. The view might be the body that acted should never do it again and that a new process should be established – something that ICISS sought to do. See Slaughter (2005).

scores very poorly on issues of impartiality, procedural justice, accountability, representativeness (let alone right-authority and the rule of law).[52]

Legitimacy, NATO and the UN

Kofi Anan reminded us of the 'unique legitimacy' provided by the United Nations when 'States decide to use force to deal with broader threats to international peace and security' (that is, beyond self-defence).[53] The UN and UN system provide three means for legitimizing such intervention – 60 per cent of the UNSC with no vetoes; 66.67 per cent of the General Assembly under the 'Uniting for Peace' procedure or, as I have pointed out, 50 per cent of the judges of the International Court of Justice. Those who want to leap from a presumed veto in the UNSC to illegal action outside the UN rarely mention (and never attempt) the second while actively avoiding the third.[54] But if a proposed action cannot secure the requisite levels of support in any of those forums, is it likely to be either wise or legitimate?[55] If not, is the problem the worthiness of the beneficiary or possibly the means adopted? Can any other body provide legitimacy to an action that cannot secure the UN's unique legitimacy in one of these three ways?[56]

This is where the 'illegal but legitimate' claim is most likely to be deeply offensive to non-NATO countries. It appears to support the legitimacy of a group of powerful states to determine that they may invade other countries.

Very few states outside NATO would consider that NATO was a legitimate body to decide to intervene.[57] It does not pass any descriptive standard of legitimacy – those who are subject to the potential power of NATO do not consider it justified. Nor does it pass any of the common normative standards for legitimacy – from the seventeenth century requirement of the consent of those over whom the power is exercised to the eighteenth century requirement of democratic choice. But one need not look beyond NATO. Such intervention outside the UN charter is explicitly

52 Thakur (2010), p. 25.

53 United Nations Secretary-General (2002).

54 I do not see the ICC as a fourth route, even if it gains jurisdiction over the crime of aggression after 2017 through securing sufficient signatures. In this context, I note Murphy's view that the ICC would not have found NATO leaders guilty of the crime of aggression had it had its post-2017 jurisdiction. See Sean D. Murphy (2009). The criminal process takes too long (years, cf. the days it took for the ICJ to convene in 1999) and requires a higher standard of proof and allowing a number of defences. One of these was noted by Robert Jackson at Nuremberg – that there might be an honest belief that an illegal war was legal.

55 Peters (2009). My suggestion is to seek a course of action that will secure approval by one of these three methods – thereby avoiding the kinds of unreasonable demands that stood in the way of Serbian agreement at Rambouillet and which were not achieved after two months of bombing (see below).

56 Johnstone (2003).

57 Ayoob (2004).

rejected by the treaty establishing NATO.[58] For any NATO member taking its treaty seriously, such a decision is clearly beyond power and wholly illegitimate.

Justification

This is not to say that an illegal act can never be justified. I have long stated that 'I will not surrender my conscience to any set of laws'. (Though I have also made it clear this is less likely than the very high threshold of consent required – unanimity of those to whom it is addressed compared to the bare majority plus one found in most democratic institutions).

Most simply put, there are norms other than law and that those norms may trump laws. If the law directs me to do or refrain from an act and my ethical values point me in the other direction, then I have a difficult decision that will ultimately be resolved by my ethics rather than the law. Some ethical values will direct me towards compliance – including respect for the way in which it is made, the general value of sticking to law even when you disagree with it and the damage to institutions if I do not (an effect which is magnified if I have power or influence), the precedent value, the office one holds (those who enforce the law have a particularly high responsibility to observe the law's constraints on such enforcement), reduced time and availability to do other good works and any particular duties arising from the office you hold. In my case that is because I am an officer of the court and might have to relinquish my practising certificate. But those who have a role in enforcing the law have a particularly great responsibility to exercise that role subject to law.

This is what the IICK said:

> The Commission concludes that the NATO military intervention was illegal but legitimate. It was illegal because it did not receive prior approval from the United Nations Security Council. However, the Commission considers that the intervention was justified because all diplomatic avenues had been exhausted and because the intervention had the effect of liberating the majority population of Kosovo from a long period of oppression under Serbian rule.[59]

In using the undefined and unexplained word 'legitimate', the Commission distracts from the argument they are trying to make. There are two promising avenues:

58 United Nations (1945). See Article 1: 'The Parties undertake, as set forth in the Charter of the United Nations, to settle any international dispute in which they may be involved by peaceful means in such a manner that international peace and security and justice are not endangered, and to refrain in their international relations from the threat or use of force in any manner inconsistent with the purposes of the United Nations'.

59 Independent International Commission on Kosovo (2000), p. 2.

1. Stating their moral views that override a duty to follow the law that had been agreed to by all nations.
2. Creating an argument from necessity – presumably because of the imminent danger to civilians.[60]

The IICK does not state moral views that might justify breaking the law.[61] Stating what they would like the law to be in the future is not an effective substitute. There are many legal changes that one would like and would happily follow if enacted. But in only a very tiny minority of cases would we consider it appropriate to act as if the preferred changes were in place. It is interesting that they do not use mass atrocities against civilians. This may be because the level of violence and civilian casualties was within what would be expected in a guerrilla war of this kind and/or because the level of suffering increased considerably after the commencement of the bombing.

The two claims suggested by the Commission as justification are: (i) the exhaustion of diplomatic channels and (ii) the securing of effective independence after a long period of oppression.[62] The first is a process claim addressing a constraint on intervention but not a justification of the intervention itself. The second is presumably the substantive justification but there is a question of what could be achieved without war (autonomy) and the justification of going to war for more (effective independence). The Kosovars were entitled to have their human rights protected but it was a big stretch to claim a right to effectively secede.

Both raise issues on which the IICK take pro-NATO positions with which I disagreed at the time and find even less justified now. These relate to whether the negotiations led by the United States at Rambouillet were a genuine attempt to secure a diplomatic settlement and the late inclusion of two conditions.

Search for a Solution or a Justification for War?

IICK outlines the issue very well.

For many Europeans, the Rambouillet meetings were expected to be 'Europe's Dayton', culminating in a diplomatic solution to avert the prospect that would provide a solution without recourse to war. Within US policy-making circles, some officials apparently shared this optimism. But there were clearly other key American players who saw the Rambouillet process quite differently. One objective was to help reticent European NATO members justify an armed intervention to their domestic constituencies, and thus build a tighter coalition in favour of what was by then being viewed as an almost certain recourse to force. Others on the US side wanted primarily to unite the various disparate Kosovar Albanian positions,

60 See Koskenniemi (2002); Slaughter (2005).

61 For a discussion on morality and formal laws see Koskenniemi (2002).

62 Independent International Commission on Kosovo (2000), p. 2.

thereby strengthening the normative case for intervention, which would take place regardless of Serbia's stance. At various points during the process, Madeleine Albright and James Rubin made statements confirming this one-sided view of the process.[63]

The reasons behind US and NATO inflexibility extended beyond the issue of Kosovo. NATO was seeking to clarify its longer-term mandate after the end of the Cold War, and the upcoming fiftieth anniversary scheduled for April 1999 was to be a key step in this process.[64]

As far as I am concerned, if diplomatic channels are to be exhausted, there must have been a genuine attempt at a 'diplomatic solution' – what 'many Europeans' expected.[65] The latter description of the process does not seem to be a genuine attempt and hence no exhaustion of diplomatic channels. To unite one side of a conflict in favour of war is more akin to war mongering – whether it was to unite the different Kosovar positions (some of whom were not nearly as committed to war as the KLA) or to bring in the doubters in NATO. The last-mentioned set of reasons is the worst of all – pressing for a war for an ulterior motive is totally unacceptable – especially when that motive is to have a war to justify retaining an alliance.

The IICK seems aware that this approach is problematic (to say the least) and uses words that seem to disingenuously deflect blame from the American administration. They mention a view 'within US policy-making circles' held by 'some officials' that was consistent with a European view that would seek the genuine solution without which war would be unjustified.[66] These are irrelevant as to responsibility and justification if the Secretary of State has a totally different policy and approach. That is the policy and approach on which the justification of the US-led war must be based.

Two Unreasonable Conditions

A subsequent article by James Rubin in the *Financial Times* further undermines the American position and any claims to a just war.[67] He indicates that the biggest problem was not getting the Serbians to sign but the KLA to do so. He was very worried about the distinct possibility that the former would sign and the latter would not. Two provisions were added that avoided this embarrassment.

First, as the IICK notes, the KLA was publicly promised 'an international conference after three years to determine the "final settlement of Kosovo", taking into account "the will of the people" but also the "opinions of relevant

63 Independent International Commission on Kosovo (2000), p. 55.

64 Independent International Commission on Kosovo (2000), p. 57.

65 Also see Chomsky (2005).

66 Independent International Commission on Kosovo (2000), p. 55.

67 Rubin (2000).

authorities''.[68] Privately, the US signed a 'side-letter which confirmed that Kosovo could hold a referendum on independence after three years'.[69] Rubin emphasises that the effective promise of secession was made.

Second, 'Annex B' was added which provided that NATO rather than UN troops would enter FRY with very wide powers. NATO troops would have free reign to travel through Serbia, to be immune from its laws and have the right to arrest and detain anyone, be funded by FRY, and, interestingly enough for those familiar with American revolutionary history, the right to be billeted wherever they wanted. IICK seem to excuse these wide powers by saying that they were not fully discussed at Rambouillet and were 'widely viewed in retrospect as a blunder'.[70] However, the consequences would be entirely clear: NATO troops would be in the whole of Serbia, not just Kosovo, and could arrest Milosevic and any of his officials – for which privilege the Serbians would pay.

As I argued at the time, neither of these conditions would have been agreed to by any sovereign nation – making a war fought for them unjustified. They were not included in UNSC Resolution 1244 and the first was explicitly excluded by the G8 Memorandum appended to it. On this basis, it would appear that the war was fought over two war aims not justifiable as a matter of principle and not achieved in practice.

Some Examples of Likely Justifications for Illegal Use of Force

While there are not many occasions where the use of force could be justified even though it was contrary to international law, there are some examples. Vietnam in Cambodia is probably the clearest actual example – even though it was obviously marred by self-interest and an unwillingness to pull back. Whether or not one sees this as justified, one can imagine some counterfactual examples in which we would now have no doubt in saying were justified.

The easiest is a counterfactual following De Lay's famous recommendation in Rwanda. What if the Canadians and French agreed to go beyond their mandate and destroyed known weapons caches and moved against those who had planned the massacre? The emerging right of humanitarian intervention may have legally justified these actions – but lawyers would probably have advised that a court of competent jurisdiction was not likely to endorse the acts. Those governments could have legitimately said: we believe it is legal and are willing to be sued in the ICJ, *or*, we are not sure that this is legal but it is morally justified and we will do so.

This is in line with my long-stated view[71] that the country engaging in such acts should be clear on the basis on which they are acting – either saying that they

68 Independent International Commission on Kosovo (2000), p. 56.

69 Independent International Commission on Kosovo (2000), p. 56.

70 Independent International Commission on Kosovo (2000), p. 56.

71 Sampford (2001).

believe that their action is legal and inviting anyone else to sue them *or* that they have been advised that the proposed action is, or could quite possibly be, illegal but that they are acting on a stated moral principle that is more important than international law.

An Inappropriate Reason

There is also evidence of a totally inappropriate reason for the escalation of the war:

> NATO believed that a relatively short bombing campaign would persuade Milosevic to sign the Rambouillet agreement. That was a major mistake. NATO also underestimated the obvious risk that the Serbian government would attack the Kosovo Albanians. NATO had to expand the air campaign to strategic targets in Serbia proper, which increased the risk of civilian casualties.[72]

It is not clear why NATO's mistake meant that they 'had to expand' the war. It seems that NATO, particularly USA and UK, felt that it just had to win to preserve credibility. This is not a justification for a war or an escalation of it. This is a particularly dangerous mode of reasoning and by no means uncommon. Proportionality is a critical criterion, not only in just war theory but all modern justifications for war developed by ICISS and IICK. If the intervening state claims that a particular end justifies limited force, the failure of the force to achieve that end does not justify extra force to win the war. It is, of course, possible that the identified end may justify more force than originally intended. However, once the 'dogs of war' are unleashed the intervening state often feels that it has to win to save face, to secure its honour and to avoid having to admit its initial mistake. It might be seen as an international version of 'honour killings'.

When 'winning of the war' becomes an end for the intervening states, it may displace the end of civilian protection. This is why the ICISS emphasis is such an improvement on IICK and other versions of an emerging right of humanitarian intervention. The ICISS confers no right to states to intervene (a right to go to war that might be seen to escalate as the means to win the war they have a right to wage). Instead, it insists that the rights are human rights of civilian populations. States do not have rights but responsibilities to protect those civilian populations. The first responsibility is that of the 'home' state where the populations reside. Other states then have responsibilities to assist the home state where it is unable to fulfil its primary responsibilities and, in some cases, a responsibility to act without the home state's consent where the home state will not provide that protection or is, itself, the threat.

72 Independent International Commission on Kosovo (2000), p. 2.

Goldstone's Proposed Norms

The IICK proposed a set of norms ('framework of principles') governing humanitarian intervention to be adopted by the General Assembly, UNSC interpretations of the existing UN Charter and eventual amendment of the Charter. These recommendations were not adopted, while a version of the ICISS's 'R2P' was adopted unanimously by the General Assembly. Accordingly, discussion of them is largely moot. I will address them because the norms they propose go to the heart of the problems with the Commission and its Report – and because it is not clear that they would validate the Kosovo War.

The IICK set three 'threshold' principles and seven 'contextual' principles. I will list them in order and set beside them queries over whether they would justify the Kosovo war.

Threshold Principles[73]

1. Triggers of humanitarian intervention were either (a) severe and sustained violations of international human rights and/or humanitarian law on a sustained basis or (b) civilian suffering from 'failed' or 'failing' states.[74]
2. The overriding aim of all phases of the intervention involving the threat and the use of force must be the direct protection of the victimized population. The method of intervention must be reasonably calculated to end the humanitarian catastrophe as rapidly as possible, and must specifically take measures to protect all civilians, to avoid collateral damage to civilian society and to preclude any secondary punitive or retaliatory action against the target government.
   Comment: Some of the attacks on civilian infrastructure did not do anything to protect the Kosovars but sought to inflict significant harm on Serb civilians as an indirect way of changing Serb policy. Many would see this as punitive and contrary to the principle.

Contextual Principles

3. There must be a serious attempt to find a peaceful solution to the conflict. This solution must ensure that the pattern of abuse is terminated in a reliable and sustainable fashion, or that a process of restoring adequate governance is undertaken.
   Comment: As indicated above, I do not think that the Rambouillet process can be characterized as such. Adding unreasonable conditions to secure

73 See Independent International Commission on Kosovo (2000), p. 66.

74 I am glad to say that state 'failure' was parenthesised – see Sampford (2011).

KLA signature and Serbian refusal is not a serious attempt to find a peaceful solution.

4. Recourse to the United Nations Security Council (UNSC), or the lack thereof, is not conclusive. This is so if approaching the Council fails because of the exercise of a veto by one or more of the permanent members; or if the failure to have recourse to the UNSC is due to the reasonable anticipation of such a veto, where subsequent further appeal to the General Assembly is not practical.
   Comment: My main concern is with the principle itself. There are two bodies that have the legitimate authority to authorize the use of force other than in self-defence – the UNSC and the General Assembly (GA). The principle suggests that the inability to secure authorization from those legitimate authorities is a reason to do that which is not authorized. This is like a policeman saying that he broke in because he could not get an arrest warrant – effectively a plea of guilty rather than a justification. A subsidiary point is the use of the term 'not practical'. As the IICK acknowledge, the reason NATO did not go to the GA was because they did not think they could get the vote through. In either case, it would have been much better to have taken the required action to the UNSC and/or GA. It is unclear whether they would not have secured a reasonable motion that excluded the two conditions that were omitted from the final UNSC resolution. There is also the problem that the US had, in the eyes of many, abused an earlier mandate for the use of force, repeatedly bombing Iraq using UNSC Resolution 678 in 1991.[75]
5. Before military action is taken, lesser measures of mediating and coercive action, including sanctions, embargoes and non-violent methods of peace observation, must have been attempted without success. Further delay must be reasonably deemed to significantly increase the prospect of a humanitarian catastrophe.
   Comment: In this case, there was a fairly high degree of success with the more limited measures implemented following the October 1998 Holbrooke agreement. The problem was the KLA took advantage of the ceasefire. Even then the level of casualties was fairly low for a civil war during 1998 and much lower during the period between Holbrooke and the commencement of the bombing – after which the suffering of the civilian population worsened.
6. Any recourse to the threat or use of force should not be unilateral, but enjoy some established collective support that is expressed both by a multilateral process of authorization and the participation of countries in the undertaking.
   Comment: My objection to this is to the principle itself. The fact that a group of countries decide to attack another does not make it legitimate. If the waging of aggressive war is a crime, increasing the number of aggressors does not lessen the crime; it merely adds conspiracy to the charges.

75 Discussed at length in Sampford (2001).

7. There should not be any formal act of censure or condemnation of the intervention by a principle organ of the United Nations, especially by the International Court of Justice or the UNSC.
   Comment: I agree entirely with the principle and have highlighted the possibility of securing authorisation via the ICJ instead of the UNSC. However, where the belligerents refuse to accept the jurisdiction of the ICJ, this either means that the principle is meaningless or the principle is flouted.
8. There must be even stricter adherence to the laws of war and international humanitarian law than in standard military operations. This applies to all aspects of the military operation, including any post cease-fire occupation.
   Comment: There is a strong case that this principle was breached. More importantly, NATO refused to allow ICTY access to information that would allow it to make a judgment.
9. Territorial or economic goals are illegitimate as justification for intervention, and there should be a credible willingness on the part of intervening states to withdraw military forces and to end economic coercive measures at the earliest point in time consistent with the humanitarian objectives.
   Comment: The independence of Kosovo was a territorial goal of NATO and its prime institutional beneficiary, the KLA. The economic coercive measures were continued after the war to try to force Milosevic's ouster. While wishing nothing but ill to Milosevic, this is a clear violation of the stated principle. It is noted that these two aims were included at Rambouillet to secure KLA agreement and Serb refusal and which were not included in the UNSC resolution. Pursuit of these aims was an attempt to secure what they could not achieve by war and had not been authorized by the UNSC – leading to further distrust of the USA, NATO and a greater reluctance to give them authority to act in future.
10. After the use of armed force has achieved its objectives, there should be energetic implementation of the humanitarian mission by a sufficient commitment of resources to sustain the population in the target society and to ensure speedy and humane reconstruction of that society in order for the whole population to return to normality. This implies a rejection of prolonged comprehensive or punitive sanctions.
    Comment: The subsequent action of the USA and NATO is in clear breach of this principle. Indeed, they promised to support reconstruction in the region (including Serbia) and not only broke that specific undertaking but continued economic sanctions.

Goldstone and the Rule of Law

Goldstone is right to say that it is not possible to make interventions subject to the rule of law in the sense that like cases are treated alike. He says that this is because there will be no intervention unless that intervention accords with the self-interest of the states. This actually points to the great danger – if interventions will only be taken if it is in the national interest of the intervener to do so, then it may be that the main reason for doing so will be state interest. Goldstone would have been on much stronger ground citing the just war principles of proportionality (the relationship between the harm done by the war compared to the harm averted) and likelihood of success (against major powers). This reflects the point that not all laws can be effectively enforced against all persons even within sovereign states. This reasoning is highly offensive domestically and much more offensive internationally than some Westerners imagine – undermining respect for international law.

One has to be careful in adopting rules that can, as a matter of practice, only be applied to some groups and not others. The norm will have a false universality in form while being targeted in practice at the weak. One has to be even more careful where it is only some of the weak who are targeted. As I pointed out in *Sovereignty and Intervention*, Western approaches to Yugoslavia were a mass of contradictions. Croatia could secede from Yugoslavia but Krajina could not secede from Croatia. If the reason was that Croatia was a province with a constitutional right to secede and Krajina was not, why should Kosovo be given the right to secede that was not granted in the constitution? If Croatia could ethnically cleanse Krajina, why could not Serbia ethnically cleanse Kosovo?

Accordingly, if a norm cannot be more or less equally enforced, one must:

- consider whether potential damage to the international law generally is trumped by the evil that can actually be prevented;
- ensure that it is equally enforced when it can be and not merely applied against those who are disfavoured;
- intervenors who think the norm is worth killing for must accept that it applies to them. This could be by recognising that it would justify intervention by others if they breach that same norm but it is altogether much more civilised to accord jurisdiction to a court of competent jurisdiction to determine if they are in breach;
- accept that they are bound by all the laws of war and accept the compulsory jurisdiction of the ICJ and ICC with regard to that war.

The IICK's comments might be appropriate if there is a right of states to intervene. If they have a contingent right to intervene, it is a right that they may choose to exercise. And if several states or groupings of states share that right to intervene then there is no responsibility for any state or international body to exercise that right. If, however, the rights belong to the victims and other states have a responsibility to protect them, there is much less room, if any, for choice. This is because most rights include a right of waiver:[76] responsibilities do not. This

76 There are some exceptions. Jury duty is both a right and a duty in the US as is voting in Australia.

leads to the key reason why the ICISS approach, establishing a 'Responsibility to Protect' is so superior to the IICK – and why its norms have been adopted.

Conclusion: Why R2P is Preferable

R2P has been preferred[77] for a number of reasons. I will repeat two.

First, R2P insisted on 'right authority' – an element of just war theory glossed over by IICK. This is the true meaning of legitimacy. 'Right authority' could be provided by the UNSC or the GA 'uniting for peace'. As I pointed out in *Sovereignty and Intervention* the ICJ could also provide it – or at least the willingness of the interveners to accept suit from which they would have little to fear in the most genuine of cases, through which the law could develop.

Second, R2P is based on the rights of those to be protected not the rights of claimed protectors to intervene. This involves recognition of the 'Feuerbachian' inversion of the relationship between sovereigns and subjects proposed by the Enlightenment.[78] Until then, subjects had to prove their allegiance to their sovereigns. After the democratic revolutions from the eighteenth century onwards, states had to justify themselves to their citizens. Converting a (state) right to intervene into a responsibility to protect reflects this inversion and extends it to the international sphere. This is an important step in the 'global enlightenment' I first argued we must develop in 1999.

Despite its clear endorsement by the GA at the World Summit in 2005, R2P remains controversial. That controversy is boosted because of the hangover from Kosovo, the attempts by one of the ICISS commissioners to claim that it applied to Iraq and mission creep in Libya that many saw as going beyond UNSC Resolution 1973. One way in which fears may be allayed is for R2P to distance itself from IICK with its skewed membership, its flawed principles and the conclusion of 'illegal but legitimate'.

References

A. Acharya (2011) 'Norm Subsidiarity and Regional Orders: Sovereignty, Regionalism, and Rule-Making in the Third World', 55, *International Studies Quarterly* 95.

J. Austin and S. Austin (1861) *The Province of Jurisprudence Determined*, 2 edn, J. Murray, 1861.

77 Richard Falk, who was on the Kosovo Commission but not the ICISS, is one who prefers the former though he does see them as complementary. See Falk (2003).

78 I so call it to reflect the way that Ludwig Feuerbach suggested that, *pace* the Christian belief that God created man in his own image: it was quite possible that man had created God in his own image. See Sampford (2012).

M. Ayoob (2004) 'Third World Perspectives on Humanitarian Intervention and International Administration', 10, *Global Governance* 99.

N. Chomsky (2005) 'Simple Truths, Hard Problems: Some Thoughts on Terror, Justice and Self Defence', 80, *Philosophy and Public Affairs* 5.

P. Fabienne (2010) *Political Legitimacy*, The Stanford Encyclopedia of Philosophyavailable at http://plato.stanford.edu/archives/sum2010/entries/legitimacy/ (accessed 27 March 2013).

R. Falk (2003) 'What Future for the UN Charter System of War Prevention?', 97, *The American Journal of International Law* 590.

R. Falk et al. (eds) (2012) *Legailty and legitimacy in Global Affairs*, OUP.

Independent International Commission on Kosovo (2000) *Executive Summary*, The Kosovo Report Council on Foreign Relations available at http://www.cfr.org/kosovo/independent-international-commission-kosovo-kosovo-report-executive-summary/p25962 (accessed 23 March 2013).

Independent International Commission on Kosovo (2000) *The Kosovo Report: Conflict, International Response, Lessons Learned*, OUP.

I. Johnstone (2003) 'Security Council Deliberations: The Power of the Better Argument', 14, *European Journal of International Law* 437.

H. Kelsen (1945) *General Theory of Law and State*, Harvard University Press.

H. Kelsen (1989) *Pure Theory of Law*, Peter Smith.

M. Koskenniemi (2002) 'The Lady Doth Protest Too Much: Kosovo, and the Turn to Ethics in International Law ', 65, *Modern Law Review* 159.

S.M. Lipset (1960) *Political Man: The Social Bases of Politics*, Doubleday.

M. Weber (Trans H Gerth) (1958) 'The three types of legitimate rule', 4, *Berkeley Publications in Society and Institutions* 1.

A. Peters (2009) 'Humanity as the A and Ω of Sovereignty', 20, *European Journal of International Law* 513.

J. Rubin (2000) *Financial Times* 7 October 2000.

G. Ryle (1949) *The Concept of Mind*, Hutchinson.

C. Sampford and M. Palmer (2005) 'The Theory of Collective Response', in M. Halperin and M. Galic (eds) *Protecting Democracy: International Response*, Lexington Books.

C. Sampford (2003) 'Get New Lawyers', 6, *Legal Ethics* 185.

C. Sampford (2005) 'More and More Lawyers But Still No Judges', 8, *Legal Ethics* 16.

C. Sampford (2011) 'Failed States and the Rule of Law', 1, *Jindal Journal of International Affairs*.

C. Sampford (2012) 'A tale of two norms', in Angus Francis and Ramesh Thakur (eds) *The Laws of Protection: Protection of Civilians and the Responsibility to Protect*, United Nations University Press.

C. Sampford (2001) 'Sovereignty and Intervention', in T. Campbell and B.Leiser (eds) *Human Rights in Theory and Practice*, Aldershot 335.

S.D. Murphy (2009) 'Criminalizing Humanitarian Intervention', 41, *Case Western Reserve Journal of International Law* 341.

J. Shea and Major General W. Jertz (17 May 1999) *NATO's Role in Kosovo*, Press Conferenceavailable at http://www.nato.int/kosovo/press/p990517b.htm (accessed 27 March 2013).

A. Slaughter (2005) 'Security, Solidarity, and Sovereignty: The Grand Themes of UN Reform', 99, *The American Journal of International Law* 619.

D. Sternberger (1968) 'Legitimacy', in D.L. Sills (ed.) *International Encyclopedia of the Social Sciences*, Macmillan 244.

R. Thakur (2010) 'Law, Legitimacy and the United Nations', 11, *Melbourne Journal of International Law* 1.

UN Security Council (2011) *Security Council resolution 1973 (2011) [on the situation in the Libyan Arab Jamahiriya]*, S/RES/1973(2011) available at http://www.unhcr.org/refworld/docid/4d885fc42.html (accessed 27 March 2013).

United Nations (1945) *Charter of the United Nations, 24 October 1945*, 1 UNTS XVI.

United Nations Secretary-General (2002) *Address to the General Assembly*, 9 December.

UNSC (1999) *Security Council Resolution 1244 (Kosovo)*, S/RES/1244 (1999).

Chapter 9
Refugees and Military Intervention in the Name of the Responsibility to Protect

Angus Francis

Introduction

Resolution 1973 is the first Security Council resolution authorising military intervention for the purposes of protecting civilians in the name of the Responsibility to Protect ('R2P') principle.[1] Specifically, the resolution condemns the attacks on civilians and gross human rights abuses taking place in Libya and authorises member states of the UN to 'take all necessary measures ... to protect civilian populations under threat of attack' short of a foreign occupation force. R2P-language is found throughout the document, beginning with the responsibility of the Libyan authorities to protect the civilian population through to the determination of the Security Council to 'ensure the protection of civilians and civilian populated areas'.[2]

Reference to the R2P principle in Resolution 1973 reflects its steady rise within the UN system since it was first expounded by the International Commission on Intervention and State Sovereignty (ICISS) over a decade ago.[3] After endorsement by the international community in the 2005 outcome document of the high-level meeting of the General Assembly,[4] the UN Secretariat has pressed on with operationalisation of the principle through appointment of a Special Adviser on R2P,[5] a Secretary-General's report setting out an agenda for the implementation of R2P[6] and moves to create a joint office on genocide prevention and the promotion of the R2P principle.[7] Meanwhile, the General Assembly has continued its 'consideration' of R2P,[8] while the Security Council has more aggressively reaffirmed the principle in Resolution 1674 on the Protection of Civilians in Armed Conflict,[9] and now in Resolution 1973.

1 UN Security Council Resolution S/RES/1973 (2011).

2 See also UN Security Council (22 February 2011); UN News Service (25 February 2011).

3 International Commission on Intervention and State Sovereignty (2001).

4 UN General Assembly (24 October 2005).

5 Secretary-General Ban Ki-moon (21 February 2008).

6 Secretary-General Ban Ki-moon (12 January 2009).

7 Luck (2010), p. 351.

8 UN General Assembly (23 July 2009).

9 UN Security Council Resolution S/RES/1674 (2006), para. 4.

Clearly, the mass exodus from the violence in Libya was a factor in the Security Council's determination to invoke R2P and authorise military intervention under Chapter VII of the UN Charter. Both Resolution 1973 and Resolution 1970, adopted on 26 February 2011 for the purposes of referring the Libyan situation to the International Criminal Court and imposing an arms embargo and smart sanctions on the Libyan regime,[10] refer expressly to the plight of refugees and foreigners forced to flee the violence. Soon after anti-government protests in mid-February elicited a violent government crackdown on dissent,[11] the United Nations High Commissioner for Refugees (UNHCR) reported thousands of people arriving at the Tunisian and Egyptian borders.[12] This number continued to rise as violence escalated.[13] Soon close to 100,000 people had fled the violence into neighbouring countries.[14] At the end of February, UNHCR reported 14,000 people crossing the Libyan-Tunisian border in one day alone.[15]

The UNHCR reported on 27 March 2011 that of the 381,888 people to have fled the violence in Libya, 193,783 fled to Tunisia (including 19,541 Tunisian, 23,184 Libyans and 145,476 others), 156,471 to Egypt (including 79,020 Egyptians, 32,679 Libyans and 44,772 others), 15,647 to Niger (including 14,698 Nigerien and 949 others), 9,987 to Algeria, 3,200 to Chad and 2,800 to Sudan.[16] Of the first boat arrivals in Europe beginning in late March, there were Eritreans, Somalis, Ethiopians and Sudanese, but no Libyans.[17] The UNHCR also expressed concern for Libyan nationals and others unable to escape the country, and for the thousands of refugees from other parts of Africa residing in Libya as evidence began to emerge that they were being associated with pro-government foreign mercenaries.[18]

The plight of persons fleeing Libya was highlighted in the lead up to Resolution 1973. The issue was raised by the UN High Commissioner for Human Rights, Navi Pillay, before the UN Human Rights Council at the beginning of a special session held in Geneva on 25 February 2011 that ended in a recommendation that Libya's membership in the Council be suspended.[19] The Secretary-General also focused on the growing crisis of refugees and displaced persons fleeing into Tunisia and Egypt when he called on the Security Council to consider immediate steps against the Libyan regime[20] and when he addressed the General Assembly on the occasion

10 UN Security Council Resolution S/RES/1970 (2011); UN Security Council Resolution S/RES/1973 (2011).

11 Amnesty International (2011); Human Rights Watch (2011); Karrar-Lewsley (2011).

12 UN News Service (23 February 2011).

13 UN High Commissioner for Refugees (27 February 2011); UN Office for the Coordination of Humanitarian Affairs (OCHA) (28 February 2011).

14 UN High Commissioner for Refugees (27 February 2011).

15 UN News Service (1 March 2011).

16 UN High Commissioner for Refugees (29 March 2011).

17 UN High Commissioner for Refugees (29 March 2011).

18 UN High Commissioner for Refugees (2 March 2011); UN High Commissioner for Refugees (22 February 2011).

19 UN Human Rights Council (25 February 2011); UN News Service (25 February 2011).

20 Secretary-General Ban Ki-moon (25 February 2011).

of Libya's suspension from the Human Rights Council.[21] At the regional level, the African Commission on Human and Peoples' Rights referred to the 'massive displacement of the population afraid for their lives' when passing a resolution calling on the African Union and the international community to take action for the protection of the Libyan population.[22]

Thus, the mass displacement of refugees and other persons was at the forefront of the international community's collective consciousness as it moved toward military intervention in Libya in March 2011. At the time of writing, international military action in Libya is ongoing. This chapter examines the likely effectiveness of the military action in Libya as a means of preventing or responding to refugee flows in light of earlier humanitarian crises. In addition, this chapter considers what new directions might be presented by the international community's express reliance on the R2P principle in this instance.

Earlier Crises Involving Refugee Flows and Military Intervention

There have been a number of humanitarian crises involving actual or potential refugee flows where international military intervention was at issue.[23] This chapter discusses just two: Rwanda (1994) and Kosovo (1998–89). These two crises, more than any others, spurred a fundamental rethink of the international community's approach to intervention in the face of mass atrocities and the role that intervention plays in preventing or responding to mass displacement.

Rwanda

On 5 October 1993, the Security Council adopted resolution 872 (1993) establishing the United Nations Assistance Mission for Rwanda (UNAMIR).[24] This followed the Arusha Peace Agreement entered into between the Government of Rwanda and the Rwandese Patriotic Front on 4 August 1993. The agreement made express provision for the repatriation of Rwandan refugees that had fled the civil war.[25] A report of the UN Special Rapporteur of the Commission on Human Rights on extrajudicial, summary or arbitrary executions, published one week after the signing of the agreement, gave an ominously dire view of the human rights situation in Rwanda, citing evidence of inter-communal violence bordering on genocide.[26]

UNAMIR's mandate included monitoring the cease-fire agreement, monitoring the security situation, assisting with mine clearance, assisting in the co-ordination of

21 Secretary-General Ban Ki-moon (1 March 2011).

22 African Commission on Human and Peoples' Rights (1 March 2011).

23 Roberts (2011), p. 220.

24 UN Security Council Resolution S/RES/872 (1993).

25 National Legislative Bodies (1993).

26 Report of the Independent Inquiry into the actions of the United Nations during the 1994 genocide in Rwanda, S/1999/1257 (15 December 1999), p. 6.

humanitarian assistance activities, investigating and reporting on incidents regarding the police and gendarmerie and monitoring the process of repatriation of Rwandese refugees and resettlement of displaced persons to verify that it was carried out in a safe and orderly manner.[27] Despite reports of growing violence, the mobilisation of armed militia, a stalling peace process and evidence of imminent widespread attacks on Tutsi, UN Headquarters refused to approve coercive intervention operations by UNAMIR on the grounds they went beyond its mandate – which envisaged UNAMIR as a neutral mediator in a civil war. The genocide of Tutsi and moderate Hutus began after the assassination of the Rwandan President on 6 April 1994.

An independent report commissioned by the Secretary-General concluded that the UN response before and during the genocide was fundamentally flawed.[28] UNAMIR was not resourced, planned or instructed in a way that took account of the deep and worsening ethnic divisions and violence within the country. The mission was planned without even awareness of the above-mentioned report of the Special Rapporteur or other human rights reports, all of which pointed to an extremely volatile situation and contained indications of the risk of genocide. UNAMIR was given a weakened mandate largely due to the Security Council's hesitancy to support new peacekeeping operations in the aftermath of Somalia, and the Secretariat doggedly maintained the neutral role of UNAMIR and the mission's existing mandate despite the deteriorating security situation. Rather than reinforce the mission, the Security Council decided on 21 April 1994 to reduce UNAMIR to a minimal force. At the same time, the Council refused to formally acknowledge the mass killings in Rwanda as 'genocide'. The genocide ended in July after the Rwandese Patriotic Front gained control over the whole of Rwanda. It is estimated that more than 800,000 people were killed, 1.5 million internally displaced and 2 million forced to flee to the neighbouring countries of Congo, Tanzania, Uganda and Burundi.[29]

This is the background against which UN efforts to protect refugees and IDPs fleeing the violence in Rwanda in 1994 must be assessed. The UN's weak response before and during the genocide not only failed to prevent the killings that led to mass displacement, but also compromised the quality of protection offered to those persons forced to flee. The Security Council's Resolution 912 (1994) passed on 21 April 1994 that condemned the deaths and displacement was empty comfort given the lack of political will to reinforce the mission.[30] Equally, the Council's eventual decision in May to expand the UNAMIR force to 5,500 and to extend its mandate to include 'to contribute to the security and protection of displaced persons, refugees and civilians at risk in Rwanda, including through the establishment and maintenance, where feasible, of secure humanitarian areas',[31]

27 UN Security Council Resolution S/RES/872 (1993), para. 3.

28 Report of the Independent Inquiry into the actions of the United Nations during the 1994 genocide in Rwanda, S/1999/1257 (15 December 1999).

29 UN High Commissioner for Refugees (2000).

30 UN Security Council Resolution S/RES/912 (1994).

31 UN Security Council Resolution S/RES/918 (1994).

was hamstrung by the failure of member states to provide sufficient troops. Also, the French-led Operation Turqoise in July 1994, which was authorized by the Security Council under Chapter VII of the Charter to establish a safe zone in south-west Rwanda with the aim of 'contributing, in an impartial way, to the security and protection of displaced persons, refugees and civilians at risk',[32] was too little, too late, and reportedly had the effect of protecting Hutu militia as much as innocent refugees.[33] Lastly, the international response to the mass influx of refugees into neighbouring countries was unplanned and fatally undermined by the Security Council's refusal to authorize an international force to demilitarize the refugee camps, sparking widespread regional instability and conflict.[34]

Kosovo

The Kosovo Liberation Army and the Federal Republic of Yugoslavia (FRY) engaged in armed conflict from February 1998 to June 1999. The conflict could not have come as a surprise to the international community. Over 350,000 Kosovar Albanian refugees had sought protection in Europe between 1989 and 1998 as Serbian repression of Albanians in Kosovo intensified. Added to this, numerous reports by NGOs and Special Rapporteurs highlighted the ongoing and systematic repression of Kosovar Albanians in the decade preceding the war. But the international community's attention was focused on ensuring the successful conclusion of the Dayton Agreement, which did not mention Kosovo for fear of antagonising Milosevic. After Dayton, the EU formally recognised FRY as including Kosovo. Subsequently, Germany and other European countries repatriated thousands of Kosovar Albanian refugees. These actions had the cumulative effect of legitimating Serbian oppression in Kosovo, while also driving the resistance movement within Kosovo to violence.

Approximately 1,000 civilians were killed and 400,000 internally displaced during the first phase of the Kosovo conflict between February 1998 and March 1999. During the second phase – after the NATO air campaign intervened in March 1999 – an estimated 10,000 civilians were killed (the vast majority being Kosovar Albanians killed by FRY forces) and approximately 863,000 refugees fled the country and an additional 590,000 were internally displaced. There was also widespread rape, torture and destruction of property. Most of the refugees sought sanctuary in refugee camps or with host families in Albania, Macedonia, Montenegro and Bosnia and Herzegovina. Around 80,000 were evacuated to the United States, Australia and other countries in Europe.

The mass deportation of Kosovar Albanians was clearly carefully planned and orchestrated by Serb forces. The patterns of arbitrary executions corresponded with the pattern of refugee flows, indicating that killings were used as a means of intimidation to

32 UN Security Council Resolution S/RES/929 (1994), paras 2 and 3.

33 Loescher (2001), p. 307.

34 Loescher (2001), p. 310.

facilitate mass forced evictions.[35] Moreover, 'the pattern of the logistical arrangements made for deportations and the coordination of actions by the Yugoslav army, paramilitary groups and the police show[ed] that this huge expulsion of Kosovo-Albanians was systematic and deliberately organized'.[36] While reports suggest that only a small fraction of Kosovar Albanians fled as a direct result of the NATO bombing raids, the Independent Commission on Kosovo concluded that NATO bombing created an environment that made the mass deportation operation feasible.[37]

What could the international community have done better to protect civilians and refugees? For starters, it could have done *something* to prevent the war. The failure to confront the intransigent Belgrade regime over Kosovo at an early stage of the evolution of the conflict and the eagerness of European countries to repatriate Kosovar Albanian refugees en masse legitimated ongoing repression. The international response to the outbreak of open conflict was slow. It was not until 23 September 1998 that the Security Council passed a resolution demanding a cease-fire, the withdrawal of Yugoslav forces 'used for civilian repression', international monitoring, access for humanitarian agencies and the safe return of refugees and displaced persons (expressing deep concern at the flow of refugees into Albania, Bosnia Herzegovina and other European Countries).[38]

The threat of NATO air strikes was required to bring Serbian President Slobodan Milosevic to the negotiating table where he agreed to pull back security forces, allow access for aid groups and accept an international monitoring team of 2,000 civilian observers. Yet repression and conflict continued, leading to the withdrawal of the monitors. On 24 March 1999, NATO aircraft began the bombing campaign against Yugoslavia without specific authorization of the Security Council. While stopping short of suggesting that the NATO bombing campaign provoked the FRY campaign of 'ethnic cleansing', the Independent Commission on Kosovo observed that NATO underestimated the obvious risk that the Belgrade authorities would use the war as a pretext to attack and expel the Kosovar Albanian population. Moreover, the fact that NATO refused to commit ground troops meant that the alliance was policing from 15,000 feet and was unable to stop the expulsion and killings of civilian Albanians.[39]

There was also no contingency planning for a mass outflow of refugees despite the obvious risks of ethnic cleansing. Why not? Aside from underestimating the risk of mass expulsion, in the lead up to the war the international community was fixated on the 'right to remain' and the 'right to return' of Kosovar Albanians. This was a natural extension of the policies of developed countries of containing refugee flows in the country or region of refugee origin, characterised in this instance by a preference for emergency relief and assistance to internally displaced persons (IDPs)

---

35 Independent International Commission on Kosovo (2000), Annex 1.

36 Independent International Commission on Kosovo (2000), Executive Summary.

37 Independent International Commission on Kosovo (2000), 'The Cleansing of Kosovo'.

38 UN Security Council Resolution S/RES/1199 (1998).

39 For discussion of the shortcomings of the Kosovo intervention strategy, see Thakur 2006, pp. 213–5.

in Kosovo (evidenced by UNHCR operations at the time) and the swift repatriation of Kosovo refugees in conditions far from safe. This objective was also evident in Security Council resolutions which championed the 'right to return'.[40]

The end result of these developments was an ad hoc and reluctant response to the refugee crisis by the international community. Macedonia refused to admit thousands of refugees gathering at its border unless it had assurances of help from other states, while most West European governments initially proposed solutions directed at keeping the refugees in the region. The French Government, for example, claimed that relocating refugees outside the region would merely facilitate the Serb policy of ethnic cleansing. Worried that the Macedonian Government would withdraw support for NATO's military campaign, the USA and its allies eventually initiated 'burden-sharing' schemes guaranteeing onward passage to third countries as an incentive for Macedonia to admit refugees.[41] Even still, the vast majority of refugees from the crisis remained within the region.

In summary, the crises in Rwanda and Kosovo were characterised to differing degrees by a failure of regional and international preventive measures; mixed signals from the international community that had the effect of legitimating state oppression and radicalising resistance; a failure of the international community to understand the political context and the risks of mass atrocities, including genocide and mass forced deportations; an under-resourced and inadequately mandated peacekeeping mission (in the case of Rwanda) or none at all (Kosovo); and a lacklustre and inhumane international response that failed to stop killings and mass expulsions. These factors had a direct bearing on the extent of mass displacement and the protection of refugees and IDPs.

What has the international community learned from these and other tragedies, and how has the R2P concretised the international community's response? How is military intervention for humanitarian purposes conceived and operationalised within the emerging R2P paradigm? Where does refugee protection fit within this broader agenda? These questions are discussed in the next part of this chapter. The final part then considers the likely effectiveness of the Libyan intervention as a response to refugee flows in light of earlier crises, taking into account the fact that the intervention has been undertaken in the name of the R2P principle.

The R2P Principle and Refugee Protection

Following the humanitarian failures of the 1990s, 'a newly energized international conscience'[42] led to a fundamental shift in the international community's response to mass atrocities. Of most importance was the elaboration and acceptance of the R2P

40 UN Security Council Resolution S/RES/1199 (1998), p. 2; UN Security Council Resolution S/RES/1244 (1999), p. 1.

41 *The Kosovo refugee crisis: An independent evaluation of UNHCR's emergency preparedness and response*, 2000, p. x.

42 Thakur (2009).

principle in paragraphs 138 and 139 of the 2005 World Summit Outcome Document [hereinafter Outcome Document].[43] The first element of the R2P principle reaffirms that each state has the responsibility to protect its populations from genocide, war crimes, ethnic cleansing and crimes against humanity.[44] It is based on the notion of 'sovereignty as responsibility', which defines sovereignty as imposing obligations on states to protect 'the safety and lives of citizens'.[45] The second element is that the international community recognises a shared responsibility to use peaceful means to help protect populations from mass atrocities. In the event peaceful means prove inadequate or national authorities manifestly fail to protect their populations from atrocities, the international community expresses its preparedness to take collective action through the Security Council in accordance with the UN Charter.[46]

The Secretary-General has established a three-pronged strategy for implementing the R2P principle, referred to as the 'three pillars'.[47] They are: prevention; capacity building; response and intervention. Pillar 1 affirms the primary responsibility of the state to prevent mass atrocity crimes by fostering respect for human rights and diversity and tolerance, building legal, political and civil society institutions that ensure greater protection, and observing international humanitarian law and refugee law.[48] Pillar 2 calls on the international community to take a more active role in preventing mass atrocities, including through exerting pressure on states to comply with their international obligations and by assisting states to build capacity.[49] Early warning and assessment are also an important part of the preventative strategy advocated by the Secretary-General.[50]

Pillar 3 sets out the pacific measures the international community may take under Chapters VI and VIII of the Charter in response to a state's manifest failure to protect against mass atrocities, including investigation by on-site missions, reminding authorities that acts of incitement could be referred to the International Criminal Court under the Rome Statute and sanctions.[51] Lastly, Pillar 3 outlines the basic precondition for international coercive action through the Security Council and Chapter VII: a state must refuse to accept international prevention and protection assistance, commit egregious crimes and violations relating to R2P and fail to respond to less coercive measures.[52]

---

43 UN General Assembly (24 October 2005).

44 UN General Assembly (24 October 2005), para. 138.

45 International Commission on Intervention and State Sovereignty (2001), p. 13; the idea of 'sovereignty as responsibility' is developed in the work of Francis Deng, see Deng (2010), p. 368.

46 UN General Assembly (24 October 2005), para. 139.

47 Secretary-General Ban Ki-moon (12 January 2009).

48 Secretary-General Ban Ki-moon (12 January 2009), paras 13, 15–17, 20, 21, 27.

49 Secretary-General Ban Ki-moon (12 January 2009), paras 28, 35–48.

50 Secretary-General Ban Ki-moon (12 January 2009), Annex; Secretary-General Ban Ki-moon (14 July 2010).

51 Secretary-General Ban Ki-moon (12 January 2009), pp. 22–5.

52 Secretary-General Ban Ki-moon (12 January 2009), p. 25.

In addition to promoting the R2P principle as an overarching protection norm, significant steps have been made in the 'protection of civilians' agenda in the UN system, as expressed in Secretary-General reports to the Security Council,[53] Security Council resolutions,[54] presidential statements[55] and UN peacekeeping mandates.[56] Specific measures include: extending the mandate of UN peacekeeping operations to permit peacekeepers to protect civilians under imminent threat of violence; highlighting the protection needs of especially vulnerable groups (women, children, refugees and internally displaced persons, humanitarian workers); pushing for compliance with international human rights, international humanitarian and refugee law; ensuring better conflict prevention; stressing the multi-disciplinary nature of peace-building; seeking greater co-operation with regional actors; maintaining the separation of combatants and armed elements from civilians in IDP and refugee camps; working on disarmament and demobilisation; and ensuring timely intervention in cases of genocide, crimes against humanity and war crimes.[57]

What is the place of refugee protection in these ambitious undertakings? It is clear refugees fall within the scope of the R2P principle as a matter of international law. Case law shows that the definition of refugee is not restricted to individualized persecution, but extends to persons fleeing attacks on a racial, political, religious, ethnic or other group.[58] The relevance of the R2P principle to

53 Secretary-General (1999); Secretary-General (2001); Secretary-General (2002); Secretary-General (2004); Secretary-General (2005); Secretary-General (2007); Secretary-General (2009).

54 UN Security Council Resolution S/RES/1265 (1999); UN Security Council Resolution S/RES/1296 (2000); UN Security Council Resolution S/RES/1674 (2006); UN Security Council Resolution S/RES/1738 (2006); UN Security Council Resolution S/RES/1894 (2009).

55 UN Security Council Presidential Statement 2004/46; UN Security Council Presidential Statement 1996/6; UN Security Council (2002); UN Security Council (2004); UN Security Council (2003); UN Security Council (2005); UN Security Council (2009); UN Security Council (2009).

56 UN Peacekeeping Mandate Darfur (UNAMID); UN Peacekeeping Mandate Afghanistan (UNAMA); UN Peacekeeping Mandate Central African Republic (MINURCAT); UN Peacekeeping Mandate Democratic Republic of Congo (MONUC); UN Peacekeeping Mandate Haiti (MINUSTAH); UN Peacekeeping Mandate Liberia (UNMIL); UN Peacekeeping Mandate Sudan (UNMIS); UN Peacekeeping Mandate Cote d'Ivoire (UNOCI).

57 Secretary-General (1999); Secretary-General (2001); Secretary-General (2004); UN Security Council Resolution S/RES/1265 (1999); UN Security Council Resolution S/RES/1296 (2000); UN Security Council Resolution S/RES/1674 (2006); UN Security Council Resolution S/RES/1738 (2006).

58 See for example, *Salibian v Canada* [1990] FCJ 454 (Canada, Federal Court of Appeal); *Knezevic v Ashcroft*, 367 F.3d 1206; 2004 US App. LEXIS 10162 (US Court of Appeals for the 9th Circuit); *S v Federal Ministry of the Interior*, Austrian Administrative Court, 26 January 1994, 93/01/0034; *Hagi-Mohammed v Minister for Immigration and Multicultural Affairs* [2001] FCA 1156.

refugee protection is reflected by the fact that key R2P documents contain express or implied references to the issue of refugees. The ICISS report refers to the destabilizing effects of refugee flows on neighbouring countries.[59] The High-level Panel's report highlights the importance of observing international refugee law.[60]

While the Outcome Document does not expressly refer to refugees, the word 'populations' in paragraphs 138 and 139 should be read in light of paragraph 133, whereby states commit themselves to safeguard 'the principle of refugee protection' and 'to upholding [their] responsibility in resolving the plight of refugees'. This reading is supported by Security Council Resolution 1674 (2006), which reaffirms paragraph 138 and 139 of the Outcome Document, and also recalls:

> … the particular impact which armed conflict has on women and children, including as refugees and internally displaced persons, as well as on other civilians who may have specific vulnerabilities, and stress[es] the protection and assistance needs of *all* affected civilian populations [emphasis added].[61]

The Secretary-General's 2009 Report on the Implementation of the R2P principle engages with refugee protection at a number of points. Firstly, it recognises the historical role played by asylum in protecting persons from mass atrocities.[62] Secondly, it recognises that the R2P principle requires mainstreaming of refugee protection in the work of UN agencies. Thirdly, the report encourages ratification and implementation of the 1951 Refugee Convention.[63] Finally, UNHCR is recognised for 'obtaining grants of asylum and protecting refugees' and thereby serving 'numerous potential victims of crimes and violations relating to the responsibility to protect'.[64]

Similarly, prominence has been given to the protection of refugees and IDPs in the Security Council's thematic resolutions on protection of civilians. Resolution 1265 of 1999 refers to the vulnerability of refugees and IDPs during armed conflict and reaffirms the 'primary responsibility of States to ensure their protection'.[65] Resolution 1296 of 2000 specifically requests the Secretary-General to bring to its attention situations where refugees and IPDs in conflict situations are vulnerable to the threat of harassment or where their camps are vulnerable to infiltration by armed elements.[66] Resolution 1674 of 2006 expresses the Security Council's commitment to ensure peacekeeping mandates contain clear guidelines regarding

---

59 International Commission on Intervention and State Sovereignty (2001), paras 1.20, 4.35, 4.36, 6.31, 8.15.

60 Secretary-General's High Level Panel (2004), p. 73.

61 UN Security Council (20 July 2004), para. 4 and Preamble.

62 Secretary-General Ban Ki-moon (12 January 2009), para. 35.

63 Secretary-General Ban Ki-moon (12 January 2009), para. 17.

64 Secretary-General Ban Ki-moon (12 January 2009), para. 35.

65 UN Security Council Resolution S/RES/1265 (1999).

66 UN Security Council Resolution S/RES/1296 (2000), para. 14.

protection of civilians and 'the creation of conditions conducive to the voluntary, safe, dignified and sustainable return of refugees and internally displaced persons'.[67] Resolution 1894 of 2009 requests the Secretary-General to provide more detailed information on the protection needs of refugees and IDPs in his reports on country-specific situations.[68]

It is clear, then, that the distinct protection needs of refugees and other displaced persons have been given significant attention in the UN discourse on both R2P and protection of civilians. How have these developments played out in the first R2P/POC military intervention – Libya, 2011? What is the likely effect of the military intervention in Libya as a response to the mass outflow of refugees and other displaced persons from the conflict? What new directions are presented by the R2P principle?

The Libyan Intervention

Some of the key failures of the interventions in Kosovo and Rwanda are disturbingly evident in the Libyan intervention, including: a failure of international preventive measures; mixed signals from the international community with respect to Libya's atrocious human rights record; a failure of the international community to appreciate the risks of mass atrocities by the Libyan regime; and an international response that risks failing to stop killings and mass refugee flows as soon as is possible.

Beginning with the neglect of international preventive measures, the following words written to describe Kosovo in the lead up to the outbreak of war in 1994 could equally apply to the Libyan regime before the crackdown in February 2011:

> From the 1980s onwards, Kosovo exhibited all the signs of a catastrophe waiting to happen. Here was an authoritarian society exposed to pressures for liberalization and democratization ... An active Diaspora ... was becoming increasingly radical. These are the conditions that typically give rise to 'new wars'.[69]

For at least as long, if not longer, Libya has displayed the same hallmarks of an authoritarian regime that has brutally repressed voices seeking greater freedoms. Not surprisingly, dissenters have been driven to radical protest. The two crises share an authoritarian core and a repressed and increasingly radicalised periphery.

Yet the international community's preventive initiatives in Libya in recent years have been poorly co-ordinated and undermined by the lack of a uniform approach to the Libyan regime. On the one hand, UN bodies, including the Human

67 UN Security Council Resolution S/RES/1674 (2006), para. 16.
68 UN Security Council Resolution S/RES/1894 (2009), para. 32.
69 Independent International Commission on Kosovo (2000), Part 1.

Rights Committee and a number of Special Rapporteurs, have actively pursued Libyan authorities over reported forced disappearances, extrajudicial, summary or arbitrary executions, the systematic use of torture and cruel, inhuman or degrading treatment or punishment and flagrant breaches of the right to freedom of opinion and expression.[70] But these efforts were largely neutralised by Libya's refusal to engage with UN human rights treaty bodies, as well as by the infamous elections of Libya to the chair of the UN Commission on Human Rights in 2003 and to the UN Human Rights Council in 2010.[71]

Mixed signals from the international community in terms of bilateral and regional endorsement of the Libyan regime have also not helped the cause of human rights in the country. The US's gradual rapprochement with Libya since it expressed solidarity with the US-led 'War on Terror'[72] has muffled US criticisms of the regime's human rights record and indicated to the Libyan authorities that their internal policies were off – or at least seriously downsized – on the bilateral agenda. Equally, the willingness of European countries to engage Libya to prevent the departure of sub-Saharan asylum seekers and irregular migrants to Europe[73] has further legitimated the Libyan regime. It is deplorable in this respect that some of the most serious human rights abuses perpetrated by the Libyan authorities in recent times have been against refugees detained in Libya pursuant to European containment policies.[74]

These observations support the further suggestion that prevention and capacity building with respect to a state's responsibility to protect its population against mass atrocities must span bilateral, regional and multilateral relationships, and must be based on a comprehensive, principled and uniform human rights approach that does not sideline rights in favour of the strategic or security interests of states. The Libyan situation is also further confirmation that greater efforts are required to ensure UN human rights bodies feed into early warning mechanisms being developed by the UN Secretariat to identify risks of genocide and other mass atrocity crimes.[75] Given the detailed international reporting of Libya's flagrant human rights abuses and repressive policies, the widespread protests and violent crackdown in February 2011 should not have caught the international community 'on the hop'.

Another worrying similarity between Libya and earlier crises is the exclusive reliance on air strikes. While some form of military intervention was necessary

70 UN Human Rights Council (21 July 2010).

71 For NGO criticisms of these elections, see, Reporters Without Borders (12 May 2010).

72 United States Congressional Research Service (2011).

73 Amnesty International (2010), p. 4.

74 UN Human Rights Council (21 July 2010), para. 10.

75 The Secretary-General's 2009 and 2010 reports on R2P recommend the establishment of a Joint Office that would 'institutionalize the collaboration' between the Secretary-General's Special Adviser on the Prevention of Genocide and his Special Adviser responsible for R2P: Secretary-General Ban Ki-moon (12 January 2009), p. 33; Secretary-General Ban Ki-moon (14 July 2010), para. 17.

after the Libyan regime refused to comply with Resolution 1970, the insistence on a high-altitude, low-casualty air war risks once again shifting the burden of risk and harm to the civilians who the intervention is meant to protect.[76] In the case of Kosovo, air strikes helped create an environment in which Serb forces could forcibly deport most of the ethnic Albanian population. While there are important differences – the Libyan forces lack the same level of co-ordination and brutal effectiveness and do not harbour the same intent of deporting an entire contingent of the population – the displacement of Libyan nationals escalated with on-ground conflict after the commencement of air strikes.[77]

Conclusion

Despite these concerns, there is a glimmer of hope that R2P is having a beneficial impact on the protection of persons fleeing the conflict in Libya. The fact that the Libyan intervention has been in the name of the R2P principle seems to have fostered greater international goodwill towards the victims of the conflict – including refugees. Most notably, Resolution 1973 praises the generous response of Egypt and Tunisia, and also contains an appeal from the Security Council for greater international support and assistance for the host countries. This is a welcome development as it adds much needed political impetus to the UNHCR's appeals for international solidarity and burden-sharing. In fact, the UNHCR has previously expressed the hope that the R2P principle would do just that.[78] But the litmus test will be the response of European countries to the direct arrival of refugees, especially the solidarity and burden-sharing extended by other European countries to the frontline states such as Malta and Italy.[79]

References

African Commission on Human and Peoples' Rights (1 March 2011) *Resolution on the Human Rights Situation in the Great Socialist Peoples' Libyan Arab Jamahiriya*, ACHPR/RES.181 (EXT.OS/IX).

Amnesty International (2010) 'Seeking safety, finding fear: Refugees, asylum-seekers and migrants in Libya and Malta', 14 December, available at http://www.amnesty.org/en/library/info/REG01/004/2010 (accessed 6 September 2011).

76 For a discussion of this in relation to the Kosovo crisis see, Thakur (2006), p. 214.

77 UN High Commissioner for Refugees (22 March 2011); UN High Commissioner for Refugees (25 March 2011).

78 UN High Commissioner for Refugees (30 June 2006).

79 UN High Commissioner for Refugees (29 March 2011).

Amnesty International (2011) 'Death toll mounts as Libyan security forces target protesters' 18 February, available at http://www.amnesty.org.au/news/comments/24855/ (accessed 6 September 2011).

F.M. Deng (2010) 'From "Sovereignty as Responsibility" to the "Responsibility to Protect"', 2, *Global Responsibility to Protect* 353.

Human Rights Watch (2011) 'Libya: Security Forces Kill 84 Over Three Days', 18 February, available at http://www.hrw.org/en/./2011/02/18/libya-security-forces-kill-84-over-three-days (accessed 6 September 2011).

Independent International Commission on Kosovo (2000) *The Kosovo Report*, OUP.

International Commission on Intervention and State Sovereignty (2001) *The Responsibility to Protect*, available at http://www.iciss.ca/report-en.asp.

T. Karrar-Lewsley (2011) *Human-Rights Groups Say Dozens Have Died in Libya*, 18 February edn Wall Street Journal, available at http://article.wn.com/view/2011/02/18/HumanRights_Groups_Say_Dozens_Have_Died_in_Libya/ (accessed 6 September 2011).

G. Loescher (2001) *The UNHCR and World Politics: A Perilous Path*, OUP.

E.C. Luck (2010) 'The Responsibility to Protect: Growing Pains or Early Promise?', 24, *Ethics & International Affairs* 349.

National Legislative Bodies (1993) *Peace Agreement between the Government of the Republic of Rwanda and the Rwandese Patriotic Front*, UNHCR, available at http://www.unhcr.org/refworld/docid/3ae6b4fcc.html.

Report of the Independent Inquiry into the actions of the United Nations during the 1994 genocide in Rwanda, S/1999/1257, (15 December 1999), available at http://www.securitycouncilreport.org/atf/cf/.6D27./POC%20S19991257.pdf (accessed 6 September 2011).

Reporters Without Borders (2010, 12 May) 'Human Rights Council's credibility threatened by Libya's probable election as member', available at http://en.rsf.org/libye-human-rights-council-s-credibility-12-05-2010,37456.html (accessed 6 September 2011).

A. Roberts (2011) 'Refugees and Military Intervention', in A. Betts and Loescher (eds) *Refugees in International Relations*, OUP 213.

Secretary-General's High Level Panel (2004) *The Report of the High-Level Panel on Threats, Challenges and Change*, United Nations, available at http://www.cfr.org/un/report-secretary-generals-high-level-panel-threats-challenges-change-2004/p22331 (accessed 6 September 2011).

Secretary-General (1999) *Report to the Security Council S/1999/957*, available at http://www.un.org/Docs/sc/reports/ (accessed 6 September 2011).

Secretary-General (2001) *Report to the Security Council S/2001/331*, available at http://www.un.org/Docs/sc/reports/ (accessed 6 September 2011).

Secretary-General (2002) *Report to the Security Council S/2002/1300*, available at http://www.un.org/Docs/sc/reports/ (accessed 6 September 2011).

Secretary-General (2004) *Report to the Security Council S/2004/431*, available at http://www.un.org/Docs/sc/reports/.

Secretary-General (2005) *Report to the Security Council S/2005/740*, available at http://www.un.org/Docs/sc/reports/ (accessed 6 September 2011).

Secretary-General (2007) *Report to the Security Council S/2007/643*, available at http://www.un.org/Docs/sc/reports/ (accessed 6 September 2011).

Secretary-General (2009) *Report to the Security Council S/2009/277*, available at http://www.un.org/Docs/sc/reports/ (accessed 6 September 2011).

Secretary-General (Ban Ki-moon) (21 February 2008) *Secretary-General Appoints Edward C. Luck of United States Special Adviser SG/A/1120*, BIO/3963, available at http://www.un.org/sg/ (accessed 6 September 2011).

Secretary-General (Ban Ki-moon) (12 January 2009) *Implementing the Responsibility to Protect: Report of the Secretary-General A/63/677*, available at http://www.un.org/sg/ (accessed 6 September 2011).

Secretary-General (Ban Ki-moon) (14 July 2010) *Early warning, assessment and the responsibility to protect: Report of the Secretary-General A/64/864*, available at http://www.un.org/sg/ (accessed 6 September 2011).

Secretary-General (Ban Ki-moon) (1 March 2011) *Secretary-General's remarks to the General Assembly on Libya*, available at http://www.un.org/apps/sg/sgstats.asp?nid=5116 (accessed 6 September 2011).

Secretary-General (Ban Ki-moon) (25 February 2011) 'Remarks to Security Council Meeting on Peace and Security in Africa', UN News Service, available at http://www.un.org/apps/news/story.asp? (accessed 6 September 2011).

R. Thakur (2006) *The United Nations, Peace and Security*, CUP.

R. Thakur (2009) 'Next word on intervention', 31 July edn. *The Japan Times*, available at http://search.japantimes.co.jp/cgi-bin/eo20090731rt.html (accessed 6 September 2011).

UN Security Council Presidential Statement 1996/6, available at http://www.un.org/Docs/sc/unsc_pres_statements (accessed 6 September 2011).

UN General Assembly (24 October 2005) *World Summit Outcome GA Res. 60/1*, available at http://www.un.org/depts/dhl/resguide/r60.htm (accessed 6 September 2011).

UN General Assembly (23 July 2009) *At the Opening of the Thematic Dialogue of the General Assembly on the Responsibility to Protect*, available at http://www.un.org/ga/president/.

UN High Commissioner for Refugees (2000) *The Rwandan genocide and its aftermath, The State of the World's Refugees*, available at http://www.unhcr.org/pubs/sowr2000/ch10.pdf (accessed 6 September 2011).

UN High Commissioner for Refugees (30 June 2006) '8th Annual Forum on Human Rights, Dublin, Ireland: Global Human Rights Protection – the way forward. Erika Feller, Assistant High Commissioner – Protection: Keynote address – "Towards a culture of protection"', available at http://www.unhcr.org/refworld/docid/44aba8d54.html (accessed 6 September 2011).

UN High Commissioner for Refugees (2 March 2011) *Update no 1: Humanitarian Situation in Libya and the Neighbouring Countries*, available at http://www.unhcr.org/ (accessed 6 September 2011).

UN High Commissioner for Refugees (2011, 22 February) *UNHCR fears for the safety of refugees caught in Libya's violence*, available at http://www.unhcr.org/ (accessed 6 September 2011).

UN High Commissioner for Refugees (22 March 2011) *Fighting in eastern Libya leaves thousands internally displaced*, available at http://www.unhcr.org/refworld/docid/4d8b01d52.html (accessed 6 September 2011).

UN High Commissioner for Refugees (25 March 2011) *Increased displacement in eastern Libya*, available at http://www.unhcr.org/refworld/docid/4d8c959a2.html (accessed 6 September 2011).

UN High Commissioner for Refugees (27 February 2011) *UNHCR emergency teams supporting Tunisians and Egyptians to respond to tens of thousands fleeing violence in Libya*, available at http://www.unhcr.org/ (accessed 6 September 2011).

UN High Commissioner for Refugees (29 March 2011) *Italy, Malta receive first boats from Libya, stretching asylum capacity*, available at http://www.unhcr.org/refworld/docid/4d92e7bc2.html (accessed 6 September 2011).

UN Human Rights Council (21 July 2010) *Compilation prepared by the Office of the High Commissioner for Human Rights in accordance with paragraph 15 (b) of the annex to Human Rights Council resolution 5/1: Libyan Arab Jamahiriya A/HRC/WG.6/9/LBY/2*, available at http://www.unhcr.org/refworld/publisher,UNHRC (accessed 6 September 2011).

UN Human Rights Council (25 February 2011) *Report of the Human Rights Council on its fifteenth special session A/HRC/S-15/1*, available at http://www.unhcr.org/refworld/type,SESSIONALREPORT (accessed 6 September 2011).

UN News Service (1 March 2011) *Tunisian border at crisis point as tens of thousands flee Libyan violence, UN Reports*, available at http://www.un.org/apps/news/story.asp? (accessed 6 September 2011).

UN News Service (23 February 2011) *Vital to keep borders open for people fleeing Libya, UN agency stresses*, available at http://www.un.org/apps/news/story.asp? (accessed 6 September 2011).

UN News Service (25 February 2011) *Ban calls on Security Council to consider immediate steps to stop killings in Libya*, available at http://www.un.org/apps/news/story.asp? (accessed 6 September 2011).

UN News Service (25 February 2011) *UN rights council recommends suspending Libya, orders inquiry into abuses*, available at http://www.un.org/apps/news/story.asp? (accessed 6 September 2011).

UN Office for the Coordination of Humanitarian Affairs (OCHA) (28 February 2011) *Libyan Arab Jamahiriya: Humanitarian Presence*, available at http://www.un.org/apps/news/story.asp? (accessed 6 September 2011).

UN Peacekeeping Mandate Darfur (UNAMID) 'African Union/United Nations Hybrid operation in Darfur', available at http://www.un.org/en/peacekeeping/missions/unamid/ (accessed 6 September 2011).

UN Peacekeeping Mandate Afghanistan (UNAMA) 'United Nations Assistance Mission in Afghanistan', available at http://unama.unmissions.org/default.aspx (accessed 6 September 2011).

UN Peacekeeping Mandate Central African Republic (MINURCAT) 'United Nations Mission in the Central African Republic and Chad', available at http://www.un.org/en/peacekeeping/missions/minurcat/ (accessed 6 September 2011).

UN Peacekeeping Mandate Cote d'Ivoire (UNOCI) 'United Nations Operation in Côte d'Ivoire', available at http://www.un.org/en/peacekeeping/missions/unoci/ (accessed 6 September 2011).

UN Peacekeeping Mandate Democratic Republic of Congo (MONUC) 'United Nations Organization Mission in the Democratic Republic of the Congo', available at http://www.un.org/en/peacekeeping/missions/monuc/ (accessed 6 September 2011).

UN Peacekeeping Mandate Haiti (MINUSTAH) 'United Nations Stabilization Mission in Haiti', available at http://www.un.org/en/peacekeeping/missions/minustah/ (accessed 6 September 2011).

UN Peacekeeping Mandate Liberia (UNMIL) 'United Nations Mission in Liberia', available at http://www.un.org/en/peacekeeping/missions/unmil/ (accessed 6 September 2011).

UN Peacekeeping Mandate Sudan (UNMIS) 'United Nations Mission in the Sudan', available at http://www.un.org/en/peacekeeping/missions/unmis/ (accessed 6 September 2011).

UN Security Council (2003) *Statement by the President of the Security Council S/PRST/2003/27*, available at http://www.un.org/Docs/sc/unsc_pres_statements (accessed 6 September 2011).

UN Security Council (2004) *Statement by the President of the Security Council S/PRST/2004/46*, available at http://www.un.org/Docs/sc/unsc_pres_statements (accessed 6 September 2011).

UN Security Council (20 July 2004) *Statement by the President of the Security Council S/PRST/2004/27*, United Nations, available at http://www.un.org/Docs/sc/unsc_pres_statements (accessed 6 September 2011).

UN Security Council (2005) *Statement by the President of the Security Council S/PRST/2005/25*, available at http://www.un.org/Docs/sc/unsc_pres_statements (accessed 6 September 2011).

UN Security Council (2009) *Statement by the President of the Security Council S/PRST/2009/1*, available at http://www.un.org/Docs/sc/unsc_pres_statements (accessed 6 September 2011).

UN Security Council (2009) *Statement by the President of the Security Council S/PRST/2009/9*, available at http://www.un.org/Docs/sc/unsc_pres_statements.

UN Security Council (22 February 2011) *Press Statement on Libya, SC/10180 AFR/2120*, available at http://www.un.org/News/Press/docs/2011/sc10180.doc.htm (accessed 6 September 2011).

UN Security Council (2002) *Statement of the President S/PRST/2002/6*, available at http://www.un.org/Docs/sc/unsc_pres_statements (accessed 6 September 2011).

UN Security Council Resolution S/RES/872 (1993), available at http://www.un.org/Docs/sc/unsc_resolutions.html (accessed 6 September 2011).

UN Security Council Resolution S/RES/912 (1994) 21 April, available at http:// www.un.org/Docs/sc/unsc_resolutions.html (accessed 6 September 2011).

UN Security Council Resolution S/RES/918 (1994) 17 May, available at http:// www.un.org/Docs/sc/unsc_resolutions.html (accessed 6 September 2011).

UN Security Council Resolution S/RES/929 (1994) 22 June, available at http:// www.un.org/Docs/sc/unsc_resolutions.html (accessed 6 September 2011).

UN Security Council Resolution S/RES/1199 (1998) 23 September, available at http:// www.un.org/Docs/sc/unsc_resolutions.html (accessed 6 September 2011).

UN Security Council Resolution S/RES/1244 (1999) 10 June, available at http:// www.un.org/Docs/sc/unsc_resolutions.html (accessed 6 September 2011).

UN Security Council Resolution S/RES/1265 (1999), available at http:// www.un.org/Docs/sc/unsc_resolutions.html (accessed 6 September 2011).

UN Security Council Resolution S/RES/1296 (2000), available at http:// www.un.org/Docs/sc/unsc_resolutions.html (accessed 6 September 2011).

UN Security Council Resolution S/RES/1674 (2006), available http:// www.un.org/Docs/sc/unsc_resolutions.html (accessed 6 September 2011).

UN Security Council Resolution S/RES/1738 (2006), available at http:// www.un.org/Docs/sc/unsc_resolutions.html (accessed 6 September 2011).

UN Security Council Resolution S/RES/1894 (2009) 11 November, available at http:// www.un.org/Docs/sc/unsc_resolutions.html (accessed 11 December 2011).

UN Security Council Resolution S/RES/1970 (2011), available at http:// www.un.org/Docs/sc/unsc_resolutions.html (accessed 5 January 2012).

UN Security Council Resolution S/RES/1973 (2011), available at http:// www.un.org/Docs/sc/unsc_resolutions.html (accessed 5 January 2012).

United States Congressional Research Service (2011) 'Libya: Background and US Relations', 18 February 2011, RL33142 (accessed 5 January 2012).

Chapter 10
The Responsibility to Protect: Retrospect and Prospect

Ramesh Thakur

Introduction

The birth and continuing evolution of the responsibility to protect (R2P) – the mobiliser of last resort of the world's conscience to avert, prevent and stop mass killings – is a clear illustration of how the United Nations has provided an essential space in which powerful normative and policy agendas have been articulated. Until the twentieth century, state sovereignty included the right to go to war and an unchallengeable monopoly on the lawful use of force domestically. Gradually by the time of the creation of the United Nations in 1945 and more rapidly thereafter, the right to use force internationally was progressively restricted to self-defence against armed attack or under UN authorisation. Historically, individual states had also intervened inside sovereign jurisdictions to stop the slaughter of kith and kin or co-religionists. Under the impact of the Holocaust and starting with the Genocide Convention in 1948, the international community asserted the collective right to stop supposedly sovereign states killing large numbers of civilians inside their borders.

Even so, for 350 years – from the Treaty of Westphalia in 1648 until 1998 – sovereignty functioned as institutionalised indifference. International interventions in Kosovo and East Timor in 1999 broke that mould and were the backdrop to UN Secretary-General Kofi Annan's search for a new norm. Both the Rwanda genocide and the Srebrenica massacre happened on his watch as head of UN peacekeeping. After becoming Secretary-General, instead of collective gnashing and wailing during atrocities followed by a traumatic repeat afterwards, yet again, of promises of 'Never Again', he pushed for a new doctrine to take timely and effective action. With Canada's help, an international commission formulated the innovative principle of the responsibility to protect (R2P). In 2005, world leaders unanimously agreed that where governments were manifestly failing in their sovereign duty, the international community, acting through the United Nations, would take 'timely and decisive' collective action to honour the international responsibility to protect people against atrocities.

As formulated by the International Commission on Intervention and State Sovereignty (ICISS), R2P redefines sovereignty as responsibility and locates the responsibility in the first instance with the state. If, but only if, the state is unwilling or unable to honour the responsibility, or is itself the perpetrator of atrocities, then the residual responsibility to protect victims of atrocity crimes shifts to the international community of states, acting ideally through the Security Council.[1] In an interview with *Time* magazine, Liberia's President Ellen Johnson Sirleaf, Africa's first elected woman president, said: 'Look at how we have gone from [a stance] of non-interference in our internal affairs to respect for the principle of the responsibility to protect'.[2]

Traditional warfare is the use of force by rival armies of enemy states fighting over a clash of interests: us against them. Collective security rests on the use of force by the international community of states to defeat or punish an aggressor from within the community, whoever that may be: all against one. Peacekeeping involves the insertion of neutral and lightly armed third-party soldiers as a physical buffer between enemy combatants who have agreed to a ceasefire: us as a buffer between formerly fighting enemies. R2P refers to the use of military force by outsiders for the protection of victims of mass atrocities inside sovereign territorial jurisdictions: us against perpetrators, as protectors of victims of mass atrocities.

Is R2P well-meaning enough to be attractive for its promise of making a difference, yet so vague as to be potentially threatening by being open to abuse? Is it in danger of falling prey to the fatal organisational paradox syndrome, where the effort to preserve the fragile diplomatic consensus in the international community is privileged over the call to protect vulnerable populations that led to the consensus being forged in the first place? That is, can the global consensus on R2P, necessary for the world to be able to translate it from noble principle to actual deeds, be stopped from fraying only at the cost of the integrity of R2P that precludes the need to act? Alternatively, is R2P a norm in search of a self-justifying crisis?

Faced with these tensions and competing imperatives, will the R2P centre hold? Revulsion at the murder of large numbers of civilians in a range of atrocity crimes – the drowning of the ceremony of innocence – has led to a softening of public and governmental support for the norms and institutions that shield the perpetrators of atrocity crimes from international criminal accountability. The failure to act can indeed be interpreted as, the best, lacking the courage of their conviction while, the worst, engaging in mass murder with passionate intensity. 'Mobilising political will' is a more prosaic way of saying that the best need to rediscover and act on their convictions.

I will first situate R2P in the context of the so-called 'challenge of humanitarian intervention' in the 1990s and trace the displacement of the challenge with the responsibility to protect and its adoption by world leaders in 2005, then bring it up to date with the report of the Secretary-General in January 2009, before outlining, as the main task of this chapter, the unfinished agenda of operationalising the norm.

1 International Commission on Intervention and State Sovereignty (2001).

2 Look across Africa and see the major changes that are happening (2009).

From the 1990s Challenge of Humanitarian Intervention to the 2005 World Summit

The ICISS report consolidated a number of disparate trends and borrowed language first developed by Francis M. Deng and Roberta Cohen to help address the problem of internally displaced persons (IDPs). 'Humanitarian intervention' was not a twentieth-century innovation.[3] The attributes and exercise of sovereignty have softened significantly since 1945. The use of force, both domestically and internationally, was an acknowledged attribute of state sovereignty and war itself was an accepted institution of the Westphalian system with distinctive rules, etiquette, norms and stable patterns of practices to govern armed conflicts.[4] Today, there exist numerous and significant restrictions on the authority of states to use force either domestically or internationally. A further challenge to the Westphalian order came with the adoption of new standards of conduct for states in the protection and advancement of international human rights. Over time, the chief threats to international security have come from violent eruptions of crises within states, including civil wars, while the goals of promoting human rights and democratic governance, protecting civilian victims of humanitarian atrocities and punishing governmental perpetrators of mass crimes have become more important.

The proliferation of complex humanitarian emergencies after the end of the Cold War, and the inappropriateness of the classical tenets of UN peacekeeping for dealing with them,[5] highlighted the inherent tension between the neutrality and impartiality of traditional peacekeeping and the partial consequences of peace enforcement. Finally, under the impact of globalisation, national frontiers are becoming less relevant in determining the flow of ideas, information, goods, services, capital, labour and technology. The cumulative effect of these changes has posed significant conceptual, policy and operational challenges to the notion of state sovereignty that is considerably less sacrosanct today than in 1945.

The crucial actors promoting and shepherding R2P through the maze of UN politics can be broken down into norm entrepreneurs, champions and brokers. As a *norm entrepreneur*, the UN Secretary-General is a unique international actor with distinctive characteristics and bases of authority and influence, albeit with limitations.[6] The other two norm entrepreneurs critical to the R2P story are Lloyd Axworthy and Gareth Evans, the activist foreign ministers of Canada and Australia who set up and co-chaired ICISS respectively. R2P's state *champion* from start to finish was Canada, a country strongly committed to UN-centred multilateralism, with a history of close engagement with the world organisation, political credibility in both North and South and a proud tradition of successful global initiatives. The *norm broker* was ICISS.

3 For a study of humanitarian interventions in the nineteenth century, see Bass (2008).
4 See Holsti (1996).
5 See Thakur and Thayer (1995).
6 See Chesterman (2007); Thakur (2006), Ch. 14.

The Secretary-General's High-Level Panel on Threats, Challenges and Change, which included Evans, reaffirmed the importance of the terminological change from 'humanitarian intervention' to 'the responsibility to protect'. China's formal paper on UN reforms noted that: 'Each state shoulders the primary responsibility to protect its own population ... When a massive humanitarian crisis occurs, it is the legitimate concern of the international community to ease and defuse the crisis'.[7] In the US, the Gingrich-Mitchell task force too endorsed the responsibility to protect.[8] In his own report before the World Summit, Annan made an explicit reference to ICISS and R2P as well as to the High-Level Panel.[9]

R2P was one of the few substantive items to survive the negotiations at the World Summit in New York in September–October 2005. The document marks a clear, unambiguous acceptance by all UN members of individual state responsibility to protect populations from genocide, war crimes, ethnic cleansing and crimes against humanity. Member states further declared that they 'are prepared to take collective action, *in timely and decisive manner*, through the Security Council ... and in cooperation with relevant regional organisations as appropriate, should peaceful means be inadequate and national authorities are manifestly failing to protect their populations' (emphasis added).[10]

The Status of R2P in 2009

Ban Ki-moon succeeded Kofi Annan as Secretary-General a bit over a year after the 2005 World Summit's endorsement of R2P. Ban has not been shy of adopting R2P as his own cause, not worried that he will merely be advancing his predecessor's legacy. Drawing on Special Adviser Edward Luck's wide-ranging consultations and reflections, in January 2009 Ban published his report on implementing R2P.[11] While not adding much to the substance of what was said in 2001, it did flesh out in greater and clearer detail many of the ideas of the ICISS report. It noted explicitly that all peoples inside a state's territorial jurisdiction, not just citizens but also non-national residents and visitors, must be protected by a state (para. 11.1). It clarified and elaborated some things, for example the fact that because force is the last resort it does not mean we have to go through a sequential or graduated set of responses before responding robustly to an urgent crisis (para. 50).

The report was effective in packaging R2P in the language of three pillars: the state's own responsibility to protect all peoples on its territory, international

7 Position Paper of the People's Republic of China on the United Nations Reforms (2005), Part III.1.

8 US Institute of Peace (2005), p. 15.

9 Annan (21 March 2005), paras 122–35.

10 World Summit Outcome, adopted by UN General Assembly Resolution (2005), paras 138–40.

11 Ki-moon (2009).

assistance to help build a state's capacity to deliver on its responsibility and the international responsibility to protect. But the report was over the top in elaborating on the metaphor by insisting that the 'edifice' of R2P will tilt, totter and collapse unless all three pillars are of equal height and strength (para. 12). The most important element – the weightiest pillar – has to be the state's own responsibility. And the most critical is the international community's response to fresh outbreaks of mass atrocity crimes.

Mercifully, the report did not retreat from the necessity for outside military action in some circumstances. But it diluted what was the central defining feature of R2P.[12] Its added value is it crystallised an emerging new norm of using international force to prevent and halt mass killings by reconceptualising sovereignty as responsibility. It aims to convert a shocked international conscience into timely and decisive collective action. The use of force by the UN against a state's consent will always be controversial and contested. That is no reason to hand over control of the pace, direction and substance of the agenda of our shared, solemn responsibility to the R2P skeptics. How do we build *international* capacity and will to protect at-risk populations when state authorities are complicit either through incapacity or, more culpably, direct complicity?

The General Assembly held a very well-attended debate on R2P on 23, 24 and 28 July 2009. It was called for by the president of the Assembly, Father Miguel D'Escoto Brockmann of Nicaragua, who in his background note described R2P as 'redecorated colonialism'.[13] In his opening remarks, he referred to 'the consecrated cornerstones ... enshrined in the UN Charter and in international law', including 'sovereignty and non-intervention, that should not be subverted'. He warned of the risk of R2P, its 'laudable motives' notwithstanding, being misused 'to justify arbitrary and selective interventions against the weakest states'; of lack of enforceable accountability on the abusers of R2P; and of double standards selectivity in its application.[14] He cited the case of Iraq as an example of R2P being abused – seemingly unaware of the irony that it took place more than two years before R2P was adopted. Ed Luck emphasised that R2P seeks to 'discourage unilateralism, military adventurism and an over-dependence on military responses to humanitarian need'.[15] Navi Pillay, the High Commissioner for Human Rights, urged that: 'We should all undertake an honest assessment of our ability to save lives in extraordinary situations' like Rwanda in 1994. It was good to have the likes of Nigeria, South Africa and Japan to speak in support of R2P.[16]

The debate was addressed by 94 speakers and included 19 statements from Africa, 21 from Asia and 16 from Latin America and the Caribbean. Almost all reaffirmed the 2005 consensus and statement on R2P, expressed opposition

12 The same mistake is made by Bellamy (2009), pp. 111–28.

13 Quoted in Macfarquhar (2009).

14 UN General Assembly (2009).

15 Luck (2009), p. 3.

16 UN (2009).

to any effort to reopen it and insisted that its scope be restricted to the four crimes of genocide, crimes against humanity, war crimes and ethnic cleansing. Most supported the Secretary-General's three-pillar strategy based on the 2005 consensus. Several expressed reservations about selectivity and double standards in the implementation of R2P and criticism of past Security Council failures to act, with some urging voluntary self-restraint in the use of the veto when faced with atrocity crimes. There was near-unanimity in accepting state and international responsibility to prevent atrocities through building state capacity and will and providing international assistance (Pillars 1 and 2) and in grounding these fundamental obligations in the UN Charter, human rights treaties and international humanitarian law (IHL). Most affirmed that should other measures not be adequate, timely and decisive coercive action, including the use of force, is warranted by the Charter to save lives. Few speakers rejected the use of force in any circumstance and only Cuba, Nicaragua, Sudan and Venezuela sought to roll back the 2005 consensus.[17]

Several speakers referred to such 'root causes' as poverty and underdevelopment. Many talked of the need for a proper balance of responsibilities between the General Assembly and the Security Council in developing and implementing the new norm. Some speakers, for example the representatives of Japan and Singapore, pointed to a linkage between R2P and the agenda of international criminal prosecution. Yet several kept coming back to the core of the R2P norm: that in extremis, something needed to be done to avoid a shameful repeat of Rwanda-type inaction. Thus Ghana's delegate, pointedly noting that the principle of non-interference can be abused just like that of intervention, said that R2P attempts to strike a balance between non-interference and non-indifference. Guinea-Bissau's delegate called for the 'gap between what was said in 2005 and the ability to act now' to be closed. In a marked change from its strong opposition to R2P in 2001, even India's Ambassador Hardeep Singh Puri emphasised that 'A State's responsibility to protect its citizens was among the foremost of its responsibilities'.[18]

It is hard to describe the debate as anything other than a resounding success for the R2P principle, and for advocates and victims working to prevent atrocity crimes by all means necessary within the Charter regime that governs international relations. The pro-R2P interventions by the delegates of East Timor and Rwanda were especially poignant. The latter said that 'the 2005 World Summit Outcome, coupled with the Secretary-General's report and today's debate, made it much less likely that such horrific events [as the 1994 genocide] would be repeated anywhere in the future'.[19]

---

17 Helpful summaries have been provided by two civil society organisations: Global Centre for the Responsibility to Protect (2009); International Coalition for the Responsibility to Protect (2009).

18 UN General Assembly (23 July 2009).

19 UN General Assembly (23 July 2009).

From Words to Deeds, Principle to Practice

R2P is a call to action on prevention, intervention and post-conflict reconstruction. The first danger is that of rollback: a shamefaced edging back from the agreed norm of 2005, a form of buyer's remorse. The need exists for continued advocacy and activism by civil society and concerned governments to remain steadfast and hold all governments' feet to the fire of individual and collective responsibility to protect at-risk populations. Some regimes that fear the searchlight of international attention being shone on their misdeeds will try to chip away at the norm until only a façade remains. The advocates of R2P cannot allow them to succeed. Better that the serially abusive regimes live with this fear of international intervention than that their people fear being visited by death and disappearance squads.

A second, opposite danger of rollback comes from the aggressive humanitarian warriors who gave 'humanitarian intervention' such a bad name in the first place. Developing countries' histories and their peoples' collective memories are full of past examples of trauma and suffering rooted in the white man's burden. The weight of that historical baggage is simply too strong to sustain the continued use of the language of humanitarian intervention.

Another danger from over-enthusiastic supporters is misuse of the concept in non-R2P contexts. A group of retired NATO generals used it to justify the first use of nuclear weapons to prevent nuclear proliferation.[20] Others have used the label to refer to action to halt the spread of HIV/AIDS or to protect indigenous populations from climate change.

Conceptual and Theoretical Refinement

The original ICISS report failed to make a forceful distinction between state incapacity, on the one hand, and state complicity through unwillingness or perpetration, on the other hand. The distinction is fine in principle but enormously consequential for policy.

The protection of victims from mass atrocities requires different guidelines and rules of engagement than traditional warfare, collective security and peace operations, as well as different relationships to civil authorities and humanitarian actors. The differences need to be identified, articulated and incorporated into officer training manuals and courses.[21] For example, recalling the tragedy of Rwanda in 1994: how does a UN peace operation, sent to supervise a peace agreement and process, recast its task on the fly to prevent an unfolding genocide?

The relationship between R2P and the protection of civilians in armed conflict could do with theoretical and conceptual clarification.[22] The latter has been a

20 Naumann et al. (2007).

21 Holt and Berkman (2006).

22 See Global Centre for R2P (January 2009).

regular item on the Security Council's agenda since 1999 when it received the first Report of the Secretary-General on the subject. Some states fear that the agenda risk being politicised unnecessarily with the intrusion of R2P. The two agendas are complementary and mutually reinforcing, neither synonymous with nor unrelated to each other. They share legal underpinnings, normative weight and Security Council commitments under human rights, international humanitarian and refugee laws. The protection of civilians in armed conflict embraces (i) all measures to protect the safety, dignity and integrity of all human beings, but only (ii) in times of war. The first part is thus considerably broader and less precise than the four specific acts under R2P. But R2P is broader in being concerned with the prevention and protection of atrocity crimes in all circumstances, not merely during armed conflict.

Each context requires its own specific protection actions against threats to the people at risk there. The UN can provide the normative mandate at the global level for their protection and the forces necessary for intervention if need be. By its very nature, a mandate is a brief, high-level policy document that cannot address the details of on-the-ground operational reality in each specific context. The action to prevent and rebuild has to be undertaken by UN agencies acting collaboratively with local civil society actors, NGOs and representatives of the Red Cross and Red Crescent Movement. They can be brought together in a distinct protection cluster to assess needs and priorities for each vulnerable group requiring protection and identifying, in advance, the custom-tailored responses for prevention and rebuilding.[23]

The map lines that delineate statehood can become blurred by the bloodlines of nationhood.[24] More research is needed on the question of whether groups who constitute a minority in one country and are targeted for killings or ethnic cleansing based on their group identity are owed any responsibility by their kin state. Inter-ethnic conflict and genocide have demonstrated the dangers of failing to protect people targeted by their fellow citizens. How can kinship ties across borders strengthen greater pan-national identity across borders without challenging territorially defined national security? The general international opinion around the world in 2008 was that Russia invoked R2P to camouflage highly traditional geopolitical calculations in launching military action against Georgia in defence of its interests in South Ossetia.[25] Unilateral intervention by a 'kin state' can lead to conflict within and between states. How can R2P be applied to the protection of persons belonging to national minorities? Whose responsibility is it to protect such persons? A sensible answer might come from the formula that France uses to describe its relationship with Quebec in Canada: *ni ingérence ni indifférence* (neither interference/intervention nor indifference).

23 See Murthy (2008).

24 See Kemp et al. (2011).

25 See Global Center for R2P (19 August 2008).

The question of protecting members of the kin group in neighbouring or distant locations outside the territorial borders is conceptually linked also to the question of protecting one's citizens who come under attack overseas. The United States invaded Grenada ostensibly with the goal of protecting US citizens, and Israel has sometimes exercised the right to use its military forces to rescue nationals from foreign trouble spots and dangers. With increased volumes of international travel, growing numbers of people risk being caught in foreign zones of danger. Can a state be said to have a duty to protect its nationals abroad? Sovereignty as responsibility cannot be confined narrowly to just one function of the state. If a state has the responsibility to protect citizens and foreigners alike on its territory, does it not also have the correlative duty to protect its individual citizens caught in danger on foreign soil when mass atrocities – that would shock the international community's conscience and activate the international responsibility to protect – are not involved but the host government is unwilling or unable to protect them, or is itself the source of harm to them?

Nor is sovereignty as responsibility necessarily limited to the domestic realm. Rather, the reality is one of systemic brittleness where shocks cascade across sectors and between countries. The contemporary international system exhibits systemic risks and vulnerabilities, both horizontally from one sector to another (the subprime crisis, mortgage meltdown and individual banks' crisis led inexorably to a global financial crisis), and vertically from firms and nations to the world. Sovereignty understood and jealously guarded as financial autonomy behind political frontiers becomes a risk multiplier for the system of sovereign states.[26] Conversely, systemic resilience lies in supranational regulatory/surveillance mechanisms, co-ordinating mechanisms, and sanctioning mechanism sans sovereignty. In other words, sovereignty entails global responsibility for the extra-territorial impacts of national decisions.

Yet another item on the research agenda would be to examine past cases of iconic examples of horrific atrocities and genocidal killings in the twentieth-century history, including the Holocaust, Bangladesh, Cambodia, Rwanda and the Balkans. Conversely, there are some iconic cases of 'bad' interventions, such as that to remove the Marxist Allende regime in Chile, that could also be studied with respect to what, if any, difference R2P would or might have made. This would apply especially if legitimacy criteria could be approved by consensus.

How can the generals and presidents responsible for mass atrocities be brought to justice? Discussion and analyses of the protection of civilians and the prosecution of perpetrators have mostly proceeded along separate lines. In fact, they are two sides of the same coin.[27] The problem is mass atrocities. The inter-related twin tasks are to protect the victims and punish the perpetrators by building domestic and international institutional capacity and political will. Both require

26 This argument is hardly new, having been made, for example, by the late Susan Strange more than a decade ago; Strange (1999), pp. 345–54.

27 See Thakur and Popovski (2008), pp. 39–61.

substantial derogations of sovereignty, the first with respect to the norm of non-intervention and the second with respect to sovereign impunity up to the level of heads of government and state. At the same time, both require sensitive judgment calls: the use of external military force to protect civilians inside sovereign jurisdiction should first satisfy legitimacy criteria rooted largely in just war theory, while the prosecution of alleged atrocity criminals should be balanced against the consequences for the prospects and process of peace, the need for post-conflict reconciliation and the fragility of international as well as domestic institutions.

Regional Peacekeeping and R2P

There has also been renewed interest in regional peacekeeping, that is, peace operations undertaken by regional organisations such as the North Atlantic Treaty Organisation (NATO), the African Union and the Economic Community of West African States (ECOWAS).

Already in 1992, UN Secretary-General Boutros Boutros-Ghali called in *An Agenda for Peace* for greater involvement of regional organisations in UN activities regarding peace and security. His proposed division of labour envisioned using regional arrangements for different mechanisms such as preventive diplomacy, peacekeeping, peacemaking and post-conflict peace-building. Since then, formal co-operation between regional organisations and the UN has been consolidated further.

The UN Security Council also has given more attention to regional organisations. In July 2004, after the second meeting between the Security Council and regional bodies, the Council invited regional organisations 'to take the necessary steps to increase collaboration with the United Nations in order to maximise efficiency in stabilisation processes, and encouraged enhanced cooperation and coordination among regional and subregional organisations'.[28]

The Secretary-General's High-Level Panel urged that, if the Security Council is to be more active and effective in preventing and responding to threats, it needs to utilise Chapter VIII provisions more, and more productively. Its report advised the UN to promote the establishment of such regional and sub-regional groupings, particularly in view of their important contributions to peace and security. Their efforts neither contradict those of the UN, nor absolve the United Nations of its primary responsibility for the maintenance of international peace and security. Regional action should be organised within the framework of the UN Charter and be consistent with its purposes and principles; and the UN and regional organisations should work together in a more integrated fashion than hitherto.[29]

Kofi Annan accepted the broad thrust of this analysis.[30] At the sixth high-level meeting between the UN and regional organisations in July 2005, he affirmed

28 UN Security Council (20 July 2004).

29 High-Level Panel on Threats (December 2004), paras 270–273.

30 Annan (2005), paras 213–5.

that strengthening UN relations with regional and other intergovernmental organisations is a critical part of the effort to reform the multilateral system. The aim is to create 'a truly interlocking system that guarantees greater coordination in both policy and action' with partnerships that 'build on the comparative strengths of each organisation'.[31]

The reasons for the popularity of regional peacekeeping are not hard to fathom. They offer a solution to the UN's lack of capacity to meet the growing demand. National and intergovernmental actors have a bigger stake in ensuring security and stability in their own region. They are less riven by heterogeneity of forces in skills, equipment and doctrines. They are more sensitive to local mores and nuances and better placed to receive and recognise early warning signals of imminent flare-ups. Against this, of course, there is the risk of regional actors, especially a regional hegemon, pursuing their vested interests instead of the regional public good. And they are vulnerable to cross-infection by rivalry among regional powers.

Most importantly for present purposes, they lack institutional policies on the protection of civilians in armed conflict and knowledge of and training in the relevant principles of international humanitarian law.[32] Victoria Holt and Tobias Berkman noted that none of the African Union, European Union, ECOWAS and NATO had a well-developed concept of the protection of civilians for their military missions.[33] There is the very real risk, therefore, that regional peace operations will neither be aware nor be able to adhere to international standards such as R2P and IHL. The risk of variable standards across different regional operations needs to be acknowledged and addressed. The verisimilitude among regional actors can only be offset by incorporating the rules of IHL and analyses of R2P into national legislation, military manuals and peacekeeping courses. In turn, this requires the development of joint standards for regional and UN operations, common principles for accountable governance, harmonisation of institutional concepts of protection of civilians in armed conflict and the adoption of appropriate governance protocols between the United Nations and regional organisations.[34] Otherwise, there will be a debilitating fragmentation of multilateral responses to conflict.

Test Cases

Myanmar: Feel Good, Do Harm

This extensive research agenda will help to build a case load of R2P-type situations as a guide to future deliberations, evidence-based analyses and robust action. In the meantime, it is in the field with actual test cases where the rubber has already hit

31 UN (25–26 July 2005).

32 See Bateman and Hammer (2007).

33 Holt and Berkman (2006), p. 183.

34 Bateman and Hammer (2007), pp. 7–8.

the road insofar as the norm-implementation gap is concerned. Five in particular are worth discussing here: Myanmar, Gaza, Sri Lanka, Kenya and Libya.

In 2008, with Burma's deadly Cyclone Nargis, principles, politics and practicality converged in counselling caution in invoking R2P. There is no *morally* significant difference between large numbers of people being killed by soldiers firing into crowds or the government blocking help being delivered to the victims of natural disasters. *Conceptually*, the shift from the crime of mass killings by acts of commission such as shooting people and acts of omission such as preventing them from getting food and medical attention is a difference of degree, not kind. *Legally*, the four categories where R2P apply are genocide, war crimes, ethnic cleansing and crimes against humanity. The original ICISS report had explicitly included 'overwhelming natural or environmental catastrophes' causing significant loss of life as triggering R2P if the state was unable or unwilling to cope, or rebuffed assistance (para. 4.20). This was dropped by 2005. But 'crimes against humanity' was included and could perhaps apply to the Burmese generals' actions in blocking outside aid.

Politically, however, we cannot ignore the significance of the exclusion of natural and environmental disasters in 2005. Clearly, the normative consensus on the new global norm did not extend beyond the acts of commission of atrocity crimes by delinquent governments. To attempt to reintroduce it by the back door today would strengthen suspicion of Western motivations and reinforce cynicism of Western tactics. The UN must base its decisions on the collectively expressed will of its member states, not on that of an independent commission or individual member states.

Practically, there is no humanitarian crisis so grave that it cannot be made worse by military intervention.[35] Unappealing as they might be, the generals are in effective control of Burma. The only way to get aid quickly to where it was most needed was with the co-operation of the authorities. If they refused, the notion of fighting one's way through to the victims is ludicrous. The militarily overstretched Western powers had neither the capacity nor the will to start another war in the jungles of Southeast Asia. If foreign soldiers are involved, it does not take long for a war of liberation or humanitarian assistance to morph into a war of foreign occupation in the eyes of the local populace.

If the invocation of R2P does not help in the immediate emergency, may indeed cause even more determined opposition and intensify the backlash against R2P, then the painfully forged consensus on the R2P norm will fracture without any material help being provided to the displaced and distressed. That is, help

35 An investigation by a group of 84 local and international organisations concluded that 'A UN-backed offensive to destroy a Hutu rebel group in eastern Democratic Republic of Congo has had disastrous humanitarian consequences, with more than 1,000 civilians killed, 7,000 raped, and 900,000 forced from their homes'. The organisations collectively described the human cost of the attempt to defeat the Democratic Forces for the Liberation of Rwanda as 'unacceptable and disproportionate to the results it has achieved' (Rice 2009).

will be less forthcoming to the next group of victims of large-scale killings. The correct equation thus is that invoking R2P in Burma would have endangered lives elsewhere tomorrow without saving any and possibly even delaying help for the Nargis victims today. Feeling good about one's own moral superiority by accusing others of privileging a norm over saving lives is a peculiar form of self-indulgence that perpetuates the killing fields without alleviating anyone's suffering.

Diplomatic pressure was better exerted on the basis of humanitarian principles enshrined in a number of UN General Assembly resolutions than on the coercive language of military intervention for which no one had the stomach and few had the capacity. In the end, Secretary-General Ban's use of the bully pulpit, good offices and personal on-the-spot diplomacy did make a difference that may not have been enough to satisfy the habitual UN critics but was nonetheless critical in helping many in distress through relaxing some curbs on international relief efforts.

Gaza

A related danger is seeking remedy in R2P when better or more appropriate tools and instruments are available for dealing with the crisis to hand. A good example of this occurred in 2008–09 when Israel launched a three-week offensive in Hamas-ruled Gaza, putatively in response to rocket attacks from Gaza against civilian targets in Israel. There were issues of *international and UN Charter law* involved: the well-established rights to self-defence against armed attack and to resist foreign occupation, the validity of these justifications for the resort to violence by Israel and Palestinians and the limits to the exercise of these rights. There were issues of *international humanitarian law*: regardless of whether the use of force itself is lawful or not, the conduct of hostilities is still governed by the Geneva laws with respect to proportionality, necessity and distinction between combatants and civilians. There were charges and counter-charges, including by responsible UN officials and special rapporteurs, of the possible commission of *war crimes*.[36] In the midst of all this, the invocation of R2P did not seem to be the most pressing or most relevant contribution to the solution. At the same time, the debate over Gaza also raised the further question of occupying powers' responsibility to protect all peoples living under their occupation, be they Palestinians or Iraqis or Afghans.

Sri Lanka

In May 2009, there was fresh debate over the relevance and applicability of R2P to Sri Lanka in the closing stages of the government's successful military campaign against the Liberation Tigers of Tamil Eelam (LTTE). Sri Lanka was waging a military offensive against a guerrilla army that had fought a brutal war against the

36 See the Goldstone Report: United Nations Human Rights Council (15 September 2009). See also, Falk (2009); McGreal (2009).

legitimate state for 26 years, killed up to 80,000 people and assassinated an Indian prime minister as well as a Sri Lankan president. The Tigers were among the most ruthless terrorist organisations and designated as such by more than 30 countries. They pioneered the use of women suicide bombers, invented the explosive suicide belt, killed many civilians including Tamils, recruited child soldiers and often raised funds from the Tamil Diaspora through extortion. Post-conflict recovery and progress was not possible until they had been decisively defeated on the battlefield.

Civilians were held against their will by the Tigers, not the army. Many who tried to flee were shot by the Tigers – an act of depravity against their own to which even Hamas and Hezbollah, other practitioners of the art of using civilians as human shields, have not stooped. Tellingly, there were no reports of civilians trying to flee from the Sri Lankan forces to the Tigers. A movement that began as the protector of the nation's oppressed Tamil minority had mutated into their killers. Along the road, it is the Tigers who fought for a solely military solution to the three-decade conflict, spurning the few opportunities that were presented for a political settlement through dialogue and negotiations, including through Indian and Norwegian mediation; they insisted on being the sole representative of the Tamil population and cause, liquidating all rival challengers; and they lost international goodwill after 9/11 as the global tolerance for terrorism as a tactic collapsed, regardless of the justice of the cause.

Yet, even if true – and, as always, much of this was contentious and furiously contested – this did not obscure the humanitarian tragedy of large-scale civilian deaths and shelling of civilian targets such as schools and hospitals in the shrinking area still held by the Tigers as government troops closed in. Government claims of zero civilian casualties caused by their firepower are simply not credible. Around 7,000 civilians died in 2009 alone.

To what extent did R2P apply to the Tigers, the government and the international community for evacuating – by land, sea and air – the civilians caught in the crossfire? R2P places the responsibility first and foremost on the state itself. Given the Tigers' nature and record, it was not unreasonable for the government to build the capacity and demonstrate the determination to defeat the Tigers as part of its responsibility to protect. R2P proponents cannot advocate the international use of force against government troops engaged in atrocities against civilians, but not permit governments to use military force to protect their people from atrocities perpetrated by terrorists. Pacifists can denounce all use of force. But those who accept that the use of force is sometimes necessary cannot deny that option to governments engaged in fighting a brutal insurgency that kills civilians without compunction.

Had the Tigers been amenable to letting civilians caught in the crossfire escape, outsiders could legitimately have asked for another pause or ceasefire in order to help evacuate civilians. Another means for avoiding a bloodbath was for the Tigers to surrender. Absent this, it was hypocritical and wrong – morally, politically and militarily – of Westerners to fault Sri Lanka. Ceasefires are not neutral in their impact on the warring sides. The Tigers used previous pauses to rest, recover, regroup, recruit, rearm and return to terrorism. Another 25 years of war would have killed many more civilians.

There is also the moral hazard of validating the tactic of taking civilians hostage as human shields. Calls for a cease-fire, without materially helping the Tamil civilians, infuriated the government and reduced space for those making the calls to establish their bona fides with the government for how best to move from a civil war into a post-conflict peace-building environment. Those who choose to be referees and award penalties against one team cannot switch to playing coach of that team.

These considerations help to explain the outcome of the Human Rights Council deliberations towards the end of May.[37] Switzerland, supported by 12 Western countries, had tabled a censorious resolution calling for unfettered access to 270,000 civilians detained in government-run camps and an investigation of alleged war crimes by both sides. China, Cuba, Egypt and India were among 29 developing countries who supported a Sri Lanka-sponsored resolution, describing the conflict as a domestic matter that did not warrant 'outside interference', praising the defeat of the Tigers, condemning the rebels for using civilians as human shields and accepting the government's argument that aid groups should be given access to the detainees only 'as may be appropriate'. While Colombo was jubilant, Western diplomats and human rights officials were said to be shocked by the outcome at the end of the acrimonious two-day special session, saying it called into question the whole purpose of the Human Rights Council.

Where R2P does apply to the government is in its preventive and rebuilding components. The fact remains that the Tigers were the after-product of systematic and institutionalised discrimination by the Sinhalese majority against the Tamil minority that quickly degenerated into oppression and then killings. Calls for equal treatment when ignored escalated into demands for autonomy and, finally, a homeland. A military victory, while necessary, will not guarantee a peaceful future for a united Sri Lanka. The responsibility to reconstruct and rebuild, with international assistance, shows the way forward. The best time for the state to adopt measures of accommodation and power sharing within a federal framework is in the flush of military victory, when no one can accuse it of weakness. The Sri Lankan Tamils as well as the international community will mark the government's noble magnanimity. Conversely, should there be vulgar triumphalism, gloating and an atavistic return to oppression and killings, Sri Lanka will suffer a reprise of the brutal civil war.

Kenya

If the above three are doubtful examples of R2P provenance, Kenya and Libya are the only two positive markers for R2P up to the time of writing. When post-election violence broke out in Kenya in December 2007–January 2008, Francis Deng, Special Representative of the Secretary-General for the Prevention of Genocide, urged the authorities to meet their responsibility to protect the civilian population.[38] Archbishop Emeritus Desmond Tutu interpreted the African and

37 This paragraph is based on Philp (2009).

38 UN Secretary General (28 January 2008).

global reaction to the Kenyan violence as 'action on a fundamental principle – the Responsibility to Protect'.[39] Called in to mediate, Kofi Annan drew on R2P:

> I saw the crisis in the R2P prism with a Kenyan government unable to contain the situation or protect its people … I knew that if the international community did not intervene, things would go hopelessly wrong. The problem is when we say 'intervention', people think military, when in fact that's a last resort. Kenya is a successful example of R2P at work.[40]

Libya

The language of R2P refers to state inability or unwillingness as the catalyst to the international responsibility to protect being activated. But when security forces, meant to protect people, are instead let loose in a killing spree, the state itself becomes the prime perpetrator of atrocities. With precisely such an unfolding scenario during the 'Arab Spring' of 2011, Libya became the place and time to redeem or renege on R2P's solemn pledge. After 42 years of autocratic rule, Colonel Muammar Gadhafi was using deadly violence to crush and kill people rebelling against his harsh dictatorship. He and son Saif vowed to fight to the last drop of their blood and deployed air, sea and land forces.

In poignant testament to its tragic origins and normative power, R2P was the dominant discourse around the world – from Asia and Africa to Australia, Europe and North America – in debating how to respond to the crisis in Libya. Three sets of issues were involved: military capacity, legal authority and political legitimacy.

Military operations entailed four activities: surveillance and monitoring, humanitarian assistance, enforcement of the arms embargo and enforcement of no-fly and no-drive zones. Only the West has the military assets and operational capability for these tasks. But NATO was not prepared to take any military action on its own authority for an out-of-area operation. Only the UN Security Council has the legal authority to mandate the international use of military force other than in self-defence against armed attack.

On 22 February, the Security Council called on Libya 'to meet its responsibility to protect its population'. The Human Rights Council did the same on 25 February while suspending Libya's (indefensible) membership. Ban Ki-moon and his special advisers on genocide prevention and R2P warned of egregious violations of human rights and international humanitarian laws while reminding Libya of its R2P obligations.[41]

When these early appeals were ignored, on 26 February the Security Council voted unanimously, demanding an end to the violence in Libya which 'may amount to crimes against humanity'. It took note of the condemnation by the

39 Tutu (2008).

40 Kofi Annan in an interview with Roger Cohen: Annan (2008), p. 52.

41 See UN (2 April 2011).

African Union, the Arab League and the Organization of Islamic Conference of the incitement to hostility and violence against civilians. Resolution 1970 imposed sanctions on Libya, forbidding the sale of arms, freezing the assets of Libya's leaders and imposing a travel ban on them. It affirmed Libya's R2P obligations and referred Gadhafi to the International Criminal Court (ICC).

With no pause in Gadhafi's attacks against the popular rebellion, calls intensified for a no-fly zone, not the least from rebels under aerial attack. The risks of mission creep – a deepening quagmire leading to nation-building – would have arisen only if ownership of the uprising was appropriated from the Libyans by the West, as would happen with ground troops. But no one was asking for foreign boots on the ground. Legal authorisation from the UN Security Council was restricted to the four military tasks listed above. On 17 March, Security Council Resolution 1973 authorised the use of 'all necessary measures', short of an invasion and occupation, 'to protect civilians and civilian-populated areas': the first UN-sanctioned combat operations since the 1991 Gulf War. Resolution 1973 was passed by a 10–0 vote within 24 hours of being introduced, contrary to prevailing expectations that the moment for action had passed and the world once again had watched haplessly from the sidelines. It took NATO over a year to intervene in the Balkans in 1999 with air power. In Libya, it took just one month to mobilise a broad coalition, secure a UN mandate to protect civilians, establish and enforce no-fly and no-drive zones, stop Gadhafi's advancing army and prevent a massacre in Benghazi.

Putting all options on the table as the riposte to planes, bombs and tanks was a pusillanimous response too shameful to stomach. The game-changer was the juxtaposition of R2P as a powerful new galvanizing norm; the defection of Libyan diplomats who joined the chorus of calls for immediate action to protect civilians; and the request for a no-fly zone by the Arab League. The key decision was made by President Barack Obama at a White House meeting of top officials on 15 March. His speech on 28 March spelt out the rationale and terms of Libyan engagement very much in the language of R2P.[42]

There were many risks and dangers. The military operations could prove inconclusive, draining and inflaming the region further. Obama's pivot from no action to intervention suggests that US policy was reactive, not strategic. There were inconsistencies in the muted response to protests and uprisings in Bahrain and Saudi Arabia where vital US geopolitical and oil interests are directly engaged. Every government has the right to fight an armed uprising. How, exactly, can R2P be implemented to protect civilians without intervening in a civil war? Who were the rebels? What did they stand for? For whom did they speak? How much popular support did they command? With humanitarian protection, the balance of risks had to be shifted back from civilians to soldiers in comparison to Kosovo, Iraq and Afghanistan.

These were the 'unknown unknowns', in former US Defense Secretary Donald Rumsfeld's memorable phrasing. Against them, the risks of no action were the

42 Obama (28 March 2011).

'known knowns'. Gadhafi would have prevailed and embarked on a methodical killing spree of rebel leaders, cities and regions. The decisive factor for many was the threat, entirely credible, to hunt down opponents house by house, room by room, without mercy or pity. The recapture of Benghazi would have marked the end of the rebellion against Gadhafi's rule. Had the world shirked its responsibility, Libya could have been the graveyard of the new R2P norm and the UN might as well have sounded the last post for it. Instead, the UN-mandated intervention had the potential to mark the beginning of the end for Gadhafi. It also marked a pivotal rebalancing of interests and values by the Arabs, the West and the UN. For the first time in half a century, the West aligned itself with the Arab peoples' aspirations for dignity, democracy and respect instead of humiliation and brutalisation.

R2P gave Obama the necessary intellectual and normative tool to act. He decided to side with pro-interventionist advisers against the traditional, realpolitik definition of US interests in favour of an alternative, values-accommodating definition of the Libyan crisis that was closer to his instincts and consistent with the narrative that won him the White House. The Arab League and Franco–British urgings gave him political cover and international legitimacy. In Iraq in 2003, Washington had done all the pushing but doors had stayed firmly shut in most capitals. In Libya, Washington was the reluctant follower, not the ardent suitor for military intervention.

Resolution 1973 restricted military action to protecting Libya's civilian population from attacks by its own government. It prohibited occupying or dismembering the country. Any final settlement of the conflict must be political, not military. Thus Libya was not the same as Iraq or even Afghanistan. The international community was as sensitive as Americans to fears of Western occupation of yet a third Muslim country. Obama's insistence that the US would not deploy ground troops aligned military means to the limited ambitions and objectives: humanitarian protection, not regime change. In contrast to the Bush doctrine, under Obama the US would act in concert with others, not alone; coax, persuade and heed, not impose its will, on others; and set clear limits on goals and means.

Conclusion

In the old world order, international politics, like all politics, was a struggle for power. The new international politics will be about the struggle for the ascendancy of competing normative architectures based on a combination of power, values and ideas. In his Libya speech on 28 March 2011, Obama explained that the US is 'reluctant to use force to solve the world's many challenges. But when our interests and values are at stake, we have a responsibility to act'.[43] Atrocity crimes on the scale of the Holocaust, the Cambodian killing fields and the Rwanda genocide are

43 Obama (28 March 2011).

rare events in human history. This is why R2P in its intervention avatar will be needed but rarely, in extremis. But when such horrific events do occur, standing on the sidelines leaves an indelible stain on our collective conscience that not all the perfumes of Arabia can remove. This is why we must not shy away from implementing R2P when it is justified and necessary.

One possible means of entrenching the norm in public and policy discourse would be to cite paragraphs 138 and 139 of the *Outcome Document* in the preambular paragraphs of all relevant Security Council resolutions creating or renewing UN peace operations, while the operative paragraphs could contain the protection of civilians in armed conflict as part of the mandate of UN missions. This could help to generate the sort of norm entrapment that is familiar from the human rights literature. Norm-violating governments can choose to deny the validity of global norms and reject critics as agents or stooges of ignorant or ill-intentioned foreigners. But if vulnerable and subjected to sufficient pressure, they may begin to make tactical concessions in order to mollify domestic and international critics, lift aid suspensions and so on. The discourse has shifted from denying to accepting the validity of the norm, but rejecting specific allegations of norm-violation by questioning the facts and evidence presented by critics, or else insisting that these are isolated incidents and the cases will be investigated and perpetrators will be punished, and so forth. By such a process of 'self-entrapment',[44] the war for human rights is won though many battles might remain to be fought.

Similarly, every time that a state protests that R2P is not applicable to it, that critics have misunderstood the facts or not taken due account of the context, it acknowledges and reinforces the global norm even while questioning its applicability in the specific case to hand. Similarly, much as imitation is the sincerest form of flattery, Russia's invocation of the R2P norm in its 2008 invasion of Georgia was a tribute to the moral power of R2P.

History proves that sovereignty and the norm of non-intervention notwithstanding, regional and global powers have intervened, repeatedly, in the affairs of weaker states.[45] R2P offers developing countries better protection through agreed and negotiated-in-advance rules and roadmaps for when outside intervention is justified and how it may be done under UN authority rather than unilaterally. It will thus lead to the 'Gulliverization' of the use of force by major global and regional powers, tying it with numerous threads of global norms and rules. Absent R2P, they have relatively more freedom, not less, to do what they want. R2P is rooted in human solidarity, not in exceptionalism of the virtuous West against the evil rest.

44 Risse (2000), p. 32. In a subsequent refinement with colleagues, Risse developed the five-stage spiral model of norm generation, diffusion and domestication by the target state: repression, denial, tactical concessions, prescriptive status (when the state accepts the international norm and incorporates it into domestic legislation), and rule-consistent behaviour. Risse and Sikkink (1999), pp. 17–35.

45 Krasner (1999); Weiss and Don Hubert et al. (2001), pp. 49–77.

By the same token, however, Westerners need to recognise and accommodate developing country sensitivities. Developing country viewpoints rarely get an airing in the dominant Western mainstream media, let alone a respectful hearing with the possibility of their being right. The crisis over 'humanitarian intervention' arose because too many developing countries concluded that, intoxicated by its triumph in the Cold War, a newly aggressive West was trying to ram its values, priorities and agenda down their throats. Even today, differences within both camps notwithstanding, the global North/South divide is the most significant point of contention for 'the international community'.[46] With regard to the use of force, for example, advocates of the right to non-UN authorised humanitarian intervention in essence insisted that the internal use of force by the rest would be held to international scrutiny, but the international use of force by the West could be free of UN oversight and control. For developing countries, the United Nations was a key instrument for protection of vulnerable nations from predatory major powers; for many Westerners, it was acting to thwart forceful action to forestall or stop the killing of vulnerable people.

The nature and sites of armed conflict have changed,[47] with corresponding changes in the respective understandings of armed group violence in the global North and South. For most Westerners 'war' has become a remote abstraction far removed from their daily experience. Not so for many developing countries, especially in Africa. The majority of armed conflicts involve challenges to national integration or to the government's authority. Westerners are incapable of comprehending the framework within which their developing country counterparts must cope with such challenges; most developing country leaders can empathise with one another on this point. While to Western minds intervening to stop the bloodletting is restoring order around the periphery, to developing countries international intervention is a direct threat to territorial integrity. Related to this is the terrible moral hazard of encouraging ethno-national groups everywhere to demand independence and back it with violence that provokes state retaliation, which then promotes external intervention.

R2P is much more fundamentally about building state capacity than undermining state sovereignty. The scope for military intervention under its provenance is narrow and tight. The instruments for implementing its prevention and reconstruction responsibilities on a broad front are plentiful. R2P is principally about protecting developing country peoples by collective international means. The 2005 Outcome Document meets the minimum requirement of the call to action of classical humanitarian intervention while protecting the bottom-line interests of the weaker developing countries and thereby assuaging their legitimate concerns. It navigates the treacherous shoals between the Scylla of callous indifference to the plight of

46 See Thakur (2008). The most recent manifestation of this came when the majority of the African Union, the Arab League and the Nonaligned Movement expressed reservations about the ICC indictment of the President of Sudan on 4 March 2009. For an analysis of 'international community' as a contested concept, see Ellis (2009), pp. 1–26.

47 Mack (2005).

victims and the Charybdis of self-righteous interference in others' internal affairs. As argued by Mohamed Sahnoun, the other co-chair of the original international commission, in many ways R2P is a distinctly African contribution to global human rights.[48] Similarly, India's constitution imposes R2P-type responsibility on governments in its chapters on fundamental rights and directive principles of state policy.[49] Developing countries, not Western ones, are the likely targets of international military interventions. That is, if they are the principal beneficiaries and victims of putting R2P into practice, they should be the lead debaters on its merits and dangers. Contrary to what many developing country governments might claim, it is rooted as firmly in their own indigenous values and traditions than in abstract notions of sovereignty derived from European thought and practice. Many traditional Asian cultures stress the symbiotic link between duties owed by kings to subjects and loyalty of citizens to sovereigns, a point made by civil society representatives who accordingly conclude that, far from abridging, R2P *enhances* sovereignty.[50]

In responding to the rapidly unfolding crisis in Libya in March 2011, the Security Council acted with unprecedented speed in approving two resolutions, the first (1970) to impose sanctions and, when this was ignored by Gaddhafi, a second (1973) to authorise limited military operations. That China and Russia chose not to veto, and Brazil and India not to oppose, is testament to the normative power and attraction of the responsibility to protect in galvanising international action.

Secretary-General Ban Ki-moon has been impressively firm and consistent on R2P, leading from the front. He noted that Resolution 1973 'affirms, clearly and unequivocally, the international community's determination to fulfil its responsibility to protect civilians from violence perpetrated upon them by their own government'.[51] R2P has moved closer to being solidified as an actionable norm. Its future will be shaped by the course of events in Libya.

References

K. Annan (2008) 'How Kofi Annan Rescued Kenya', *New York Review of Books* 14 August, 51.

K. Annan (2005) *In Larger Freedom: Towards Development, Security and Human Rights for All: Report of the Secretary-General*, UN: A/59/2005, 21 March 2005.

G.J. Bass (2008) *Freedom's Battle: The Origins of Humanitarian Intervention*, Knopf.

Maeve Bateman and Michael Hammer (2007) 'Don't call me, I'll call you?', 107 *Briefing Paper*.

48 Sahnoun (2009).

49 I argued this in Thakur (2007).

50 See World Federalist Movement (2009), p. 8. 'At almost every roundtable, civil society emphasized how R2P principles already resonate with pre-existing cultural values'.

51 UN (12 April 2011).

A.J. Bellamy (2009) 'Realizing the Responsibility to Protect', 10, *International Studies Perspectives* 111.

S. Chesterman (ed.) (2007) *Secretary or General? The UN Secretary-General in World Politics*, CUP.

D.C. Ellis (2009) 'On the Possibility of "International Community"', 11, *International Studies Review* 1.

R. Falk (2009) *Israel's war crimes*, Le Monde Diplomatique (English edition), available at http://mondediplo.com/2009/03/03warcrimes (accessed 25 October 2010).

Global Center for R2P (19 August 2008) The Georgia-Russia Crisis and the Responsibility to Protect: Background Note, available at http://www.globalr2p.org/pdf/related/GeorgiaRussia.pdf.

Global Centre for R2P (January 2009) *The relationship between the responsibility to protect and the protection of civilians in armed conflict*, Policy Brief, available at http://globalr2p.org/pdf/GCR2PPolicyBrief-ProtectCivConflict.pdf (accessed 25 October 2010).

Global Centre for the Responsibility to Protect (2009) *Implementing the Responsibility to Protect – The 2009 General Assembly Debate: An Assessment*, Global Centre for the Responsibility to Protect available at http://www.GlobalR2P.org/ (accessed 25 October 2010).

Challenges and Change (HLP) High-Level Panel on Threats (December 2004) *A more secure world: our shared responsibility*, United Nations, A/59/565.

K.J. Holsti (1996) *War, the State, and the State of War*, New Internationalist, CUP.

V.K. Holt and T.C. Berkman (2006) *The Impossible Mandate? Military Preparedness, the Responsibility to Protect and Modern Peace Operations*, Stimson Center.

International Coalition for the Responsibility to Protect (2009) *Report on the General Assembly Plenary Debate on the Responsibility to Protect*, ICRtoP, available at http://www.responsibilitytoprotect.org/.

International Commission on Intervention and State Sovereignty (2001) *The Responsibility to Protect*, International Development Research Centre.

W. Kemp et al. (eds) (2011) *Blood and Borders: The Responsibility to Protect and the Problem of the 'Kin State'*, United Nations University Press.

B. Ki-moon (2009) *Implementing the responsibility to protect: Report of the Secretary-General*, UN: A/63/677, 12 January 2009.

S. Krasner (1999) *Sovereignty: Organized Hypocrisy*, Princeton University Press.

'Look across Africa and see the major changes that are happening' (2009) *Time Magazine* 13 July.

E.C. Luck (2009) *Remarks to the General Assembly on the Responsibility to Protect*, available at http://www.un.org/ga/president/63/interactive/protect/luck.pdf (accessed 25 October 2010).

N. Macfarquhar (2009) 'Memo from the United Nations: When to Step In to Stop War Crimes Causes Fissures', *New York Times* 22 July.

A. Mack, et al. (2005) *Human Security Report 2005: War and Peace in the 21st Century*, OUP.

C. McGreal (2009) 'Demands grow for Gaza war crimes investigation', *Guardian* 13 January.

J. Murthy (2008) 'Mandating the Protection Cluster with the Responsibility to Protect: A Policy Recommendation Based on the Protection Clusters Implementation in South Kivu, DRC', *Journal of Humanitarian Assistance*, available at http://jha.ac/2007/10/05/mandating-the-protection-cluster-with-the-responsibility-to-protect (accessed 25 October 2010).

K. Naumann et al. (2007) *Towards a Grand Strategy for an Uncertain World: Renewing Transatlantic Partnership*, Noaber Foundation.

B. Obama (28 March 2011) *Remarks by the President in Address to the Nation on Libya*, available at http://www.whitehouse.gov/the-press-office/2011/03/28/remarks-president-address-nation-libya (accessed 25 October 2010).

C. Philp (2009) 'Sri Lanka forces West to retreat over 'war crimes' with victory at UN', *The Times* 28 May.

Position Paper of the People's Republic of China on the United Nations Reforms (2005) 7 June 2005, Responsibility to Protect, available at http://news.xinhuanet.com/english/2005-06/08/content_3056817_3.htm (accessed 25 October 2010).

X. Rice (2009) 'UN-backed Congo military offensive a 'humanitarian disaster', *Guardian* 13 October.

T. Risse (2000) 'Let's Argue!: Communicative Action in World Politics', 54, *International Organization* 32.

T. Risse and K. Sikkink (1999) 'The socialisation of international human rights norms into domestic practices: introduction', in Thomas Risse, Stephen C. Ropp and K. Sikkink (eds) *The Power of Human Rights: International Norms and Domestic Change*, CUP 17.

M. Sahnoun (2009) *Africa: Uphold Continent's Contribution to Human Rights, Urges Top Diplomat*, allAfrica.com available at http://allafrica.com/stories/printable/200907210549.html (accessed 25 October 2010).

S. Strange (1999) 'The Westfailure System', 25, *Review of International Studies* 345.

R. Thakur (2006) *The United Nations, Peace and Security: From Collective Security to the Responsibility to Protect*, CUP.

R. Thakur (2007) 'The responsibility to protect revisited', *Daily Yomiuri* 12 April 2007.

R. Thakur (2008) *Towards a Less Imperfect State of the World: The Gulf between North and South*, Briefing Paper 4, Friedrich Ebert Stiftung, Dialogue on Globalization.

R. Thakur and V. Popovski (2008) 'The Responsibility to Protect and Prosecute: The Parallel Erosion of Sovereignty and Impunity', in Giuliana Ziccardi Capaldo (ed.) *Yearbook of International Law and Jurisprudence*, OUP 39.

R. Thakur and C.A. Thayer (eds) (1995) *A Crisis of Expectations: UN Peacekeeping in the 1990s*, Westview.

D. Tutu (2008) 'Taking the Responsibility to Protect', *International Herald Tribune* 19 February.

UN (25–26 July 2005) *Joint Statement by Participants in the Sixth High-Level Meeting between the United Nations and Regional and other Intergovernmental Organisations*, United Nations.

UN (2009) *Assembly President warns on doctrine to intervene on war crimes, atrocities*, available at http://www.un.org/ga/news/news (accessed 25 October 2010).

UN (2 April 2011) *Ban strongly condemns Qadhafi's actions against protesters, calls for punishment*, available at http://www.un.org/apps/news/story.asp?NewsID=37599 (accessed 5 May 2011).

UN (12 April 2011) *UN document SG/SM/13454, SC/10201, AFR/2144*, available at http://www.un.org/News/Press/docs/2011/sgsm13454.doc.htm (accessed 5 May 2011).

UN General Assembly (2009) *At the Opening of the Thematic Dialogue of the General Assembly on the Responsibility to Protect*, available at http://www.un.org/ga/president/63/statements/openingr2p230709.shtml (accessed 25 October 2010).

UN General Assembly (23 July 2009) *More than 40 delegates express strong scepticism, full support as General Assembly continues debate on responsibility to protect: General Assembly document GA/10849*, United Nations available at http://www.un.org/News/Press/docs/2009/ga10849.doc.htm (accessed 25 October 2010).

UN Secretary General (28 January 2008) *Daily Press Briefing by the Office of the Spokesperson for the Secretary-General*, available at http://www.un.org/News/briefings http://www.un.org/News/briefings (accessed 25 October 2010).

UN Security Council (20 July 2004) *Statement by the President of the Security Council S/PRST/2004/27*, United Nations, available at *www.securitycouncilreport.org/atf/cf/./RO%20SPRST2004_44.pdf* (accessed 25 October 2010).

United Nations Human Rights Council (15 September 2009) *Human Rights in Palestine and Other Occupied Arab Territories: Report of the United Nations Fact Finding Mission on the Gaza Conflict*, UN A/HRC/12/48, available at http://www2.ohchr.org/english/bodies/hrcouncil/specialsession/9/docs/UNFFMGC_Report.pdf (accessed 25 October 2010).

US Institute of Peace (2005) *American Interests and UN Reform: Report of the Task Force on the United Nations*, US Institute of Peace.

Thomas G. Weiss and Don Hubert et al. (2001) *The Responsibility to Protect: Research, Bibliography, Background*, International Development Research Centre.

World Federalist Movement (2009) *Global Consultative Roundtables on the Responsibility to Protect: Civil Society Perspectives and Recommendations for Action: Interim Report*, WFM.

World Summit Outcome, adopted by UN General Assembly Resolution (24 October 2005) UN: A/RES/60/1, 2005, available at http://unpan1.un.org/intradoc/groups/public/documents/un/unpan021752.pdf (accessed 25 October 2010).

Index

For Product Safety Concerns and Information please contact our EU representative GPSR@taylorandfrancis.com
Taylor & Francis Verlag GmbH, Kaufingerstraße 24, 80331 München, Germany

www.ingramcontent.com/pod-product-compliance
Ingram Content Group UK Ltd.
Pitfield, Milton Keynes, MK11 3LW, UK
UKHW011003180926
475701UK00004B/540
* 9 7 8 1 1 3 8 2 4 5 9 2 1 *